THE BIBLE AND THE COMMON READER

By MARY ELLEN CHASE

DAWN IN LYONESSE

A GOODLY FELLOWSHIP

MARY PETERS

SILAS CROCKETT

THIS ENGLAND

WINDSWEPT

THE BIBLE AND THE COMMON READER

THE BIBLE
AND THE
COMMON READER

By MARY ELLEN CHASE

New York
THE MACMILLAN COMPANY
1944

First Printing

A WARTIME BOOK

THIS COMPLETE EDITION IS PRODUCED
IN FULL COMPLIANCE WITH THE GOVERN-
MENT'S REGULATIONS FOR CONSERVING
PAPER AND OTHER ESSENTIAL MATERIALS.

This book is dedicated in gratitude to my students at Smith College who have enjoyed with me the reading and the study of the King James Bible, and especially to those four who have worked for Honours in that subject and who have given me constant help and encouragement:

> Dorothea Perry
> Elizabeth Brigham
> Maud Eckert Wilcox
> Mary Hoyt

CONTENTS

PART III

THE NEW TESTAMENT

FOREWORD

This book makes no claim to profound biblical scholarship. As its title clearly implies, it is written for the common reader; and from those common readers who may perhaps enjoy its pages I am myself distinguished only by the fact that I may possess more knowledge of its subject than they. I write it because for many years I have taken more delight in the Bible than in any other book I know and because I have become convinced that too few persons know how to read it. Like many another enthusiast for one thing or another, I want the fun of explaining that enthusiasm and, perchance, of inculcating it.

I owe the initial impulse which has given rise to these chapters to my students at Smith College, who, either directly by their suggestions or indirectly by their pleasure in the Bible, have urged me to write a book on its literature. For some years I have given a course in the King James Version and its influence on other English literature. Most of the girls studying with me knew painfully little of the Bible when they began to read it. I think I do not exaggerate when I say that all of them, without exception, have become its devotees, not because of their teacher, but because of itself. In many years of teaching English literature I have enjoyed no literary adventures as I have enjoyed those within the pages of the Old and the New Testament; and it is with a sense of deep gratitude and appreciation that I dedicate my book to my fellow students at Smith, who have been responsible for its conception and incalculably helpful in its fulfillment.

My book has been written, first of all, on the principle of selection. The old custom of reading the Bible from Genesis to Revelation has, I hope, been abandoned on the part of most readers. If it has not, it should be. Many portions, especially of the Old Testament, have now little meaning or value save to the theologian or the scholar. These portions, such as Leviticus, most of Deuteronomy, the Chronicles, practically all of Ezekiel, and many of the minor prophets, have been given no place in this book, partly because they are relatively undistinguished and uninteresting as literature, partly because a knowledge of them is completely unnecessary for the common reader. To treat them here would obscure my main purpose and threaten the fascinating with dullness.

I should like to warn my readers in advance that a careful reading of the four introductory chapters is not only wise but necessary unless they are already well versed in their contents, in which case they probably will find little of interest in the rest of the book. These chapters have been written as an indispensable preface to an understanding of those which follow; and a knowledge of their material will help immeasurably as background for the treatment of the biblical literature itself.

Although I was happily brought up to know as a child the stories of the Bible and to memorize innumerable passages of its literature, it was not until a few years ago that I began to make a study of it in terms of chronology and of criticism. For the many things I have learned concerning its various authors, known by name and unknown, its historical and archaeological background, its fact and its fiction, I am, of course, indebted to the many fine scholars who have made these subjects their special fields of research. I am grateful to them all, particularly to Julius Bewer for *The Literature of the Old Testament*, to Fleming James for his *Personalities of the Old Testament*, to Robert Pfeiffer for his indispensable *Introduction to the Old Testament*, to Ernest Scott for *The Literature of the New Testament*, and to Harry Emerson Fosdick for *A Guide to Understanding the Bible*. I wish also to express my gratitude to

Alfred Young Fisher, professor of English at Smith College, for his illuminating *Note* on *The Book of Job,* published, with wood engravings by Gustave Wolf, by the Cummington Press, Cummington, Massachusetts, 1944. I am giving at the close a list of other works both in scholarship and in literature, all of which have proved of the greatest interest and assistance to me. And to those who may, I hope, find pleasure in my book, I prophesy far greater pleasure in the reading of those better ones which have done so much to make possible my own.

Nor can I begin to express my thanks to my friends, Ruth and Charles Hill, Allison Grant, Eleanor Duckett, and Ruth Young, all of Smith College, whose help in reading and in criticizing my manuscript has been invaluable, and to my secretary, Gladys Nute, who has spent long and tiring hours in preparing it for the press.

In conclusion it is hardly necessary to say that I have made every effort to discover the truth behind and within the incomparable literature of which I write. The time has surely passed when to know and to love the Bible one must accept the purely legendary as intrinsic and literal truth or confuse history with fiction. The researches of the historians, the critics, and the archaeologists have clarified and strengthened rather than injured the imperishable material upon which they have worked. In taking away, they have rebuilt; in clarifying, they have illuminated. Much may be lost, but to the seeker after truth more remains. For it is the Spirit that maketh rich, and that Spirit is inviolable and immortal.

MARY ELLEN CHASE

Smith College
August, 1944.

PART I

CHAPTERS IN INTRODUCTION

I

What Is the Bible?

In the derivation of our word, *Bible*, lies its definition. It comes from the Greek word, *biblion* [1] which in its plural *biblia* signifies "little books." The Bible is actually a collection of little books, of every sort and description, written over a long period of time, the very earliest dating, in part at least, as far back as 1200 B.C. or perhaps even earlier; the latest as late as 150 A.D. In its rich and manifold nature it might be called a *library* of Hebrew literature; in its slow production over a period of many centuries it might be termed a *survey* of that literature to be understood as we understand a survey of English literature, in which we become familiar with types of English prose and poetry from Anglo-Saxon times to the twentieth century.

The Bible, in the form in which most of us wisely read it, the King James, or Authorized, Version, has been called by John Livingston Lowes "the noblest monument of English prose." It is as well the richest monument, for within its covers are to be found all types of literature, both in prose and in poetry. Here are ancient songs, written by unknown hands before the year 1000 B.C., preserved in old collections, now lost, or tenaciously bequeathed by word of mouth to succeeding generations, songs of war and of triumph, such as the famous martial song of Deborah in the 5th chapter of Judges; or in the 10th chapter

---

[1] *Biblos* was the name given to the inner bark of the papyrus; and the word *biblion* meant a papyrus roll, upon which the Bible was originally copied.

of the book called by his name the dramatic command of Joshua to the sun and the moon that they should stand still upon Gibeon and in the valley of Ajalon until the Amorites should be destroyed; or in Exodus 15 the triumphant song of Miriam, the sister of Moses, who with her women sang "with timbrels and with dances" over the destruction of Pharaoh and his hosts in the Red Sea; the revengeful song of Lamech, boasting to his terrified wives, Adah and Zillah, in the 4th chapter of Genesis; the little song to the well in the 21st chapter of Numbers, a song which the children of Israel sang in the wilderness of the desert when they thirsted for water and which is today in similar form sung by roaming Arabian tribes. Here are riddles, old perhaps as the famous riddle of the Sphinx, such as the riddle in Judges 14 propounded by Samson at his wedding feast about the honey in the carcass of the lion which he had killed with his bare hands; here are fables, exemplified in Judges 9 by Jotham's fable of the talking trees, the olive, the fig tree, the grape vine, and the bramble, and, like all fables, containing in its words a teaching for its time; here are oracles (for the great men of ancient Israel sometimes spoke in oracles as well as did the gods of ancient Greece), the beautiful oracles in Numbers 23 of Balaam, who went astride his wise and talkative ass to confound Balak, king of Moab.

These, which are among the oldest pieces of Hebrew literature, existed as folk material long before they were incorporated into the biblical narratives to give added richness to the narratives themselves. And what narratives! For the story-tellers of the Bible have never been surpassed, if equalled, by those of any later age or race, who time and time again have gone to them as to models of the art of narration. The Old Testament teems with stories: legends such as those in Genesis of the creation and of the flood, sagas like the Jacob-Joseph saga in Genesis 27–50, hero tales like those of Gideon, Jephthah, and Samson in the book of Judges, romances like much of the story of David, tragedies like the dark, ironic story of Saul, realistic stories like those many sordid incidents in King David's tempestuous and ill-governed household or in the cruel, designing lives of Ahab and Jezebel. There are short stories in the Bible, the idyllic love story of Ruth and the humorous, ironic story of Jonah sulking under his withering gourd. And there is a novel in the book of Esther, which in plot design and irony of incident has never been surpassed.

The story-tellers of the Bible, both in the Old Testament and the New, understood men and women of all sorts and in all conditions. There is literally no type of person whom they have neglected. All are here: the wise and the foolish, the rich and the poor, the faithful and the treacherous, the designing and the generous, the pitiful and the prosperous, the innocent and the guilty, the spendthrift and the miser, the players of practical jokes and their discomfited victims, the sorry, the tired, the old, the exasperated young, misled and impetuous girls, young men who lusted and young men who loved, friends who counted no cost for friendship, bad-mannered children and children well brought up, a little boy who had a headache in a hay-field, a little servant girl who wanted so much her master's health that she dared to give him good, if unpalatable, advice. Once one discovers such persons as these, still alive after many centuries, they become not only fascinating in themselves but typical of persons whom we know today, just as Mr. Micawber and Fagin are typical of the easy-going and the cruel, or as Robin Hood and Captain Blood typify two different attitudes toward daring and adventure, or as Don Quixote and Parson Adams are typical of men who, although they exist in this world, actually live in a kinder, better, more glorified one.

These stories of men and women, old and young, although they occupy a large portion of the Bible, are only one of its many literary forms. There is poetry in the Bible. In addition to the ancient songs already spoken of, there are lyrical love songs, odes, laments, hymns of all kinds, both secular and religious, dramatic monologues, and, above all else, the exalted poetry of the prophets and of the book of Job. And the poets who wrote this biblical poetry, some of them known by name, others unknown, were as distinct and individual in their method of writing and in their ways of thought as were the familiar English poets. Indeed many of them in their manner of expression and in their attitude toward life bear a striking resemblance to other poets whom we know far better than we know the poets of the Bible. Amos, for example, is like Milton in his sonorous, ringing lines; Hosea sounds the sad and minor notes of A. E. Housman; Second-Isaiah is like Shelley in his ecstasy; certain of the Psalmists are like William Blake, or Thomas Traherne, or John Donne.

There is at least one great drama in the Bible, that contained in the book of Revelation, with its majestic and awful stage settings, its celestial actors, its solemn acts and scenes. And there are a score of tragedies which, if placed in dramatic form, would rival *Othello* or *Hamlet* on Broadway.

There are great biographers among the biblical writers: Baruch, who wrote the biography of the prophet Jeremiah and whose first copy of it was cut in pieces by King Jehoiakim's pen-knife and thrown into the open fire on a cold December day; the unknown, vivid biographer of David, who rivalled Boswell in frankness and detail; the naive, almost childish chronicler, also unknown, who wrote in awed accents of King Solomon's magnificence, how he drank from cups of gold, how he spoke in proverbs, and how "he spake of trees"; and, in the New Testament, the biographers of Jesus, especially St. Luke, whose Gospel, to many readers, is more sensitive, more revealing, and more beautiful, than those of the other three writers. And the earliest autobiography of which we have record in ancient literature is that found in Nehemiah's thrilling account of how he left his service as cup-bearer to King Artaxerxes to return to Jerusalem and to rebuild the broken-down walls and gates of his fathers' city.

The best letters ever written are in the Bible, and St. Paul is the author of them, a more vivid letter writer than even Horace Walpole or Lord Chesterfield largely because he had far more important things than they to say. St. Paul is never dull. Whether he writes for a room to be made ready for him, or thanks his friends for presents, or gives his opinions on marriage or on the behaviour of women in church, or describes his utter dejection or his astounding faith, or is concerned over the collection of money or the virtue of charity, or rises to impassioned heights over the corruptible and the incorruptible, the terrestrial and the celestial, he is always vibrant with life, and his language in its force and vigour, clarity and beauty, can never be forgotten.

There are countless proverbs in the Bible, many contained in the book bearing their name, others scattered elsewhere, maxims and aphorisms, some of great antiquity, some of other origin than Jewish. Proverbs, as all know, are one of the most ancient and perennial forms of literature, reflecting the sagacity and common sense of practical men of all ages in their attempts to get on reasonably well in life. They are, in other words, the records of long and sometimes hazardous experience expressed in short sentences. Here in the Bible we have them at their best and, often unconscious of their origin, quote them over and over again as Sancho Panza, in his exasperation, quoted ancient Spanish proverbs to Don Quixote.

There are two philosophers in the Bible, both of whom give to us in mingled prose and poetry their questions and their conclusions concerning the meaning of life and the ways of God with men. They are the unknown authors of the books of Ecclesiastes and of Job, the one a skeptic, the other a tortured man of faith. Because they dealt, each in his own way, with man's great quest, his search for Reality in life, because they recognized the problems of evil and of pain, and because, like other thoughtful and honest men, they found no sure and certain answers to their questions, the books which they wrote, disparate though they are in both literary and philosophical

7

value, are surely among the most deathless of all the books of the Bible.

The Bible, then, is a collection, a library of various books, reflecting and illuminating the long life of a small, yet a great people. If it were only that, its value would be imperishable. But it is more. It is, indeed, in its most perfect of translations, the noblest monument of our English prose; and its words and phrases, images and similes have become part and parcel of our common English speech. Think for a moment how in the course of a single day spent in the homely, necessary details of living, we clarify and illuminate our talk with one another by the often unconscious use of its language. An unwelcome neighbour becomes "gall and wormwood" or "a thorn in the flesh"; a hated task, "a millstone about the neck"; we escape from one thing or another "by the skin of our teeth"; we earn our bread "by the sweat of our faces"; like Martha we become "careful and troubled about many things"; we "strain at gnats and swallow camels"; tired at night, we say that "our spirit is willing but our flesh is weak"; in moments of anger we remember that "a soft answer turneth away wrath"; intrusions upon our sleep are "the pestilence that walketh in darkness"; we warn our children to be "diligent in business" so that they may not "stand before mean men," or prophesy that if "they sow the wind, they shall reap the whirlwind," or puzzle them by knowledge "brought by a bird"; we recall that "the tongue is a little member but boasteth great things"; our pay-days mean "corn in Egypt"; words fitly spoken are "like apples of gold in pictures of silver"; the price of our generous friends is still "far above rubies," they are, in fact, "shining lights" or "the salt of the earth"; we pray that our sons may be brought safely homeward "to the haven where they would be"; we "heap coals of fire" on the heads of recalcitrant children or of harassed wives or husbands; having no servants, we are ourselves "hewers of wood and drawers of water"; we long for the time when men "shall beat their swords into ploughshares and their spears into pruning-

8

hooks"; and, after an irritating session with ration books, we are forced to remember that "better a dinner of herbs where love is than a stalled ox and hatred therewith."

The language of the Bible, now simple and direct in its homely vigour, now sonorous and stately in its richness, has placed its indelible stamp upon our best writers from Bacon to Lincoln and even to the present day. Without it there would be no *Paradise Lost*, no *Samson Agonistes*, no *Pilgrim's Progress*; no William Blake, or Whittier, or T. S. Eliot as we know them; no Emerson or Thoreau, no negro Spirituals, no Address at Gettysburg. Without it the words of Burke and Washington, Patrick Henry and Winston Churchill would miss alike their eloquence and their meaning. Without a knowledge of it the best of our literature remains obscure, and many of the characteristic features and qualities of our spoken language are threatened with extinction.

The Bible belongs among the noblest and most indispensable of our humanistic and literary traditions. No liberal education is truly liberal without it. Yet in the last fifty years our colleges have, for the most part, abandoned its study as literature, and our schools, for reasons not sufficiently valid, have ceased to teach, or, in many cases, even to read it to their young people. Students of English literature take for granted that a knowledge of the *Iliad*, the *Odyssey*, the *Aeneid*, and the *Divine Comedy* are necessary not only for the graduate schools but for cultured and civilized life, as, indeed, they are; but most of them remain in comfortable and colossal ignorance of a book which antedates Dante and, in large part, Vergil by many centuries, some of which was written before Homer, and all of which has contributed more to the humanistic civilization of the Western World than have the so-called "Classics."

To all English-speaking peoples the Bible is a national as well as a noble monument, for much of their history is securely rooted and anchored within it. In 17th century England it nurtured the Puritan revolt and paved the way for the Bill of Rights. In 17th and 18th century America it supplied not only the names of our ancestors but the stout precepts by which they lived. They walked by its guidance; their rough places were made plain by their trust in its compassionate promises. It was a lamp to their feet and a light to their path, a pillar of cloud by day and of fire by night. It was the source of the convictions that shaped the building of this country, of the faith that endured the first New England winters and later opened up the Great West. It laid the foundations of our educational system, built our earliest colleges, and dictated the training within our homes. In the words alike of Jefferson and Patrick Henry, John Quincy Adams and Franklin it made better and more useful citizens to their country by reminding a man of his individual responsibility, his own dignity, and his equality with his fellow-man. The Bible is, indeed, so imbedded in our American heritage that not to recognize its place there becomes a kind of national apostasy, and not to know and understand it, in these days when we give all for its principles of human worth and human freedom, an act unworthy of us as a people.

And, lastly, the Bible in its slow, patient evolution is the noblest record in any language of the hearts and the minds of men. Those who wrote it and those of whom it was written thought and wondered over the eternal questions of life and death, of man's lot upon this earth, and of his ultimate destiny. Amos on the Tekoan hills, the Great Isaiah by the waters of Shiloah and the Second Isaiah by those of Babylon, Job in the dust with his sententious friends, "physicians of no value" to him, St. John on the island of Patmos, Daniel by the river Ulai —these were men of dreams and of visions who struggled with the questions that beset us all. Consumed like Dante "by the Love that moves the sun and the other stars," they were intent upon the possible reaches of man's spirit even in a dry and thirsty land. In the midst of desolation and suffering, of oppression and greed, they saw hope; in war, the ways of peace; in the perennial processes of nature, the treasures of the snow, the

10

former and the latter rain, the waste places of the deep, the singing of the morning stars, they saw the mysterious ways of God with men. Because of their vision, deep calleth unto deep in their pages; and the unanalyzed perception of the meaning and value of threescore years and ten is woven into the very texture of their speech. In their two-fold recognition of wisdom, that moral and ethical code by which a just man lives his life and that intangible and spiritual Power, set up from everlasting and possessed by God in the beginning of His way, only by the understanding of which man achieves his triumph, they encompassed all the affairs, small and great, of one's sojourn on this earth.

"I myself also am a mortal man, like to all. . . . And when I was born, I drew in the common air, and fell upon the earth, which is of like nature, and the first voice I uttered was crying, as all others do. . . . For all men have one entrance into life, and the like going out. Wherefore I prayed, and understanding was given me; I called upon God, and the spirit of wisdom came to me. I preferred her before sceptres and thrones, and esteemed riches nothing in comparison to her. . . . I loved her above health and beauty, and chose to have her instead of light; for the light that cometh from her never goeth out. All good things together came to me with her, and innumerable riches in her hands. For she is a treasure unto men that never faileth; which they that use become the friends of God."[2]

[2] These words are taken from the 7th chapter of the Wisdom of Solomon from the *Apocrypha*.

Since the Apocrypha is now seldom included in editions of the Bible except for Catholic readers and since its reading should follow a reading of the Old and of the New Testament, I have thought best not to treat it in this book. I have, however, referred to it from time to time. It is a collection of historical, narrative, and poetic writings known as apocryphal books from the Greek word meaning *hidden* or *secret*, and so of uncertain origin and authority. They are late books, most of them belonging to the last three centuries B.C. Among the best ones, both from a literary and an historical standpoint, are I and II Maccabees,

11

2

The King James, or Authorized, Version of the Bible: Its History and Value

1

It is not only safe but extremely pleasant to say that probably ninety per cent of those who today read the Bible in English read it in the King James, or Authorized, Version. Doubtless their wisdom in this matter springs from custom or from chance rather than from intelligent choice, since up to the year 1885 when the Revised Version was published, the King James Version of 1611 was the only one in common use among English-speaking peoples; nor has the Revised Version in terms of circulation ever approached in number the King James. Since the publication of the Revised Edition there have been other translations: the American Standard Version in 1901, and, in later years, certain renderings, mostly of the New Testament, which have attempted, not too successfully, to translate so-called biblical language into the speech of our own day.

Together with these modern translations there have appeared several editions of the Bible, the editors of which have tried to lend a larger measure of intelligence and understanding to

---

which tell the story of the rising of Judas Maccabeus and of the wars which followed, the short stories of Tobit and of Judith, and the beautiful poetry and poetic prose of Ecclesiasticus and the Wisdom of Solomon.

The Apocrypha was translated by the King James scholars and included in the Authorized Version of 1611. It can be obtained in a small volume published by the Oxford University Press.

readers by re-arrangement of the material. Chief among these are Richard G. Moulton's *The Modern Reader's Bible*, published in small volumes from 1896 to 1907, when a single large volume appeared, and *The Bible Designed to Be Read as Living Literature*, arranged and edited by Ernest Sutherland Bates in 1936. The editors of these Bibles have unquestionably performed a service to readers by arranging the various books in historical sequence, or in order of composition, or under types of literature, and by placing the poetry in a form by which it is more clearly grasped as poetry. Mr. Bates has, moreover, eliminated from his volume certain portions of both Old and New Testaments now rarely read and, especially in the case of the Old Testament, actually of little historical, literary, or religious value. Mr. Moulton in his edition has used the Revised Version throughout; Mr. Bates has used the King James with the exception of the Revised Versions of Job, Ecclesiastes, Proverbs, and the Song of Songs, which, he claims, are "admittedly far superior" to the King James. I do not agree with him in this statement, much as I honour his work. Nevertheless, he has surely performed most admirable service to those who would read and understand the Bible.

Why this perhaps unbridled enthusiasm for the King James Version? Reasons are not wanting. First of all, that of familiarity and tradition. For three hundred years and more this English Bible of 1611 has been read, revered, and loved by countless millions of English-speaking people. For more than two hundred years in the history of our own country it held the honoured place in every Protestant household and was, in many homes, literally the one book possessed. Its familiar words, now gracious, now awful, ennobled the speech of our ancestors and echoed in the ears and in the consciences of their children, many of whose mothers, like Susanna Wesley, had taught them to read by bending with them for long, arduous hours over the first chapter of Genesis. The records of numberless towns, schools, and churches prove how its language was woven into our early civil, educational, and religious life. Imagine the consternation of our forefathers, who began and ended each day with its reading, had they been asked to confuse such a well-known passage as:

In the beginning God created the heaven and the earth. And the earth was without form and void; and darkness was upon the face of the deep, with the following from a modern translation: *When God began to create the heavens and the earth, the earth was a desolate waste, with darkness covering the abyss and a tempestuous wind raging over the surface of the waters.*[1]

But familiarity and tradition, although they may well weigh heavily with many readers, are not in themselves sufficient reasons in a day of change for cleaving to the King James Version before all others. Especially is this true in the face of the fact that in too few ears today, not to mention consciences, the old words and rhythms sound at all! The truth remains, however, and provides a more cogent reason, that the translation of 1611 has entered into our literature as no other version has yet had time or authority to do. Knowing it as many of them knew no other book, the great writers of English for three centuries have made of it a requirement for the understanding of their own works, indeed of themselves. Milton, Sir Thomas Browne, Swift, Lamb, Newman, Hazlitt, Macaulay, De Quincey, Ruskin, Dickens, George Eliot, Hardy, Emerson, Thoreau, Hawthorne, Melville, Lincoln, to name only those best known to us, have woven its words, its characters, its incidents, its imagery, its style into the very fabric of their own literature. If we would truly understand them, we must know the Bible in its one translation which they knew and honoured.

Finally, although no one should underestimate those scholars of the new versions who, for the sake of greater accuracy in translation, have spent years upon their work, one can, I think, fairly say that their accomplishment, valuable as it doubtless is

[1] From *The Bible, An American Translation,* edited by J. M. Powis Smith and Edgar J. Goodspeed, University of Chicago Press, 1927.

for the student and the theologian, offers little to the common reader of the Bible in exchange for the King James Version. A simplicity and vigour, an honesty and dignity, a stateliness, beauty, and incomparable fitness of language mark the work of the old translators which the new, even those who have made relatively few drastic changes, have been unable to achieve throughout.

The common reader for whom I write this book is, in my opinion and that of countless others, wise if he leaves the revised versions to the scholars. He is wiser if he sets aside all recent experiments in re-writing the New Testament in undistinguished and often mediocre language. I would remind him that the King James Version was written for the common readers of its day, fewer in number though they were than in our time.

"I would to God," wrote William Tyndale, translating Erasmus in 1529, "the plowman would sing a text of the Scriptures at his plowbeam. And that the weaver at his loom with this would drive away the tediousness of time. I would the wayfaring man with this pastime would expel the weariness of his journey." [2]

2

It was this same William Tyndale who in the first quarter of the sixteenth century contributed by his own translation of the Bible so much to the King James Version. For our incomparable translation is an evolution, owing many of its gifts and graces to those which came before it. It is well, therefore, to trace briefly its history and accomplishment in the light of its several predecessors; and in order to do this it is necessary to know something of the background from which it came.

When we think of the sixteenth century in England, most of us are likely to think of it in certain rather circumscribed terms. It recalls to us, first of all, those "spacious times of great

[2] I have modernized the old spelling here for the sake of clearness.

15

Elizabeth," when Shakespeare wrote his plays for the Globe and Blackfriars, when Sidney wrote his *Arcadia* and Spenser his *Faerie Queene*, when Raleigh and Drake sailed the Spanish Main, when the Armada of Philip the Second was destroyed, and when daring adventurers, convinced at last that the world was round, were crossing the oceans, even to our own shores, in search of a northwest passage or of fabulous stores of gold. But the earlier years of that century, with which fewer of us are familiar, were marked by very different things. Religious controversy, fed, on the one hand, by the personal desires of King Henry VIII, and, on the other, by the spread of Protestantism in England, was rife between the Pope and the English Church. Men's heads were cheap in those stormy days. Sir Thomas More forfeited his rather than subscribe to the Act of Supremacy which placed Henry VIII at the head of the Church; only a natural death prevented Cardinal Wolsey from the scaffold; Latimer and Ridley, because of their zeal for reform, were burned at the stake in Oxford. No other half century of English history shows such tumult in the hearts and in the minds of men. On the one hand, adherence to the doctrines and the practices of the Church of Rome, royal politics, the fears of abandoning the old for the uncertain new, the terror of heresy, the distrust of popular demands, and, on the other, the New Learning in the universities, the influence of the spread of Protestantism on the Continent, the far-reaching results of the invention of printing, introduced into England by William Caxton in 1477, the growing of national consciousness, the clamour for the use of English in the services of the Church and for the Bible in the national tongue—these questions and controversies marked the age out of which came those several translations of the Bible, forerunners and ancestors of our King James Version of 1611.

In the last years of the fourteenth century, assisted by certain of his followers, John Wycliffe, because of his conviction that the people required a Bible in their own language, had translated both the Old and the New Testament from the 4th century Latin

Vulgate of St. Jerome into the English of his day. Since, however, his translation was in manuscript, written almost a century before the introduction of printing into England, its circulation, in spite of numerous copies made, had relatively little influence, even though we read that some men would gladly give a load of hay for a few chapters of St. Paul in English. It is to William Tyndale that we owe our first printed Bible, incomplete though it was; and the years from his translation of the New Testament in 1525 mark almost a century of devoted labour.

This long story of the King James Version is a crowded one, beset by perils and even by martyrdom. Tyndale, sometimes called the Father of the English Bible, was a student at Oxford and at Cambridge, a teacher and a preacher, whose views on religion were far in advance of those current in his day. His outspoken criticism against the ignorance of the English clergy early embroiled him in trouble with Church authority. In the year 1523 he sought from the Bishop of London permission to translate the New Testament into English. Finding "that there was no rowme in my lorde of londons palace to translate the new Testament but also that there was no place to do it in all englonde," he went to Germany in 1524. He lived and worked in Hamburg and in Cologne, and later, betrayed by enemies of Luther and of all so-called heretics, he escaped to the strongly Protestant city of Worms, where in 1526 the first printing of his New Testament was completed. In England, in spite of Church and royal authority, which proscribed their use and ordered them to be burned, copies were smuggled into the country while more editions were being published by courageous booksellers in Antwerp.

Once the New Testament had been translated, Tyndale set to work upon a translation of the Old and accomplished the first five books, known as the Pentateuch, or the Five Books of Moses, as well as a translation of the book of Jonah. So far as we know, these were the only books of the Old Testament published by him. Beset by English spies, hunted by those hostile

17

to the spread of Protestantism on the Continent, Tyndale was finally convicted of heresy and condemned to death. After more than a year of painful and degrading imprisonment, he was burned at the stake on October 6, 1536 in the town of Vilvorde near Brussels, crying with his last strength, "Lord, open the King of England's eyes."

It was upon this incomplete work of Tyndale more than upon any other that the King James Version was based, and upon it also depended the versions of the several translators who followed quickly upon his death. For, once the separation from the Church of Rome had been established by Parliament in 1534, once the king was supreme in his own realm and surrounded by more liberal ecclesiastical advisers, the growing demand for a Bible in English could not be indefinitely set aside. Nevertheless, the next translator, Miles Coverdale, thought it wise to do his work outside England. His translation of both the Old and the New Testament, together with the Apocrypha, is the first printed English Bible, published probably in Zurich in 1535.

A Yorkshireman by birth, Coverdale was not without humour or diplomacy. He dedicated his volume with its uncertain fate to King Henry VIII together with his "dearest just wyfe and most vertuous Pryncesse, Quene Anne," and in his elaborate dedication compared the king to the virtuous King Josiah, who had commanded "that the lawe of God shulde be redde and taught unto all ye people." Moreover, at the bottom of his title page he included a picture of King Henry benevolently handing out the Bible to the bishops kneeling before him! No royal patronage or even license was, however, formally accorded to Coverdale, who published his Bible without authority; and yet we know that in 1537 the Coverdale Bible was printed in England.

Miles Coverdale had his oddities of translation, as we shall see when we compare some of his renderings with those of the King James Bible. For example, the beautiful first verse of Isaiah 60: *Arise, shine; for thy light is come,* is translated by

18

Coverdale: *Get thee up; be illuminated.* Yet we owe to him certain perfect lines never altered by later scholars. It is he who gave us such simple, memorable phrases and sentences as *the valley of the shadow of death; thou anointest my head with oil; they that sow in tears shall reap in joy.*

In 1537 also appeared two other translations of the Bible, now under royal license. These were the so-called Matthew's Bible, edited by a certain John Rogers, who later because of his work was executed under the Catholic Queen, Mary Tudor, and the revision of Matthew's Bible by a man called Richard Taverner, his revision being known as the Taverner Bible. Both these Bibles were in effect compilations of the work of Tyndale and Coverdale. It seems odd, and ironical, that these Bibles should have received official sanction when we remember that only the year before their publication William Tyndale, without whom neither would have had being, had been martyred at the stake!

Perhaps, indeed, the close dependence of these two revisions upon Tyndale actuated the ecclesiastical heads of England in their eagerness for a translation which might be authorized to be read in churches. Accordingly in 1539 appeared the so-called Great Bible, named because of its size, and edited largely by Miles Coverdale. Not that Tyndale's influence had in any sense been lost, for again and again Coverdale as editor of the new Bible chooses to employ Tyndale's diction and phrasing in place of his own.

This Great Bible is of importance to us, both in itself and as a predecessor to the King James Version. It was the first Bible "apoynted to the use of the churches," as the title page of the 1540 edition declares. Its rendering of the Psalms, the work of Coverdale, became that adopted for the Psalter of the Book of Common Prayer, and to this day is used in the Church of England and the Protestant Episcopal Church. It was the first English Bible given freely into the hands of the people. True it was that in the later years of the reign of Henry VIII the

19

freedom of Bible reading became again restricted under the still dark shadow of Tyndale and heresy. Women particularly, "except noble or gentle women," were by an Act of Parliament of 1543 forbidden to read it publicly or privately under pain of imprisonment. Nevertheless, the fight for its translation and for its common use had been largely won; and the Great Bible marks that triumph.

The printing of Bibles in English came to a standstill in the reign of the Catholic Queen Mary; and yet in the few stormy years of her sovereignty she apparently had too much on her hands to fret unduly over the possession of Bibles by individuals or over the reading of them in English homes, however much she strove to burn those set up in churches. Because of her persecutions many Protestant scholars, including Miles Coverdale, escaped to the Continent; and a colony of them, later to be known as Puritans, who settled in Geneva, took the next step forward in biblical translation. In 1557 one or more of their number completed a revision of the New Testament; in 1560, emboldened by the accession of Queen Elizabeth to the English throne, they published in Geneva their complete translation of both Old and New Testaments together with the Apocrypha.

This Geneva Bible, a small volume and because of its size convenient for private use, holds many things of great interest to us today. For fifty years it was the Bible used in all English homes until it was superseded by the King James Version. It was the first to be printed in our own familiar roman type, as it was the first volume in English to divide the text into verses. For the first time also italics were used to show any addition to the original text, a practice still in use today. But above all else the Geneva Bible is important to us because, in the long lineage of our King James Version, it holds, with the sole exception of Tyndale's work, the most honoured place as ancestor and predecessor. Little as most of us know of it, we read its identical words in numberless chapters and verses of our version. Dissatisfied with the Great Bible's rendering of the 23rd Psalm: *The Lord is my shepherd, therefore can I lack nothing,* its wise and sensitive translators wrote: *The Lord is my shepherd, I shall not want.* We owe the beautiful words in the 40th chapter of Isaiah directly to the Geneva Bible: *O Zion, that bringest good tidings, get thee up into the high mountain,* a sentence surely more satisfying to our ears than the wording of the Great Bible: *Go up unto the high hill, you that bringest good tidings.* And, finally, there is interest in recalling that those who in Geneva worked upon their new version marked the beginnings of that movement which in the next century was to found the Puritan colony of Massachusetts Bay.

The widespread popularity of the Geneva Bible among the common people was disturbing to the bishops of Elizabeth's Church of England. Nor did the queen herself, although the Geneva exiles had dedicated their volume to her, give it any royal approval. Moreover, the obvious superiority of many of the Geneva renderings to those of the Great Bible was steadily ousting the latter and causing a slump in the esteem formerly accorded it. And, lastly, certain marginal notes printed in the Geneva Bible sounded too ominously of Non-Conformist doctrine for Church of England ears.

Seeing these things with not a little anxiety, Matthew Parker, Archbishop of Canterbury, determined upon a new version which the Church could officially use and approve. Accordingly in 1566 he apportioned various parts of the Scriptures to some seventeen bishops, presumably chosen because of their learning, and asked them to revise the several translations, to base their work upon the Great Bible, and not to "varye much from that translacion" unless the careful study of the Hebrew and Greek demanded change.

This new Bible, published in 1568 and from its origin known as the Bishops' Bible, was in outward appearance at least the largest and most pretentious that had appeared. It was illustrated by woodcuts and, in addition to a portrait of the queen

21

on its title page, contained, with perhaps small reason, two engravings of men prominent in royal circles, the Earl of Leicester and Sir William Cecil. It cannot be said, however, that the handsome new volume put to flight the popularity of the Geneva Bible, with which it seems to have fought a losing battle throughout the rest of the century. In certain of its translations it shows an elegance of style perhaps in keeping with its appearance; and we can be thankful that our King James Version wisely decided to preserve the Geneva rendering of the familiar first verse of the 23rd Psalm: *The Lord is my shepherd, I shall not want*, rather than to accept the clumsy form of the Bishops' Bible: *God is my shepherd, therefore I can lack nothing: he will cause me to repose myself in pasture full of grass, and he will lead me unto calm waters.* We can be equally grateful, on the other hand, for certain changes and innovations which *did* wisely influence the King James scholars, such as the use of the word *charity* in the 13th chapter of I Corinthians preserved by them and the opening verse of the 1st Psalm which was taken verbatim from the Bishops' Bible.

The next English translation of the Bible was one made by Roman Catholic scholars for the use of Catholic readers. In the last quarter of the sixteenth century, through the zeal of the Jesuits and the spread of the Counter-Reformation through western Europe, certain prominent Catholics had left England in well-merited fear of persecution at the hands of an uneasy Protestant queen, who feared Catholic plots against her throne. These exiles found refuge in the French town of Douai, which afterward gave its name to the Bible translated into English by the scholars among them. Later they moved to the city of Rheims where in 1582 they printed their version of the New Testament. Returning to Douai in 1593 they set to work on the translation of the Old Testament, which was published in 1609–10. These Roman Catholic translations, as may be assumed from the history and tradition of the Catholic Church, rested largely on the Latin Vulgate of St. Jerome instead of on the original Hebrew and Greek; and both are marked by influences of Latin style and diction, even the names of characters being given in their Latin forms.

The very date of the completing of the Douai version of the Old Testament would, in all probability, preclude any influence on the King James Version, which was printed in 1611. The Rheims translation of the New Testament, however, was studied by the King James translators together with all the other earlier versions; and, although its influence was relatively slight, its contributions should not be entirely set aside. As one example among many, we owe to the Rheims New Testament the fine use of the word *adorned* in Revelation 21: *prepared as a bride adorned for her husband*, surely a more effective adjective than the *trimmed* or the *garnished* of the earlier versions. At the end of the eighteenth century the Old and New Testaments, together with the Apocrypha, were revised and then published for the first time in one volume, the form in which the Douai Bible is most generally known today among Catholic readers.

And now after a necessary survey of its predecessors and ancestors—a survey which I have tried to make as concise and as interesting as possible—we come to the most familiar as well as the greatest of all translations, the King James, or Authorized, Version of the Bible. What steps brought about its translation as the version "authorized" by the King and the Church of England? Who and what were responsible for its perfection?

When King James ascended the throne in 1603, the Bishops' Bible was nominally the standard English translation and the official version presumably used in all churches. The Bible most commonly used, however, by the people in their homes was the Geneva. This was clearly an unsatisfactory, if not unfortunate, state of affairs since the Geneva Bible, especially in the marginal notes inserted by its translators, carried a distinct and perhaps dangerous flavour of Calvinism. Nevertheless, it was a Puritan scholar who himself expressed dissatisfaction with the existing translations, the Geneva as well as the others, on the ground that

23

they were "corrupt and not aunswerable to the truth of the Originall." He was John Reynolds, a prominent Puritan and president of Corpus Christi College, Oxford; and he made his proposal, which was to mean so much to his own and future centuries, at the Hampton Court Conference held with King James in January of the year 1604.

Reynolds' proposal seems to have been received by the king with greatest enthusiasm, for by July of 1604 he had appointed fifty-four "learned men . . . having especial skill in the Hebrew and Greek tongues" to make the new translation. These scholars, chosen for their learning and intelligently including both Churchmen and Puritans, were divided into six companies of nine men each, two companies to work at Cambridge, two at Oxford, and two at Westminster; and each company or group was assigned certain portions of the Bible, for the new rendering of which each was responsible.

The names of forty-seven of these English scholars remain to us although few of them mean much more than names today. Important as they surely were in University and Church circles, a dozen or more of them being masters or presidents of colleges at Oxford and Cambridge, we know and honour them only for the great task they accomplished "in so decent a manner." The first name on the list, that of Lancelot Andrewes, means more than any of the others to most modern readers and students. Andrewes was Dean of Westminster and afterward Bishop of the sees of Chichester, of Ely, and finally of Winchester. He seems to have been a likable as well as a learned man, a favourite counsellor at Court, a man of rich personality and imagination. His sermons and certain beautiful prayers which he wrote are not entirely unknown today, nor is his reputation as one of the most learned men of his time; for his fellow scholars claimed generously that he might have been "interpreter at Babel" so great was his linguistic knowledge, and that there was not enough learning in the world "to know how learned was he."

It would be interesting indeed to know the details of this

work of translation, where and how the scholars lived, how and what they were paid for their labour. We do know the rules by which they were governed: that they were to follow the Bishops' Bible before any other version in their work; that they were to alter as little as possible the chapter divisions already established; that (apparently because of the controversy which notes in the Geneva Bible had stirred up) they were to affix no marginal notes; that they were to meet together and compare translations; and that they were to welcome suggestions of any man who might be "skilful in the tongues" and who might send "his particular Observations" to any of the groups at work.[3] How their expenses were met and whether they were actually paid for their work we do not know; but from the few existing documents it is clear that those stationed at Oxford and Cambridge received their board and lodging in the colleges free of charge. A memoir of one of the translators, Dr. John Boys, written by a friend of his, tells us that the Reverend Mr. Boys "abode all the week [at St. John's College, Cambridge] till Saturday night; and then went home to discharge his cure at Boxworth; returning thence on Monday morning." Nor do we know why a delay of three years took place between the original proposal of John Reynolds in 1604 and the actual beginning of the work of translation, which, in spite of the delay, saw its completion and publication as the King James Bible in 1611.

Perhaps the greatest of literary mysteries lies in the unanswered question of how fifty-four translators managed to infuse their work with a unity of effect which seems the result of one inspired imagination. The mystery will never be solved; but the perfect choice throughout of current English words, the rhythmic fall of phrase and clause, the unfailing escape from the heavy and sometimes pompous renderings of the older transla-

[3] These rules are given in full on pp. 199–201, *The Bible in Its Ancient and English Versions*, edited by H. Wheeler Robinson, Clarendon Press, Oxford, 1940.

tions remain. That the older versions, chiefly that of Tyndale,[4] contributed untold gifts is certainly true; and it is to Tyndale's work that we shall forever owe the simplicity, the vigour, and the economy of words that have become so familiar to us. Yet, although we rightly look upon the King James Bible as an evolution rather than a creation in its own right, granting to the earlier versions honour where honour is due, much of the miracle of creation endures.

In his fine essay, already alluded to in these pages, John Livingston Lowes has attempted to account for this perfection of literary expression, this "winnowing of words" until the perfect one is captured, this felicitous fall of phrase, this deep and ringing organ music.

And after these things I heard a great voice of much people in heaven, saying Alleluia; Salvation and glory, and honour, and power, unto the Lord our God . . . And I heard as it were the voice of a great multitude, and as the voice of many waters, and as the voice of mighty thunderings, saying, Alleluia; for the Lord God omnipotent reigneth.

He cites the fact, too little thought upon, that the salient characteristics of Hebrew and Greek diction, simplicity, clarity, and directness, have their counterparts to an unrivalled degree in our native English speech, and that for this very reason the ancient tongues became supremely translatable into our own. He reminds us, too, that our language at the period of the King James translation was in a fresh and a flexible stage, that the time was one of incomparable eagerness for life itself, and that, with the new quickening of every phase of human existence, a fresh understanding of the resources and possibilities of language gave a kind of adventurous zest to its use. And lastly he suggests that as the writers of the Old Testament wrote for the most part in a time of suffering and stress, of uncertainty and bewilderment,

[4] In spite of the fact that, according to the first of the Rules for the translators, the Bishops' Bible was to be used as the basis for their work, it actually had the least influence of all the earlier versions.

which marked the greatest of their literature with the rhythmic accents of emotion, of faith and hope, of mystery and heartbreak, so something of the spiritual stress and suffering of the sixteenth century, out of which the King James Bible grew, remained in the minds and the memories of the translators and was preserved in the cadences of English clause and phrase.

However inconclusively the perfection of the King James translation can be explained, the translation itself remains, again in Mr. Lowes' words, "the noblest monument of English prose" and the greatest single contribution of any century to our literature. And because without some measure of comparison its worth both as a translation and as a work of literature cannot easily be discerned, I am quoting here two familiar passages as they were rendered in certain of the earlier English Bibles and as they reached their final beauty and triumph in the King James. The first is from the 4th verse of the 2nd chapter of Isaiah; the second is the 7th verse from perhaps the most beautiful chapter in the entire Bible, Job 38.

I

COVERDALE:

So that they shall break their swords and spears to make scythes, sickles, and saws thereof. From that time forth shall not one people lift up weapon against another, neither shall they learn to fight from thenceforth.

GENEVA:

They shall break their swords also into mattocks, and their spears into scythes; nation shall not lift up a sword against nation, neither shall they learn to fight any more.

BISHOPS:

They shall break their swords into mattocks, and their spears to make scythes: And one people shall not lift up a weapon against another, neither shall they learn to fight from thenceforth.

KING JAMES:

They shall beat their swords into plowshares, and their spears into pruning hooks; nation shall not lift up sword against nation, neither shall they learn war any more.

II

COVERDALE:

When the morning stars gave me praise, and when all the angels of God rejoiced.

GENEVA:

When the stars of the morning praised me together, and all the children of God rejoiced.

BISHOPS:

When the morning stars praised me together, and all the children of God rejoiced triumphantly.

KING JAMES:

When the morning stars sang together, and all the sons of God shouted for joy.[5]

[5] Other interesting comparisons of the translation of famous and familiar passages in the various versions can be found in Chap. VII of *The Bible in Its Ancient and English Versions*, edited by H. Wheeler Robinson, and in the Appendix of Charles C. Butterworth's invaluable book, *The Literary Lineage of the King James Bible*, University of Pennsylvania Press, 1941.

I have changed the original spelling in these passages for the sake of clearness.

3

The Hebrew People: A Short Sketch of Their History in So-Called Biblical Times

It is, of course, impossible to understand the literature of any people without first knowing something at least of the background of that people and of those racial traits and characteristics which have made their literature distinctive and peculiar to themselves. I shall, therefore, attempt in the following pages to give a brief account of the history of the Hebrew people within those years covered by the biblical narrative, and to correlate the principal events of that history with those books of the Old Testament which record those events or which were written during certain historical periods. For purposes of clearness and convenience I am dividing this history as follows:

1. From unknown times to about 1200 B.C.
2. From the Exodus to the time of the Kingdom (about 1200 B.C. to about 1030 B.C.)
3. The One Kingdom and the Two (about 1030 B.C. to 586 B.C.)
4. The Captivity in Babylon. 586–536 B.C.
5. The Return to Jerusalem and the Years Following. 536–320 B.C.
6. Judea as a Province in Subjection. 320–63 B.C.

CANAAN

Scale of Miles

0 5 10   20   30

ZIDON

ZAREPHATH

Mt. Hermon

TYRE   DAN

Waters of Merom

RAMAH

Mt. Tabor

ENDOR

Mt. Carmel

Kishon R.

Valley of Jezreel

Mt. Gilboa

Sea of Galilee

Jordan River

GILEAD

SAMARIA

GILGAL

Jabbok R.

TIMNATH

Mt. Lebanon

SHILOH

JOPPA

BETHEL

EKRON

JERICHO

GIBEAH

ASHOD

JEBUS

GATH

ASKELON   HEBRON

ZIPH

GAZA

Dead Sea

BEERSHEBA

G R E A T   S E A
(MEDITERRANEAN)

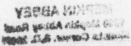

1

THE EARLIEST PERIOD OF HEBREW HISTORY

(From unknown times to about 1200 B.C.)

The Hebrews belong racially to that large group of ancient peoples known as Semites, a name which legend assigns to the descendants of Shem, the eldest son of Noah. Many nations besides the Hebrews made up the Semites, the Arabians, the Assyrians, the Phoenicians, and several lesser tribes and peoples. A comparison, given by various scholars, between the Semitic peoples as they existed in ancient times and the various tribes of American Indians is a helpful parallel; in other words, there was one great Semitic race divided into various nations and tribes, of which the Hebrews formed a relatively small group.

We first hear of the Hebrews through the pages of the book of Genesis. There we read of Abraham, the "patriarch" of the Hebrew race, of his son Isaac, and of his grandson Jacob, whose twelve sons formed the so-called Twelve Tribes of Israel. When, or if, these persons actually lived, we do not know, but together their story forms one of the greatest epics or sagas of any literature.

At some remote time they or others like them wandered with their flocks and herds over the Arabian deserts, probably their original home, until they at last drifted into the land of Canaan, which we know now as Palestine, although they knew it by no such name.[1] There, between the sea on the west and the desert wastes on the east, in a strip of land about the size of our state of Vermont, they continued their life as a nomadic people, living in tents, tending their sheep, goats, and camels, wandering by families or tribes as necessity or good sense demanded, always looking for wells of water which could supply irrigation for their crops of grain and comfort for their families and their flocks.

[1] The name *Palestine* is another form of the word *Philistine*.

31

The stories of them, written many centuries later by unknown authors, reveal them to us as a people tenacious of family and tribal loyalties and of the rights and responsibilities of the individual, quick-witted and versatile, possessed of a vivid and concrete imagination, and, above all else, worshipers of one God instead of many.

The world was already old when certain of their tribes wandered into Palestine. Great kingdoms like those of Egypt and Babylonia had already flourished in the valleys of the Nile and of the Tigris and Euphrates. The land of Palestine itself had known both Babylonian and Egyptian conquest and subjugation; but at the time of the earliest Hebrew immigrations these great ancient empires were less powerful than some centuries earlier. Nor must we imagine that the earliest Hebrew tribes wandered at will over the hills and valleys, appropriating whatever spots they chose for their flocks and herds. This land of Canaan had been occupied for many centuries by a motley people known from its name as Canaanites, who were probably a mixture of many groups and tribes, and between whom and the Hebrews we read of battles and wars. Apparently the Hebrew nomads had their problems in their new home. In the book of Genesis we are told that the "Philistines" had a revengeful and extremely uncomfortable trick of filling in the wells with earth to the dismay of Isaac. We read also that two Hittite girls, named Judith and Bashemath, whom Esau, Jacob's brother, unwisely married, became such a "grief of mind" to his distracted parents that his mother, Rebekah, claimed she was weary of her life because of them.

This earliest history of the Hebrews, their first entrance into Canaan, or Palestine, is, in fact, lost in mystery and in legend. Their actual history begins some fifteen centuries before our Christian era when a group of them left its home there, perhaps because of famine, as the old stories say, and went with their flocks and families into the pasture lands of Egypt, "the land of Goshen," to settle, still as shepherds and goatherds, within the territory of the Pharaohs. Probably at most there were but a few thousand persons among them, and they apparently continued in Egypt the life they had lived in Palestine, preserving their language, their patriarchal institutions, their strong sense of tribal or of national unity, and their religion.

But in course of time, perhaps some two hundred years after their arrival, perhaps more or less, these foreign guests and sojourners in the land of Goshen fell into trouble with their overlords, the Pharaohs. For the first time, in a life already long, they began to experience that "anti-Semitism" which was to mark the future centuries of their tragic yet triumphant existence. The book of Exodus tells us in its first chapter that a new king arose over Egypt "which knew not Joseph," and that this new king, fearing lest they multiply and join with the enemies of Egypt, "set over them taskmasters." This account is accepted as a fact by most historians since inscriptions found on ancient Egyptian monuments bear out the Exodus story. The labour which was exacted of them "in mortar and in brick" was probably in the construction of new public works in an ambitious building program of the Pharaoh, a labour insulting to their sense of freedom and destined to destroy those distinctive traits of themselves as a people, traits which apparently from the beginning had been dear to them. How long they were forced to submit to the Egyptian king we do not know; but at last a deliverer arose to free them from tyranny and to lead them out of the land of their subjection. This deliverer was Moses, their first great national leader and hero, in the story of whom, intermixed though it is with legend, their actual history as a people begins.

2

FROM THE EXODUS TO THE TIME OF THE KINGDOM

From what we know of Moses he must have been a man of great genius both as a leader and as a teacher of his people.

Somewhere about the year 1200 B.C. he stirred them up to revolt against their cruel state in Egypt, teaching them to look upon their struggle for independence as a positive article of their religious faith and inspiring them with the belief both that their God was the God of Israel and that Israel was the people of their God; in other words, his first and greatest gift to his people was to fill them with a burning sense of national unity, religious in its character.

Circumstances favoured Moses and this sense of national and religious unity which, through the force of his own personality and faith, he had been able to give his people. Seizing upon a time when Egypt was scourged by a terrible plague, he banded the Hebrews together and led them forth one night from Goshen toward that country already memorable to them as the home of their ancestors and their kindred. When they halted for rest on the shore of the shallow northern arm of the Red Sea and saw to their consternation the hosts of Pharaoh pursuing and overtaking them, an accident of nature further intensified their faith. A high wind suddenly arising left the shallow sea so low that they were able to cross it, then, suddenly changing, rolled back the waters in time to overwhelm and annihilate the chariots and horsemen of Pharaoh. This incident, never forgotten throughout the history and the literature of Israel, came to be regarded as the care of God for His people, and perhaps more than any other one event in Hebrew history bound the nation together in fervid unity and faith, a unity and a faith which Moses maintained and cherished throughout his long life as leader of his people.

The emigrants settled at a place called Kadesh on the southern borders of Palestine where there was a well, and there they remained for many years, still a pastoral people, still ranging with their flocks over the adjacent country, but keeping Kadesh as the sanctuary of their religion and as the center of their life as a people. Perhaps from the outset they thought of the conquest of Palestine; but although scattered within it were other tribes

34

of their own race and kindred, there were hostile and more powerful Canaanitish people, living in well-fortified towns with a well-established civilization of their own. The years at Kadesh strengthened their sense of national unity and religious faith; and the life that they lived there under the leadership of Moses may be considered as a period of valuable and creative growth, a period in which they formulated, under Moses, the laws under which they were governed in the interest of the whole community, and in which they steadily grew in their faith, not alone in the God of Israel but in the God of law and justice.

The many vivid stories in the book of Exodus, mingled though they undoubtedly are with legend, tradition, and folklore, tell us a great deal concerning their life in the wilderness of Kadesh. There, in the early, most difficult days of their sojourn, they were fed by the great flocks of quail common to the country and by the so-called manna from heaven. This manna, modern historians tell us, may well have been the sugary sap of the tamarisk tree, which, dripping to the earth in the heat of the day, solidifies at night, and which even today the Arabs use, under their name of *mun*, as a relish for their bread. The well at Kadesh was the shrine of their religion; and there they kept the Ark of the Covenant, the chest, or coffer, built of acacia wood and overlaid with gold, which was the symbol of the dwelling-place of their God and which was housed within the blue, scarlet, and purple curtains of the tabernacle, or tent, constructed for its safety. There, under Moses, who was inspired by mighty and awful revelations of the commands of God, the early priesthoods were established with their rites and ceremonies. There the children of Israel, like all human beings everywhere, had their doubts and their lapses, their returns to idolatry, and their seasons of repentance and faith. There, from the hillsides about Kadesh where they wandered with their flocks, they could look across stretches of country, some of which were occupied by former kinsmen of theirs, such as the Ammonites and the

Moabites, others of which were held tenaciously by the Canaan-itish tribes.

We are told by an interesting story in the 18th chapter of Exodus that Moses one day received good advice from his father-in-law Jethro, who feared lest Moses should not be able to bear alone the heavy responsibilities placed upon his shoulders and should "wear away" because of the strain upon him. Jethro therefore advised his son-in-law to select "able men, men of truth" who should act as judges of the people. Whether or not the story is true in its details, judges were chosen, men such as Joshua, and later on Gideon and Jephthah, who, upon Moses' death, acted as leaders of Israel.

The conquest of Canaan, once the settlers at Kadesh determined to set forth into the "Promised Land," was slow, beset by difficulties and even by defeat of certain of the Hebrew tribes. It became a matter of many generations before that conquest was complete. But it was carried on from the beginning with tenacious fury and always with the flaming faith that Israel's God had promised victory and triumph. For, however often the Hebrews forgot their God in times of peace, in times of war He alone became their standard as they bore the Ark in which He dwelt before them into battle. The very name *Israel*, which God had given to Jacob and therefore to themselves, means "God does battle"; and it was in these graver moments of their history, when victory or defeat hung in the balance, that the children of Israel rose to fullest stature in their consciousness of themselves as a nation and of God as their God. He was a god of storms and thunderings, to be sure, a god of revenge and of anger against apostasy and sin; but above all else He was a god of righteous war, battling for His people and, like them, relentlessly hating their enemies. With His leadership and before His fury the Canaanites were slowly pushed from their strongholds. Joshua took the city of Jericho, marching upon the city with priests blowing upon trumpets of rams' horns as they moved before the sacred Ark; Gideon conquered the Midianites; and the decisive defeat of Sisera, who headed a league of the now terrified Canaanites, was accomplished by the waters of the ancient river Kishon through the intrepid Deborah with Barak as her leader of the Hebrew tribes. From that day of Sisera's defeat, extolled by Deborah in her famous ode, when "the stars in their courses" fought with the children of Israel, the strength of the Canaanites was broken.

It is helpful, indeed necessary, in visualizing this conquest of Palestine by the Hebrew tribes to keep several facts clearly in mind. In the first place, in spite of the careful researches of numberless scholars, little is known about actual dates. The conquest must have taken many years, perhaps even two centuries or more, for even the date of the Exodus has never been perfectly established. Nor must we think of the Hebrew invaders as one great people. They were divided into small tribes and families; and in the days of the gradual conquest of Canaan they were few in actual numbers. Probably not more than a few thousand men, women, and children lived at Kadesh. Nor did they probably move as one people against the inhabitants of Palestine. It is far more likely that they accomplished their conquest by attacks of certain families and tribes, now here, now there, against certain small districts and towns. We must remember, too, that they were poorly armed with outmoded weapons, and that in military organization and equipment, to say nothing of numbers, they were in every way inferior to the Canaanites. The two advantages which they possessed were, first, a strong sense of unity in spite of tribal divisions, which unity the Canaanites lacked, and, second, always their knowledge, fostered by Moses and the leaders after him, that God was on their side.

This ancient conquest of Canaan becomes more clear to us if we keep in mind also the size of the country involved. It was very small. North to south, "from Dan to Beersheba," to quote the expression so often used in the Bible, was not more than one hundred and fifty miles. In the tapering north country its breadth from river to sea was only twenty-five miles, and in the wider south but eighty at most. It possessed in all not more than one-sixth the area of England or, as has already been said, somewhat less than the square miles of our own state of Vermont. Had it not been for ranges of hills and mountains which shut off the view, the Hebrews, inspired by their dreams of conquest around the camp-fires of Kadesh, might on a clear day from the summit of a high hill have seen almost their entire Promised Land in prospect.

As the country was small, so were its towns and strongholds, both in area and in population. A sizable Canaanitish town would cover less than six or eight acres of land and in population number probably not more than fifteen hundred people. Even Jerusalem, which remained in the possession of a Canaanitish tribe called the Jebusites until its conquest by David about 1000 B.C., was not more than fifteen acres at most within its wall.

Yet to the still half-nomadic Hebrews in the wilderness of Kadesh, on fire with their great design, it must have seemed at once a strange and a desirable land, one indeed "flowing with milk and honey." From the spies, which they without doubt sent forth in all directions, came tales of the rich grain fields of its northern valleys, of the vineyards on its terraced hillsides, of the oranges of its western coastal plains, of its high pastures watered by the rains of which they knew so little, of the incredibly diversified character of its land, now desert, now green with grass, and of the snows on its highest mountains. They must have wondered, not without fear of change, concerning the life within the terrifying walls of its towns, its stone houses in place of tents, its skilled use of metals, the tunnels which carried water to its cities, the caravans from Egypt and Mesopotamia which moved along its roads.

Those changes, which especially the old among them must have feared, came to pass once they had conquered the Canaanites and moved into their towns and villages. They were no longer a nomadic or even strictly a pastoral people. They became cultivators of corn and grapes, of olives and figs, those necessities of life of which their writers constantly speak. As one might expect from their dominant racial characteristics, they gradually absorbed not only the Canaanitish civilization but the Canaanites themselves, whom we see gradually fading out as a people; and, as one might also expect, their devotion to Jehovah as their one God suffered change as well. For the Canaanite god was Baal, the giver of corn, wine, and oil; and it was natural enough that, in order to be sure and certain of these good things of life, the Hebrews, especially in the early days of their settlement, should appropriate Baal worship, never indeed to the destruction of their own religion but sometimes to the weakening of it in the national consciousness. Nevertheless, beneath the ashes of occasional apostasy, the embers of their faith still glowed, to be fanned again into flame whenever dangers from without threatened their unity as a people and those ideals of the responsibility resting upon each individual for the good of his nation.

3

THE ONE KINGDOM AND THE TWO

The change from a relatively loose tribal organization held together by judges, or leaders, came to an end about the year 1030 B.C. with the formation of the kingdom. This revolution in Israel's form of government was made seemingly wise, if not absolutely necessary, by a new danger which threatened the tribes and demanded a closer national unity. This new danger came from the Philistines, that people which occupies so great a space and which plays so great a part in the dramatic narratives in the books of Judges and of I and II Samuel.

These Philistines were sea peoples who had settled on the southwestern coastal plain of Palestine. Originally they came from the coast of Asia Minor and the Aegean islands. They were at first concentrated in five cities near or on the Mediterranean, Gath, Gaza, Askelon, Ekron, and Ashdod, each with its own ruler. They were an energetic people, boasting a culture and a military art far superior to those of the Israelites; and it was not long before they began to press upward from their seacoast home into the hills where immediately they began to clash with the Israelitish tribes. They possessed giants like the probably legendary Goliath of Gath; they had chariots and horsemen, modern weapons and smiths to forge them, and a military precision and organization with which the Israelites could not compete. Overwhelmingly victorious in their first forays into the hill country, they destroyed the sanctuaries and temples of the Israelites and, as a crowning insult, carried off as a trophy the Ark of Jehovah.

This tragedy had the immediate effect of firing the tribes with widespread religious revival and with an almost fanatical determination to resist these enemies of Israel and of its God at any cost. Religion and patriotism joined hands, became identical. In their distress the people called upon an old man named Samuel, who lived in the village of Ramah some five miles north of Jerusalem and who was widely known both as a priest and as a wise man, or "seer." Perhaps from his knowledge of the government of neighbouring peoples, he recognized the advantages to be gained by the consolidation of loosely held tribes and families into a kingdom. At all events, relying upon his God-given talent as a seer or prophet, he chose a man named Saul, the son of Kish, of the village of Gibeah and anointed him as the first king over Israel.

In succeeding pages we shall deal more fully with the story of Saul as one of the great and ironic tragedies of all literature. Here we have to do with him only as the first king of his people. He was not a young man when he ascended the new and insecure throne of Israel, for we know that he already had a son capable of bearing arms. He was apparently a man of great physical stature, for we are told that "there was not among the children of Israel a goodlier person than he: from his shoulders and upwards he was higher than any of the people." He was also a man of prodigal enthusiasm, and he entered upon his one

40

great task of conquering the Philistines with heroism and daring. Before long, however, his impetuous nature was kindled with anger and jealousy against a young man named David, the son of Jesse, a farmer and herdsman in the village of Bethlehem. David seems to have come into the life of King Saul because of his accomplishments in music in which the king delighted and which served to arouse him from periods of depression and melancholy. An able soldier, David became in his early years of association with the king his armour bearer, the most intimate friend of his son Jonathan, and finally the husband of Saul's daughter Michal. But for at least ten of the some twenty years of Saul's reign, the king's hatred and suspicion of his son-in-law knew no bounds; and the bitter story of his kingship is marked by enmity against the growing popularity of David as a national figure, with inglorious and even treacherous schemes for David's death, and with finally his own suicide on Mt. Gilboa after a disastrous defeat at the hands of the Philistines.

David, by nature a diplomat as well as an artist and a romanticist, was quick to seize upon the advantage offered him. With the sanction of the Philistines, and perhaps even as their vassal, he set up for himself a small principality, which had as its center the town of Hebron some ten miles south of Jerusalem, and held it against the captain of Saul's army, Abner, and against the king's weak son who succeeded him. In the feud which followed between the houses of David and Saul the house of David became increasingly popular, and at least by the year 1000 B.C. David at about the age of thirty-seven was king of Israel.

In spite of human weaknesses which are almost inevitably a part of a personality so rich and vivid as was David's, he was a great king over his people, and his importance in Hebrew history is immeasurable. His first act seems to have been to seize the neighbouring town of Jerusalem, or Jebus as it was called after the Canaanitish tribe which held it, and to make it his capital. Thus into the history of the Israelitish people came that city which to future ages was to mean more in religious and even mystical significance than merely the political center and the court of their first great king. It was to Jerusalem that David with great pomp and ceremony brought the Ark of the Covenant to place it within his new citadel on that hill which was later to become the site of the first Temple.

Alarmed by the union of the Israelitish nation under David, the Philistines, with whom he had played an undeniably clever game, tried too late to subdue him. The new king quickly disposed of their power and reduced them, in their turn, to vassalage. He proceeded then to bring under his dominion the remaining recalcitrant Semitic tribes, the Moabites, the Ammonites, and others who had little to offer against the concentrated strength of his armies. Within a few years he had built up a miniature empire centered in the so-called "City of David," an empire which extended from the river Euphrates in the north to the wilderness in the south, where two centuries before those few thousands of his people had lived in their tents at Kadesh, and which, small as it may seem to us today, marked a triumph for its time.

From the tribute money paid into his treasury by the subdued peoples of Palestine, David became wealthy in a manner that Israel had never before known. His court and his harem became a by-word for luxury and splendour. Through the several gates of his new city caravans and pack-trains brought tribute money and material. He made a friend of Hiram, king of Tyre in the neighbouring province of Phoenicia, whose superior artisans he procured for the building of his house and for improving the fortifications of his new city of Jerusalem. It is very probable that this new wealth was already laying the foundations of those social and religious conditions which two centuries later were to give such grave concern to the first great prophets of Israel.

Perhaps, however, the worst sufferers from the king's newly acquired wealth were his several sons. Surely, if we can depend upon the story of their excesses and intrigues as recorded in the

42

book of II Samuel, they do not seem either to have inherited from their father his unquestionable virtues or to have managed to hold any of their own against his woeful indulgence and the lack of discipline within his household. The last years of his reign were made miserable and disillusioning by their behaviour —by the murder of Amnon by Absalom, by Absalom's revolt, and by Adonijah's treachery. And within Solomon, who succeeded him, he had surely managed to place that love of magnificence and display which was to portend dark days for the generations to follow.

No one can read carefully those vivid chapters of II Samuel which portray the reign of David without being made aware of his shortcomings both as a man and as a sovereign. And yet we must remember that he was, in point of fact, an ancient king in a primitive and a barbarous age. If he was capable of treachery toward the Philistine king of Gath, whom he unquestionably used for his own purposes, we must remember that treachery in 1000 B.C. was hardly looked upon as it is today. If he lied in certain situations, as he apparently did, we must not forget that lying in his day betokened cleverness and sometimes even triumph rather than wrongdoing. If he was harsh toward his wife Michal and cruel toward his captives, we must remember that harshness and cruelty in his age were too often interpreted as simple acts of justice and desert. He was, according to the standards of his time, a great king, more generous than most men, courageous and daring at any cost, ambitious for his people as well as for himself, capable of gaining and retaining the devotion of his rough soldiers, willing and ready to admit guilt and sin, and from first to last passionately devoted to the God of Israel.

As Moses had instilled the early tribes in Goshen and at Kadesh with a sense of their identity as a people and strengthened their common faith in the God of Israel, so David was in a very real sense the founder of the Hebrew nation and kingdom. Not until his day did the name of this people bear the slightest prestige in the world of its time. He raised it from insignificance to at least a relative glory, gave it a court, a government, and a capital at Jerusalem, and actually made of it the leading state between the ancient empires of Egypt and Assyria. Small wonder that he became the ideal king within whose royal house was born the tradition and the dream of the coming of a Messiah.

We do not know King Solomon as we know his father. The account of him in the first chapters of I Kings gives us no picture of an intensely human person as was David throughout his long life. His biographer in these chapters was apparently vastly more impressed by kingship as an institution than by the king as a man. Because of this, Solomon is presented as a magnificent figure, loving luxury, trafficking in powerful horses and chariots, drinking from vessels of gold, sending navies to far-off Tarshish for "ivory and apes and peacocks," building costly houses for his various foreign wives and altars for their strange gods, visited by amazed foreign rulers like the "Queen of Sheba," and presiding over the most gorgeous and extravagant of courts.

It is difficult in so naive an account of such splendour to discover the truth about Solomon and his reign. The wisdom which he is said to have possessed sounds a somewhat false and hollow note in the story of his forty years as king of Israel. Without doubt many legends grew up around him; and although he is said to have impressed "all the earth" with his wisdom and his riches, to have written proverbs and songs by the thousands, and to have known the ways of trees, beasts, fowls, and fishes, the story of his rule is in many ways an inglorious one. His seven hundred wives are obviously grossly exaggerated in number, but in character they did not redound to his glory, for they were foreign princesses from Egypt and elsewhere, and they apparently demanded not only temples for their gods but freedom to worship whomsoever or whatsoever they pleased.

The search for truth among the astounding biblical reports of Solomon's reign and among those things which later and sounder historians have had to say about him reveals, however, certain safe conclusions. That he was no soldier or military leader is evident in the fact that he allowed a new Syrian kingdom to rise on his northern boundary and to threaten Israel. That the passion of his life lay in building is shown not only by the biblical records but by relatively recent excavations of the archaeologists, who have also discovered that his commercial activities were large and flourishing. Nor do we need the story of the taxes and tributes which he exacted both in toil and in money to be convinced that a passion for building must needs require both capital and labour.

The conclusion, then, that the reign of Israel's third king was one largely of personal ambition is without doubt true. As a young king he may have prayed for an "understanding heart"; but he surely was not displeased at the promise of God that he should also have riches and honour. He may have desired wisdom above all things; but he surely was anything but wise in not foreseeing the misery and discontent which his heavy taxation was to bring upon his people. The supreme moment of his life may well have been when the great Temple to Jehovah with its pillars and its porches, its ornate carvings and its vessels of gold was dedicated and the sacred Ark of the Covenant at last installed under the spreading wings of the cherubim; but in order to pay for the seven years of its construction he had to go so heavily into debt that he paid his chief creditor, Hiram, king of Tyre, by turning over to him twenty cities with their people. Foreign alliances and the importation of foreign cults may have strengthened the lot of Israel for the time being in the eyes of neighbouring peoples; but they unfortunately tended to weaken the chief thing which Israel had to give to the world, her faith in her national God.

Remarkable as Solomon doubtless was as an organizer of vast projects and as an administrator in carrying them out, the projects themselves with their emphasis on wealth and splendour were injurious for the social and moral future of his people. His country was too small in actual space to support with its resources the weight of such a program. Moreover, the emphasis upon such wealth was bad in its effects upon the minds of men and women. Solomon may well have amazed and delighted the more prosperous among his subjects, but he did not benefit them; and the poor among them became steadily poorer and more discontented with their lot. When he died in 936 B.C. he might, like a future king, well have said, had he possessed the wisdom attributed to him, "After me, the deluge."

The deluge was not slow in coming. Rehoboam, the son of Solomon, was a young man of apparently little strength and less vision. Instead of taking measures to quiet the discontent aroused by the extravagant program of his father and lightening the "heavy yoke" of which his people complained, he peremptorily refused any leniency whatsoever. The biblical story quotes him as saying arrogantly to his subjects: "My father chastised you with whips, but I will chastise you with scorpions." Such an utterance, or one like it, did not go unrecompensed. A certain man named Jeroboam, who had apparently earlier opposed Solomon as an oppressor of his subjects, won the confidence of the people in the north of Israel and led a revolt against the king. This revolt resulted in a new state over which Jeroboam by popular choice was made king. From this time on the one Israelitish kingdom was divided into two: Israel in the north and Judah in the south.

To follow the complicated histories of these two kingdoms would occupy far too much space in a brief historical sketch such as this. For two centuries each continued under its own rulers, some good, some bad, of whom the books of the Kings and also of the Chronicles give us record. The northern kingdom, that of Israel, found a powerful and dangerous rival in the neighbouring kingdom of Syria. Moreover, because of the character of the country and its nearer location to the growing empire of Assyria, it was in a more perilous position for its continued existence than was the southern kingdom of Judah. Also it is doubtless true that the people of the north were more of a mixed race than were those of the south. The traditions and the religious rites of foreign peoples were, therefore, more of an imminent danger to them, as we realize when we read the terrible yet stirring story of their queen Jezebel, the wife of King Ahab, with her fanatical devotion to her Sidonian god Melkart and her slaying of the prophets of Jehovah. It was in these tumultuous days that Elijah, the Tishbite, arose with his successor, Elisha, the great "speaking prophets" of Israel, who sealed the doom of the wicked queen and who together give to us some of the most fascinating narratives of the Old Testament.

These "speaking prophets" were followed about a century later by the first of the "writing prophets," Amos, who about 750 B.C. burst upon the northern sanctuary of Jehovah at the village of Bethel with things of grave and even grim importance to say to the people gathered there for festival and feasting. Amos was a man of the south, a Judean, who kept his sheep and tended his sycamore trees alone in the wilderness of Tekoa, bordering on the Dead Sea. He, like those who were to follow him, Hosea, Micah, the Great Isaiah, and Jeremiah, were not only gravely concerned over the condition of Israel and Judah in terms of social and religious behaviour and over the dangers that threatened them from the powerful empires to the north and east, but they also, from their lives of thought and prayer, had discovered a new conception of the world, of God, and of man's relation to Him. What these men meant to the intellectual and religious development of their people will be the subject of later chapters of this book. They are mentioned now only as forming an inseparable part in the turbulent histories of the two kingdoms.

Israel met its fate almost two centuries before Judah. In the year 722 B.C. Assyria swept upon it and put an end to its existence as an Israelitish nation. The Assyrian conqueror Sargon deported many thousands of his new subjects, particularly those of the wealthy or aristocratic classes, who, he thought, might conceivably make trouble for him in his new domain. These, in accordance with the Assyrian policy of conquest, he scattered about in various parts of his empire and filled their places in Israel with foreign colonists. Unlike the people of the southern kingdom of Judah, who one hundred and fifty years later were to meet a like fate, these exiles seem to have been so quickly absorbed into the life of other races, so entirely submerged, that they lost their identity as Israelites and left not a trace behind them.

Judah, safer from foreign foes than Israel and possessing in the house of David a far more stable dynasty, continued its existence as an Israelitish kingdom through varying fortunes until 586 B.C. Certain of its kings, such as Hezekiah and Josiah, stronger men than those of Israel, gave their best to the service of their country, strengthening its religious life, cleansing the Temple of idolatry and promoting its rites and worship, and instituting necessary social and economic reforms. Certain others, such as Manasseh, were hostile to all reforms and by a policy of reaction, political intrigue, and bloodshed hastened the impending doom of their country. Through these turbulent years the great prophets of Judah, first Isaiah and then Jeremiah, played the parts, not only of prophets and poets, but of statesmen. It was they who were actually the powers behind the tottering throne of Judah, already, since the downfall of the northern kingdom, a tribute nation to Assyria. It was they who saw the darkness of the future, they who in their long lives as servants to their people advised succeeding kings in their policies toward the great encroaching powers, threatening to cancel the life of Judah as that of Israel had been cancelled. Their history is the history of their desperate labours to save their country; and, although each failed in the end, their names remain, not alone as those of exalted and God-intoxicated men, but as men of affairs and as political figures of their bitter day.

The great empire of Assyria gave way at last before the rising power of Babylonia. Her capital city of Nineveh fell in 612 B.C., an event prophesied in one of the greatest war poems of any literature, a poem preserved in the book of the prophet Nahum. By 597 B.C. Judah's downfall was assured at the hands of Nebuchadnezzar, king of Babylon, who laid siege to Jerusalem and compelled it to yield. In that year, sometimes called the year of the First Captivity, the more important of the citizens of Jerusalem were carried away into exile. Eleven years later in 586 B.C. the siege was followed by utter destruction and ruin. Many more Jews were now carried into captivity; and the existence of the kingdom of Judah, once so powerful as the corner-stone and center of David's empire, was at an end.

4

THE CAPTIVITY IN BABYLON. 586–536 B.C.

As land to cultivate and a place in which to live, Babylonia surely offered more advantages than Palestine. Instead of in a mountainous country where only incessant labour could bring forth crops of grain and grapes and olives, the exiled Jews found themselves in a rich plain watered by great rivers and cut by numberless tree-shaded canals. They found themselves also in the midst of a vast commercial civilization of which they as a people had known relatively little and surrounded by wealth of which they had never dreamed. Jerusalem in memory must have seemed small and provincial indeed when compared with the unbelievably great and magnificent city of Babylon with its miles of towered walls, its palaces, and its famous hanging gardens, or even with the ancient city of Nippur, near which they were settled, with its famous library and its stately temple.

Apparently their lot was in many ways by no means unendurable. They were generously not scattered far and wide, but allowed to remain together in families and tribes and to preserve their own clan organizations. Nor were they denied the essential practices of their ancestral religion or made to sacrifice their native Hebrew tongue. Moreover, from the beginning they were allowed free economic and social development in

49

their own localities, a concession upon which they were quick to seize as we know from at least one record of a thriving banking firm in Nippur, dated some years after their arrival there, in which several of them held most responsible positions. It was probably from their life in Babylon that they discovered and developed within themselves those dominant commercial abilities for which they were later to become distinguished throughout the world.

And yet in spite of financial prosperity and relative freedom to live as they pleased, the Jews in Babylonia were by no means happy. It is true without doubt that some among them were weaned away from Jehovah and the memory of the mountains about Jerusalem to marry Babylonian women and to exchange fast-fading thoughts of home for the material blessings of a new and rich land. But more still clung to the glory of Lebanon, the excellency of Carmel and of Sharon. Not all of them, perhaps, shared the desperate grief of the unknown writer of Lamentations, who cried out bitterly over the solitude of Jerusalem once so "full of people," over "all her pleasant things which she had in the days of old." The later poet of the 137th Psalm, who was to describe their homesickness as they wept by the rivers of Babylon and their anger against their captors ironically demanding of them songs of Zion, was perhaps in his beautiful lines a poet before he was an historian. Yet it is unquestionably true that many among the exiles longed for home, waited for the morning of their deliverance, were oppressed and troubled over many things: the humiliation of Jehovah, apparently helpless before the deities of Babylon, His apparent forgetfulness of His people, the threatened annihilation of Israel as a nation, the condition of their relatives and friends left in Jerusalem, the consciousness of their own sins, for which they believed, however, that they had received double in punishment.

During their fifty years in Babylon they seemingly did not want for prophets and poets, many of whom are now lost to us.

We can safely assume, not only from the situation in general but from references in the book of Jeremiah, that certain self-appointed prophets kept stirring up hopes of return and that at least some among them were seized by the Babylonian police and burned to death as promoters of unrest among the exiled subjects of Nebuchadnezzar. Two names stand out brilliantly against this dark half century of subjection and mental suffering: one that of Ezekiel and the other that of a young man who, because his actual name has been lost and because his poems and prophecies were included in the manuscript of the book of Isaiah, is known to us as Deutero- or Second Isaiah.

Ezekiel, whose rather long-winded and repetitious book lacks much of interest and meaning for us today, was apparently a sort of pastor to the exiled Jewish community in Babylon. He had, in fact, gone there among the exiles of the First Captivity in 597 B.C. From his many trances, ecstasies, and visions, his denunciation of sin and his sense of doom, his intolerance toward non-Israelitish people, his air of complete seriousness and his seeming lack of any humour, he is in many ways an unattractive figure, and one's imagination sees in him an uncomfortable thorn in the flesh to many of his more light-hearted parishioners. Not even the visions of the young William Blake, who as a child claimed to have seen Ezekiel, or the importance which he sustained in the studies of later ecclesiastical scholars from Jerome to Abelard can make him appealing to us. In the years between the First Captivity and the fatal siege of Jerusalem in 586 he was, however, a constant purveyor of object-lessons to the first exiles, prophesying through his visions the fall of their home city. After the fulfillment of his predictions of doom he preached the restoration of Israel in such a famous vision as that of the terrible valley of bones, in the 37th chapter of his book, where the breath of God covered the dry bones with sinews, with flesh and skin, so that they lived again, "stood up upon their feet, an exceeding great army."

Unattractive as he seems to us today (and may well have seemed to his own age), fanatic and dogmatist though he certainly was, Ezekiel, nevertheless, in his relation to the future of his people stands forth as the most powerful figure during the years of Jewish captivity in Babylonia. It was he who determined that although a nation and a people had been temporarily lost, a religion must remain. Completely dominated by a zeal for the cause of the God of Israel and entirely assured of His justice toward His chosen people, he kept alive in an alien land that faith which had made Israel. Didactic and unyielding though he was, prosaic even in the description of his heavenly visions, he was more influential in the subsequent history of the Jewish people than many a more appealing figure. For he reclaimed the Temple worship, made plans for rebuilding the destroyed sanctuaries of Jerusalem and Judea, established rites, ceremonies, and priesthoods, instituted holy days and arranged for their observance, laid emphasis alike on the holiness of God and on the duties of the pious Jew, extolled the Jewish Law as the force which must govern the community through scrupulous observance of its tenets—in a word, established within an alien empire a church and congregation devoted and bound to the idea of its survival as an ecclesiastical institution whatever might be its political fate. He has rightly been called the father of Jewish ritualism and the initial forerunner of Judaism as a religious sect.

There could hardly be a more vivid contrast between any two men than between the somewhat sour figure of Ezekiel and the young, ecstatic poet of the exile, known to us as Deutero-Isaiah. He went among the people by the rivers of Babylon with a far different message, inflaming them with faith, full of understanding of their misery and dejection, bringing them comfort and hope, stressing not the observance of the Law but the love of God, and not alone that love for one people but for all mankind. He will sing unto God a new song, a song of good tidings, of the crooked made straight and the rough places plain; he will call upon the waste places of Jerusalem to break forth into joy and to sing together because all the nations and all the ends of the earth shall see at last salvation and peace.

As a poet, Deutero-Isaiah was unexcelled among the poets of Israel; and his great contribution to Hebrew literature will be considered in a future chapter. Here we are concerned only with his presence in Babylon, probably from about the year 546 B.C. onward, and with a sudden historical event which he chronicles in his poetry and which undoubtedly gave concrete hope to his prophecies. This event was the rise of Cyrus, originally king of a small province of Media, soon through a series of wars conqueror of the Median Empire, which comprised Persia, Northern Assyria, Armenia, and part of Asia Minor. By the year 546 he had become master of practically all southwestern Asia from the Indus River to the Aegean Sea. Only Babylon stood in the way of a new and united Asiatic empire under Persian rule, and its conquest, through the weakness of Nebuchadnezzar's successors, was accomplished by Cyrus in the year 538.

Cyrus wisely adopted the policy of conciliating, by tolerance and understanding, the peoples whom he had conquered. He was generous toward customs and cultures different from his own. He recognized the various national deities worshipped within his wide empire and encouraged the continuance of national religions. His conquest in many ways marked the dawn of a better day; and after many centuries he still deserves the judgment of historians that he was "one of the most enlightened rulers the world has ever seen."

It was in Cyrus that Deutero-Isaiah saw the hope of exiled Israel, Cyrus who to him was the "shepherd," even the "anointed" of God. To the young prophet, who believed and taught that the God of Jacob was the God of the whole earth, there was no humiliation in the granting by a Persian monarch of freedom to Israel. This freedom Cyrus in the year 538 bestowed upon the exiled Jews with immediate leave to seek their fatherland once more; and in 537 B.C. the first group started on its long eight hundred mile journey to Jerusalem.

5

THE RETURN TO JERUSALEM AND THE YEARS FOLLOWING. 536–320 B.C.

There are perhaps few episodes in history at once more dramatic and more significant than this return to Jerusalem. How many exiles actually went back we do not know. It is difficult to believe that the number equalled 42,000 even with the careful figures by families enumerated in the books of Ezra and Nehemiah. There may instead, as many scholars hold, have been but a few thousands or even a few hundreds of them on this first return, others to come later and over a period of years. Many of the second and third generation must have remained in Babylon, assured of peace and prosperity under Cyrus and already, after fifty years, reluctant to exchange cultural and economic security for hardship and privation in a land known to them only by the traditions of their race and the stories of their fathers; yet to many others the almost fanatical idea of Jerusalem was enough to start them on their way.

We have no reliable source for the details of their journey across the deserts; we can only imagine it. Their leader was named Sheshbazzar, "a prince of Judah." In the long caravan, the books of Ezra and Nehemiah tell us, there were priests and singers, porters and their children, horses, mules, camels, and asses. There were doubtless halts for the observance of the Sabbath and of other holy days; there must have been frequent singing of the "songs of Zion" from the "two hundred singing men and singing women." To one looking back upon it through the centuries and realizing its significance to history, literature, and religion, it is still an impressive and extraordinary sight. For upon that march to Jerusalem went the future of the world. Upon it depended the very existence not only of the Bible as we

54

know it and of the Jewish faith, but of Christianity and the long centuries of western civilization. Had there been no return to Jerusalem, Judah would doubtless have shared at least in great measure the fate of Israel, mingled with the East and, as a united people, eventually have been lost.

Disillusionment awaited the returned exiles. Jerusalem, within and around which most of them settled, retained not even a shadow of its former glory. Its walls were razed and its buildings in ruins. Many villages and towns, devastated by the Babylonian armies, were abandoned. The Temple and the ancient shrines of their faith were desolate. Orchards and vineyards and fields had grown up to "thorns and briers." But an even worse source of disillusionment lay in the motley groups of persons, who during their absence had pressed into the once almost depopulated territory of Judah. In fifty years such peoples as the Ammonites, the Moabites, the Samaritans, and the hated Edomites, whom the prophet Obadiah so lashed in his poem of contempt and revenge, had possessed portions of the land and had intermarried with the remnant of the Jewish population left behind by Nebuchadnezzar.

The returned Jews, trained by Ezekiel in the lesson of religious isolation in Babylon and made conscious through the very circumstances of their life in an alien land of a tenacious exclusiveness, did not take kindly to the invaders of Judea. Here at home they were seemingly again strangers in a strange land. They apparently made the mistakes of returning cordiality on the part of their unwelcome neighbours with contempt and of refusing to associate with those of mixed race and mixed religion. In the writings of certain of their prophets of this unhappy period of their history, Haggai, Zechariah, and Malachi, we catch echoes of their mental distress, their anxiety over the influx of foreigners, over the prevalence of intermarriage with those not of their own race, over the smallness of their numbers.

The first years of their return were assuredly anything but happy. Drought and parasites took their crops, and the fact that they were consistently poor, even for many decades, is vouched for by the researches of the archaeologists who find no evidences until after the Greek conquest of the country two hundred years later of any material prosperity in their manner of living. They had incurred the hostility of their neighbours by their rigid exclusiveness. Their Temple lay in ruins, not to be restored for twenty years after their arrival from Babylon. They had no ruler of their own to lend dignity and hope to their existence, for, as a subject state of the Persian empire, they were ruled by a foreign governor.

Yet there were to be lights in the darkness. In the year 520 B.C. through the labours of the prophets Haggai and Zechariah the rebuilding of the Temple was begun, to be completed four years later in 516. This event to a people whose former life as a nation had fallen to a mere existence as a religious community was one of extreme importance; and the new temple became a center and a rallying-ground not only for Jewish faith but for Jewish patriotism. In the century following they were given new courage and hope as a community by the extraordinary work of two men named Ezra and Nehemiah, the first, a subject of much controversy among scholars as to his time, his work, indeed his actual identity, the second, a well-established and extremely interesting figure in Jewish history. Whether Ezra actually came from Babylon in the year 458, as many scholars assert, bringing with him a great number of his compatriots to attempt a reformation of the Judean community upon the basis of the Jewish Law, is a question which will probably never be solved; to certain other scholars he is merely a legendary figure; but that Nehemiah in the year 444 B.C. returned as governor of Jerusalem is accepted as an historical fact, and his memoirs are held to be a genuine autobiography.

Nehemiah is, indeed, one of the most vivid characters in Old Testament history. He has left behind for us in the book called by his name the story of his stay in Jerusalem, a document preserved and recorded together with other far less interesting material by the author of the Books of the Chronicles. Nehemiah was a man of vigour and of action. As cupbearer in the court of Artaxerxes, king of Persia, he heard one day from one of his Jewish brethren there of the "great affliction and reproach" of his people in Jerusalem and of the broken-down walls and burned gates of the city. He thereupon begged the king to allow him to return to Judea as the governor appointed by Persia and, his request being granted, set forth upon his mission. Whether or not he worked with Ezra (who is reputed to have been a "Scribe," or interpreter of the Law) or alone, he unquestionably brought new life and strength to the community in Jerusalem. The picture of his going forth by night to view the desolation of the city is a stirring one, as is his account of his rebuilding in fifty-two days of work "from the rising of the morning till the stars appeared" of its walls and gates. He tells us that his builders worked with their swords, spears, and bows at hand against those of the foreign population who sought to prevent the "feeble Jews" from gaining a stronghold upon the land where they had once lived and prospered.

The methods employed by Nehemiah to bring order out of chaos and to instill his people with renewed faith and courage were ruthless, not to say desperate at times. He tells us that he not only cursed and smote those Jews who had married "outlandish" women and whose children could not speak their native language, but that he pulled out their hair in fury! With his own hands he threw out-of-doors the meat offerings and tithes of corn, wine, and oil which a certain Tobiah had stored away for his own selfish use. He railed against the practice of usury and against the profanation of the Sabbath, swore to lay stout hands upon any merchant who sold his goods on holy days, uncovered hostile plots with complete disregard for his own safety, and strode about Jerusalem like a man possessed. He re-established the ordinances of religion, put in operation the Law of Moses, proclaimed assemblies and feast days, exacted the observance of rites and the collection of tithes, and above all else made his people conscious of their national religion and of its requirements. In place of an independent Jewish political state now gone, he succeeded in establishing a religious state, virtually governed by the high priest and bound by that intricate and tenacious body of laws and precepts, moral, social, and ecclesiastical, known to us as Judaism. He was rabidly intolerant of foreigners, nationalistic and despotic to the core, overbearing and tactless, and rather unpleasantly concerned over his good works being scored up to his credit both by God and by his brethren; but his shortcomings were insignificant compared with his passionate zeal for his self-appointed task and with the magnitude of his accomplishments. For he brought back to life the dying Jewish community in Palestine and assured its vitality for the future.

Nor even in these troublous days were the returned Jews entirely bereft of poetry. About the time of Nehemiah there lived, presumably in Judea if not in Jerusalem, a poet and prophet known to us as the Third Isaiah, or Trito-Isaiah. Exactly what portions of the last chapters included in the book of Isaiah were written by him is a question which has been debated by many scholars; but certain of them are so evidently reminiscent of the struggles and disillusionment of the return to Jerusalem that we are safe in assuming that these at least were composed by one inspired imagination. Trito-Isaiah was apparently an admirer of the work of Deutero-Isaiah, for, although in many ways he is a lesser poet, he has caught much of the melody and ecstasy of the former. His poetry as poetry will be considered later; but it is well to mention him now as one touched by the misery of his people, as one sent "to bind up the broken-hearted" and "to comfort all that mourn in Zion." In the beauty of his lines and the exalted imagination of his prophecies for the future of his oppressed and miserable land, he lends to his confused times the one note of romanticism in the midst of so much grim reality.

For the subsequent history of the Jewish community as a

Persian dependency we have, after the time of Nehemiah, almost no reliable information; nor does the work of Nehemiah in itself lend much knowledge of the life and events of that century which followed the Return. The intense racial and religious exclusiveness of the community and its comparative isolation from the outside world and from those lines of trade and traffic which it had known in the past and of which Trito-Isaiah had such hopes for its future made it an almost unknown factor in the great Persian Empire. That empire in its turn was doomed to decline and to final overthrow through the sudden rise of Philip of Macedon and his son Alexander who, in almost exactly two hundred years from the triumphs of Cyrus, began in 338 B.C. a series of mighty conquests. Through these conquests the seemingly insignificant province of Judea was again seized by foreign invaders. Palestine fell into the young Alexander's possession in 332, and in the year 320 one of his generals, Ptolemy I, took the city of Jerusalem, ironically enough on the day of the Jewish Sabbath. Now in place of Oriental despotism the Jews in Palestine came under the domination of western powers, to become from now on and for the space of two more centuries a minute portion of the far-flung Hellenistic world with its center at Alexandria.

6

JUDEA AS A PROVINCE IN SUBJECTION. 320–63 B.C.

The history of Palestine and particularly of the region about Jerusalem during the two and a half centuries which followed the death of Alexander in 323 B.C. is one of change and confusion. Alexander's leading generals in his conquests constituted themselves his successors and proceeded to divide his empire among themselves. Chief among these so far as Palestine was concerned were the Ptolemies of Egypt and the Seleucids of Syria with Antioch as their chief city. For over a century the Ptolemies retained the control of Palestine, ruling it on the whole with consideration, yet naturally and inevitably introducing within it the new ideas of Hellenistic culture which were making themselves dominant throughout the world of that day.

To the Jew in Palestine this Greek culture with its emphasis on the intellect of man, on his sense of beauty, his right of private judgment, with its preponderantly humanistic outlook on life, aroused suspicion. To him certain of its aspects savoured of moral degradation in spite of its passion for the beautiful. Its blindness toward his notion of the corruption of human nature, of the sense of human frailty and sin so ingrained in his religion of Judaism, made him fear and loathe it, aroused his antagonism and stimulated his instinct for the preservation of his own religion with its stern recognition of the moral law and its insistence on ceremonial observances and daily rites. He did not easily share the liberalism of many of his brethren living in the regions outside Judea, in the now Greek cities of Babylon, of Alexandria, and of Antioch, many of whom, in spite of remaining true in thought at least to the faith of their fathers, had learned to follow Greek ways and to enjoy Greek life. With increasing passion he clung to his Law and looked with increasing fear upon those foreign influences which were steadily encroaching upon his hard-won homeland and upon his ancient faith.

In 198 B.C. the Syrian king, Antiochus III, wrested Palestine from the Ptolemies of Egypt, an event which foretold disaster to the Jews in Jerusalem; for some twenty years later there succeeded him a king known as Antiochus Epiphanes, who was to bear a dark and sinister name in Jewish history. This Antiochus was an enthusiast for Hellenistic culture, which he straightway attempted to force upon his subjects in Judea. His first act was to appoint to the highest ecclesiastical office a Jew known as Jason, who had taken the Greek form of his Jewish name of Joshua, or Jesus, and who had in other more important ways been won over to Hellenistic views. Under Jason a new tide of

Greek manners and fashions swept over Judea. In the shadow of the ancient citadel of Jerusalem a Greek gymnasium was erected; Hellenized Jews were sent to participate in Greek games in the city of Tyre; young men began to follow Greek ways and to forsake the Jewish Law under which they had been born and nurtured. The conflict between those who had been won over to Hellenistic modes of life and thought and the staunch followers of the Law grew steadily more bitter until Jerusalem became a city of turbulent people.

Antiochus, seeing in this intolerable situation a flouting of royal authority, visited vengeance and punishment upon the Jews. South of the Temple area he actually built a fort in which those Jews of his own Hellenistic views might take refuge and from which they sallied forth to attack those engaged in the Temple rites. Finally, in a determination to make an end to Judaism altogether, he forbade the ancient rite of circumcision, the observance of the Sabbath, the services and sacrifices in the Temple, and destroyed the sacred books. As a culminating insult in December of the year 168 he erected upon the sacred altar of the Temple, where burnt offerings had been made, an altar to Olympian Zeus and rededicated the Temple to the Greek god. Similar altars were built throughout the cities and villages of Judea, and the Jews were ordered to pay them homage and sacrifice upon the occasions of pagan festivals. Persecution even to death was the portion of those who continued to acknowledge their loyalty to the Jewish faith.

Then began the so-called wars of the Maccabees so stirringly depicted in the Apocryphal books of that name. They were led by Judas Maccabeus, or Judas, the Hammerer, one of the five sons of a priest named Mattathias, of the Hasmonean family, who lived in the village of Modin not far from Jerusalem. This Mattathias, an old man at the time, had dared to revolt against the commands of Antiochus Epiphanes and had gathered around him a motley company ranging from pious Jews, incensed over the spread of Hellenism, to all manner of recalcitrants and des-

61

peradoes. These men, like those other outlaws whom David nine centuries before had gathered about him in his wars against Saul, now took to the hills and caves for guerilla warfare of the most desperate sort. Judas upon his father's death was made captain of this ill-assorted band, untrained and unequipped, and began his series of incredible battles against the trained armies of a powerful state.

Out of these desperate times arose the book of Daniel, written by a young Jew, who scorned the inroads of Hellenism and remained steadfast to the Law. His book, to be discussed in a later chapter as one of the most significant in the Old Testament, was written to arouse the spirits of his compatriots and to inspire them for this bitter trial of their ancestral faith. In a series of thrilling narratives and visions he lent courage to those who fought, exalted their loyalty to the God of Israel, and prophesied the ultimate downfall of His enemies.

For nearly a century the sons of the Hasmonean Mattathias and their descendants fought for an independent Jewish nation and religion. Assisted now and again by the caprices of Fate in the deaths of Syrian kings and generals and in more important claims elsewhere for their armies, they accomplished in one hundred years more than had seemed possible in the beginning of their revolt. They retook Jerusalem and restored the Temple, conquered and annexed a considerable portion of territory, won religious freedom, and, for at least a short time, attained political independence from Syria. Had the later Hasmoneans possessed the wisdom, valour, and faith of the five sons of Mattathias, more might have been accomplished toward the re-establishment of the Jewish people as a nation before the Roman Empire was to cast its mighty shadow over Palestine.

The scepter of world-empire, which in this brief historical sketch of Jewish destiny we have seen pass from Assyria to Babylon and from Persia to Alexandria, was now swiftly taken by Rome. Early in the first century B.C., having absorbed Italy, Northern Africa, and Greece, she was now fighting for the possession of Asia Minor and the lands drained by the Euphrates. Her general, Pompey, naturally turned eager eyes toward Syria and Palestine, not only for themselves but as a base of operations for conquests further east. In the year 63 B.C. he laid siege to Jerusalem; and, after three months of bloody resistance from the Jews fighting from the citadel and the Temple, the legions of Rome entered the ancient city to begin her long hold of seven centuries upon it.

The Jewish nation as a political unity, in strength or even in shadow, was at an end, but not that religion which had been the basis of national unity for twelve hundred years. That continued in Jerusalem in the rigid sect of the Pharisees, of whom we hear much in the New Testament, in the sumptuous Temple of Herod, made king of Judea under Rome in 39 B.C., until its terrible destruction under Titus a century later, in the famous schools of the Rabbis in Judea and Galilee, and in the countless Jewish communities throughout Asia Minor and the Mediterranean world, in Rome, in Greece, on the islands of the Aegean, in Babylon, and, most important of all, in Alexandria, each with its synagogue and its schools. One cannot, indeed, overestimate the strength of these communities. It was they which were in large measure responsible for the diffusion of Christianity, for it was to their synagogues that St. Paul and his fellow apostles attached themselves on their missionary journeyings. Well might King Agrippa write to the Emperor at Rome: "Jerusalem is the metropolis not only of Judea but of very many lands"; or St. Luke in the 2nd chapter of the Acts of the Apostles say that on the day of Pentecost there were at Jerusalem "Jews, devout men, out of every nation under heaven" from Parthia to Crete and from the ancient land of the Medes to the cities of Egypt.

4

The Hebrew People: Their Racial and Literary Characteristics

1

In the appealing story of Balaam, which is given in the book of Numbers, chapters 22 to 24 inclusive, and in the first of the three oracles which he spoke concerning the God of Israel and His people, he describes the children of Israel in words which are as impressive as they are accurate: *Lo, the people shall dwell alone, and shall not be reckoned among the nations.* During the twelve hundred years in which the Bible came slowly into being, these ancient words of Balaam may be looked upon as prophetic understanding of that racial individuality, that separate identity, that singularity and aloofness from other peoples which remained characteristic of the Hebrews even through the course of those long centuries of varying fortunes. Brought into contact with foreign influences though they were, Canaanitish, Philistine, Egyptian, Assyrian, Babylonian, Persian, and Hellenic, and un-questionably influenced to some extent by them as their literature here and there proves, they seem, more perhaps than any other race in history, to have been capable of preserving their substantial and tenacious identity. From the earliest books of the Bible to the last, they remain inherently the same.

The reason for this almost astonishing survival of determining and peculiar traits lay, first of all, perhaps, in the intense vitality of the race, both physical and spiritual. In spite of disasters sufficient to have shattered a people less hardy, in the midst of vicissitudes and tragedies of every sort, they seem literally never to have lacked inexhaustible powers of fortitude and of replenishment. They were vigorous and hardy in their physical makeup and unquenchably heroic in their spiritual. Their prodigal powers of endurance and of resiliency run throughout their literature. In one of their earliest masterpieces, the Song of Deborah in the 5th chapter of Judges, one is made aware in every tense and hurrying line of their sense of discipline, their sheer energy and resourcefulness, their scorn of weakness and delinquency, their devotion to physical valour and self-sacrifice, and their ability to lose themselves in almost fanatical devotion to their God and to the well-being of their nation. Precisely the same qualities dominate the proud words of Mattathias to his five sons in the 2nd chapter of I Maccabees in the Apocrypha, when a thousand years after Deborah he called upon them to avenge their wrongs and preserve their nation, and when he made captain his son Judas, who in his acts "was like a lion, and like a lion's whelp roaring for his prey." Such fire as this literally never died out of the nation. It might at times smoulder in embers, slumber seemingly in eras of too great prosperity or of too great adversity, it might seem at times to be put out by tears and suffering; but fuel for it in terms of unquenchable vitality was never really lacking, and its rekindling was inevitable.

Throughout the Bible one is made aware of the vigorous physical life of the greatest heroes and prophets: the stature of Saul, the strength of Samson, the endurance of David and his outlaws, half starving "upon the rocks of the wild goats"; the immense physical prowess of Nehemiah, building furiously his walls; Elijah running one hundred miles from Carmel to the wilderness of Beersheba and, after a night's sleep under a juniper tree and two meals cooked by an angel, running on two hundred miles more to Horeb; Jacob wrestling all night with the angel; Amos stalking from the deserts of Tekoa to the shrine at Bethel and flaming with his high purposes; Joab ascending the precipitous rock to the walls of Jebus; the "three mighty men" who burst through the hosts of the Philistines to bring water from the well of Bethlehem to David longing for a drink of it; and, in the New Testament, St. Paul, who with pride enumerates his ability as well as his willingness to endure physical sufferings, cold and hunger, weariness, beating, and shipwreck. These are but a few instances among hundreds in which the abounding physical strength and elasticity of the Hebrew race is made manifest, a strength and an elasticity which in the same and countless other instances was supplemented by equal spiritual fervour and intensity. No verse in the Bible better suggests this combination of body and spirit than that concluding the beautiful 40th chapter of Isaiah: *They that wait upon the Lord shall renew their strength; they shall mount up with wings as eagles; they shall run, and not be weary; and they shall walk, and not faint.*

In spite of the numerous stories of cruelty and revenge which dot the Old Testament narratives and which we must ascribe in large part to the primitive ethics of ancient times, the Hebrews were unquestionably centuries in advance of many other peoples in their ideals of human behaviour and of man's responsibility not only to his own conscience but to the rights of other men. Side by side with tales of terrible vengeance, many times explained, if not justified, by their earliest conceptions of God, are numberless instances of magnanimity and generosity and of condemnation of needless and gratuitous cruelty. One can never forget the spirit of David's beautiful lament over his enemy Saul or his kindness to Saul's son, Mephibosheth, "lame in both his feet." When the servants of the Syrian king, Benhadad, comforted him in his fears by telling him that the kings of the house of Israel were known to be merciful, they were apparently dealing in comparison with other monarchs of that rude age. As one reads the Old Testament chronologically, one notes a constant advance in the Hebrew conception of the attributes of God, the ethical attributes of righteousness, justice, and mercy taking the old places held by vengeance, jealousy, and hatred of Israel's enemies. The stories of Elijah and Elisha are those of men who not only denounce injustice and cruelty, but who go about looking upon men as their neighbours and performing all manner of simple kindnesses in any number of ordinary, human circumstances. And surely no more lofty conception of human behaviour and human thought can be found than in the utterances of the earliest prophets, then only in the 8th century B.C., when they make the distinction between that goodness which is of the heart and that worship which is merely outward form, between those truths which are eternal and those precepts and rules which are transitory and lifeless. *I hate, I despise your feast days,* cries Amos, speaking for God at the shrine of Bethel. *Though ye offer me burnt offerings, I will not accept them. But let judgment run down as water, and righteousness as a mighty stream.* Job later echoes those high ideals of the earlier prophets when, in the 31st chapter of the book called by his name, he enumerates in humble pride the ethical code by which he has lived his life and by which all men ought to live: the code of faithfulness to one's marital and family obligations, of justice and decency to one's servants, of mercy and charity to the poor and the fatherless, of the right estimation and use of wealth, of service to one's community, and of hospitality to the stranger and to the traveler.

In more than one way the Hebrews may seem to us, in spite of these positive traits, a singularly negative people when we consider them in relation to other races and nations of their day. They were not primarily conquerors. After their invasion of Palestine, an act urged upon them both by the promises and commands of God and by the necessity of a place in which to settle, we do not hear of many inroads upon the lands of others except for their self-preservation. Even David's miniature empire could hardly be termed the result of conquest on any large scale. They were not, like the Romans, organizers of great bodies of men, their armies always small in numbers and existing chiefly to make possible their own security. They were not builders to any great extent like practically all the other important nations of ancient times. It is only in the early days of the monarchy that we hear of extensive building and then only in the case of Solomon. Nor were they, except for the ventures of Solomon with the navies of Tyre and their much later enterprises in Babylon, primarily a commercial people. Indeed it is significant throughout their literature that they looked upon the wide ways of the sea with awe and fear rather than with familiarity and friendliness. They seem to have entirely lacked the artistic capacities of the Greeks; nor can this lack, I think, be wholly explained by the commandment in their Decalogue forbidding them to make "any graven image or any likeness of any thing in heaven above or in the earth beneath or in the waters under the earth." It was with words, not with more tangible and concrete material, that they made their immortal images! Nor were they, with all their literary genius, a race of thinkers. With the exception of the book of Job, of that of Ecclesiastes, and of certain portions of the Apocrypha, there is very little philosophy in terms of abstract or theoretical thought in the Bible. Hebrew minds were concrete and vivid but not basically speculative. They dealt in flashes of insight rather than in contemplation, in swift figures of speech rather than in logic and argument. They did not reason; they saw and felt.

Surrounded always by their enemies, tossed like some small craft in the ebb and the flow of great tides of conquest, they were from first to last a people of suffering. The Bible is, indeed, a chronicle of suffering. And although as a people they were negative in the sense that they lacked many of the gifts and accomplishments of contemporary races and civilizations, in their suffering they were positive and even prodigal. All their anguish of soul and spirit could not quench that spirit or deaden that soul. Here again their vitality asserted itself, their unquenchable, innate sense of life springing up within them. No matter how many Valleys of Baca they must pass through, they could find fresh wells which would fill their pools of despondency so that they could go on again "from strength to strength."

Their sufferings they could bear (and, one is sometimes tempted to think, even enjoy!) for they loved life with all its pain. No fact concerning them is more well-established or better illustrated than this. Their writings are vibrant with a passion for living, for the homely details of daily existence, for the frank acceptance of the pleasures and the fruits of physical life, fields and pastures with their flocks, corn and wine, the beauty of women, the joys of marriage and of children. And in noting this trait we must remember that it was doubtless deepened and strengthened within them by the fact that, until late in their history and probably under Greek influence, their religion offered them no hope of any life beyond this short and transitory existence. Those who died descended into Hell, or Sheol, a dark, unreal land of silence and of forgetfulness, a land similar to Homer's Hades where the departed lived a shadowy existence with no care and no knowledge of that which once had been. The best that could be said for such a life was that it was free from the sufferings of earth. *There,* cried Job in his torment, *the wicked cease from troubling, and there the weary be at rest.* It is small wonder that, with no hope beyond the Psalmist's threescore years and ten, a people so full of vitality should seize upon all that life offered and enjoy it to the full.

For this enjoyment to its fullest capacity, quick and alert eyes, ears, and hearts were essential; and no people in history has possessed a greater capital of these. It is significant in this connection that their earliest name for their prophets was *seers* and that throughout their prophetic books these leaders of Israel represent themselves as men who *watch* and *look* and *listen.* In such occupations they belonged to the race whence they had sprung, for Hebrew eyes seem always to have been open and Hebrew ears sensitive to the manifold and free gifts of the world about them. It is not only in the rhapsodies of their

69

Psalmists, writing five hundred years later than their earliest poets, that we are made aware of green pastures, still waters, the handiwork of God in the firmament, mountains and hills which sing and trees which clap their hands, the speech of the day and the knowledge possessed by the night, the nests of the sparrows and swallows, and the praise of streams and water brooks. In their most ancient songs none of these things escapes their eyes and ears: the stars in their courses, the bleating of the flocks, the talk of the trees, gardens by the river's side and cedars beside the waters, the strength of the unicorn and the lion, the majesty of "high places," the dew and the rain on the mountains of Gilboa. The brightness of the sky meant no more to Daniel than to Isaac when he went out "to meditate in the field at the eventide." Wine was as red and milk as white to the ancient classical poet of the Blessing of Jacob in Genesis 49 as to the epicurean author of Ecclesiastes, who, seven hundred years later, warns his readers to live joyfully and mightily all the days of their life since there will assuredly be no pleasure, nor knowledge, nor wisdom in the grave to which all must go.

This keenness of observation, this almost childlike, perennial wonder of the Hebrew mind toward the works of God in nature, is shown in a very appealing way, to cite but one example, in their love and often humorous understanding of animal life. The charming picture of Balaam's ass, who was granted the sight of an angel and who justly reproved her master for an undeserved beating, is echoed in the book of Job, where its author describes the wild ass who will not regard "the crying of the driver," and in the ass in Isaiah who knoweth his master's crib. The ostrich when she has risen to her full stature scorneth the horse; the horse in turn cries Ha, Ha! when he hears the battle trumpets; the hippopotamus can drink up a river without any haste whatever; and God Himself plays with leviathan as a man might play with a bird. Dissolute women are described as cows in the satiric scorn of Amos; kind ravens feed Elijah by the brook Kerith; the quick hands of the spider assure her a home even in kings' palaces; and the dogs who have consumed the carcass of the wicked Jezebel wisely decline to eat her feet which have run on errands of mischief, the palms of her hands which have wrought cruelty, and her head which has designed evil deeds. Birds engage their delighted attention, the voice of the turtle-dove in the spring, the songs of birds in the early morning, the wondrous way of an eagle in the air. They know where the stork builds her house, the wild dove, the swallow, and the ostrich. And they compare their trust in God to nestling beneath feathers and to chickens gathered beneath the wings of the hen.

2

Just as the Hebrews were a people of concrete and vivid imagination, a people who dealt in sense impressions and emotions rather than in abstract thinking, so their language was primarily a language of the senses and of the emotions. Hebrew scholars tell us that few abstract terms existed in ancient Hebrew and that in the construction of sentences very little subordination of clauses, such as one meets with constantly in Greek and Latin, or, for that matter, in English, was used. Instead, the use both of single words and of words in combination was concrete, almost rudimentary, sentence following sentence in simplicity, clarity, and sameness of construction. Our King James translation has beautifully kept these qualities, so that, although we are unfamiliar with the original language of the Old Testament, we can yet understand its prevailing characteristics.

When one reads, for instance, the first chapter of Genesis, one is immediately impressed by the utter simplicity both of diction and of construction: *In the beginning God created the heaven and the earth. And the earth was without form and void, and darkness was upon the face of the deep.. . . . And God called the dry land Earth; and the gathering together of the waters called he Seas: and God saw that it was good.* Throughout the Old Testament, although not always to such a marked degree, this simplicity of style predominates, especially in the narratives, the use of the co-ordinate conjunction *and* employed more than any other means for the connection of sentences and that of monosyllabic words always taking precedence over those of many syllables.

This simplicity, indeed, is likely, unless we are careful, to make us underestimate the beauty and the meaning of biblical literature. The Hebrew narrator and poet often, if not always, meant more than he actually said in words. What may sometimes seem to us an understatement, as almost incomplete narrative, did not mean that to him. He leaves us to supply by our imaginations what was latent in his own.

An excellent example of this dramatic economy of words occurs in the familiar story of the sacrifice of Isaac in the 22nd chapter of Genesis, one of the great narratives of the Old Testament. After God, in order to test the faith of Abraham, has told him to take his son, "thine only son Isaac, whom thou lovest," and offer him as a burnt offering upon one of the mountains of Moriah, we are told nothing of the feelings of Abraham faced by such a tragedy. Those are for us to supply. We are merely told that he rose up early, saddled his ass, cut wood for the fire which should consume his son, and set forth. But an even more telling omission of detail occurs between verses 3 and 4. At the close of verse 3 Abraham is on his way; at the beginning of verse 4 two full days have passed. *Then on the third day Abraham lifted up his eyes, and saw the place afar off*. If we fail to note this omission of detail, the two days' journey loses its meaning, its poignancy and pain.

And although the Hebrew poet was often more eloquent than the writer of prose, he, too, depended more upon the sound of the language itself, its melody and rhythm, the pictorial value of its single words, and its inner meaning than upon elaboration by means of unnecessary description. *The beauty of Israel is slain upon thy high places. How are the mighty fallen*, sings David in his lament for Saul and Jonathan. And the Psalmist: *I was glad when they said unto me, Let us go into the house of the Lord.* And the poet of Job: *My days are passed away as the swift ships.*

The use of similes and metaphors such as that just quoted from Job is perhaps the most characteristic and beautiful trait of Hebrew literature at its best. The realistic and concrete imagination of its writers, their sensitiveness to nature in all its manifold aspects, their feeling for their home land, their intense concern with all the details of daily life—these furnished the substance for their images, for their quick and apt comparisons of one thing with another. Job's days not only pass away as the swift ships, but they are "swifter than a weaver's shuttle," they are "swifter than a post," or they are "as the eagle that hasteth to the prey." Occasionally these figures seem overdone, almost bizarre to us, in their wealth of Oriental imagery, as, for example, in the Song of Songs where the lover compares his sweetheart's hair to a flock of goats and her teeth to a flock of sheep, and where she returns his odd compliments by declaring that his legs are as pillars of marble set upon sockets of fine gold.

But such similes are rare. For the most part, the Hebrew poet chose his comparisons from the homely details of his life in the desert and the hill country as a shepherd or as a vine dresser and farmer. The discouragement of God under the sins of His people is, in the words of Amos, "as a cart that is pressed full of sheaves"; Isaiah sees the daughter of Zion "as a lodge in a garden of cucumbers" and the house of Israel "as the vineyard of the Lord of hosts." To David, Saul and Jonathan are swifter than eagles and stronger than lions. The various Psalmists and the writers of the Proverbs over and over again reflect the life lived in a dry and thirsty land where even the shadows cast by great rocks are welcome against the heat of summer. Rocks and water are constant themes of their thought and speech. They compare God to a rock; they long for Him as they long for water and "as the hart panteth after the water brooks"; good news from a far country is "as cold water to a thirsty soul."

73

Although they wrote in Greek rather than in Hebrew, the writers of the New Testament, especially of the Gospels, constantly use such simple, concrete figures. Jesus, who spoke in Aramaic, is true to His Hebrew literary heritage when in His parables He compares the kingdom of Heaven to a man who sowed good seed in his field, or to a grain of mustard seed, or to yeast which a woman hid in a pint of meal, or to a net which is cast into the sea, or to a treasure hid in a field. To St. John in his Revelation the voice from heaven which he heard was "as the voice of many waters and as the voice of a great thunder."

Of all the parts of speech, except for the adverb, often redundant in any language, the adjective is most rare in Hebrew literature. The Hebrew writers preferred the unembellished use of concrete nouns. They had, however, their favourite descriptive words which, when adjectives seemed necessary, they used over and over again much as Homer used the same adjectives to describe the sea as *wine-dark, barren,* and *unharvested*. Our King James translation has taken care to preserve these repetitions in its choice of English words to express the Hebrew. For example, two adjectives used again and again in the Old Testament are the extremely suggestive ones, *goodly* and *pleasant*. *The lines are fallen unto me in pleasant places,* cries the Psalmist; *yea, I have a goodly heritage*. Moses' mother sees that he is a *goodly* child; Saul is a *goodly* young man; David is of a beautiful countenance and *goodly* to look upon. Saul and Jonathan were lovely and *pleasant* in their lives; the words of the pure are *pleasant* words; Daniel eats no *pleasant* bread while he mourns; Eve sees that the fatal tree in Eden is *pleasant* to the eyes; the men of Judah in the words of Isaiah are God's *pleasant* plant; and to a writer of the Proverbs the ways of wisdom are ways of *pleasantness* and all her paths are peace.

A favourite device of the Hebrew story-tellers and poets was the frequent use of the question. It was a means of securing added rhythm and stress to their sentences, variety to their style, and the suggestion, now of pathos, now of mystery, both in narrative and in poetry. Many of these questions, scattered so lavishly throughout the Old Testament, give an almost unbearable sense of sadness. *The child is not; and I, whither shall I go?* says Reuben to his brothers when he discovers that Joseph is not in the pit. Jeremiah in his angry sorrow over Zion cries: *Is there no balm in Gilead? Is there no physician there?* And in the 137th Psalm is perhaps the saddest of all questions in any literature, a question asked by the exiled Jews in Babylon and one that is echoed today throughout the world by millions of their descendants: *How shall we sing the Lord's song in a strange land?* The beauty of the 139th Psalm, with its wonder at God's mysterious ways, is increased by the poet's use of the question: *Whither shall I go from thy Spirit? or whither shall I flee from thy presence?* The magnificence of the 38th chapter of Job is actually dependent upon the fact that God speaks out of the whirlwind in a series of questions: *Where wast thou when I laid the foundations of the earth? . . . Hast thou entered into the treasures of the snow? . . . Canst thou bind the sweet influences of the Pleiades, or loose the bands of Orion?*

3

The foregoing brief treatment of some of the most distinctive traits of Hebrew literature in general should be supplemented by a short and, of course, by no means exhaustive description of the form of its poetry, since without at least a modicum of such information the reader of the Psalms, the prophetic poetry, the Song of Songs, and the most beautiful portions of Job will lack the means of understanding the way by which the Hebrew poets attained their distinctive effects. The most striking feature of Old Testament poetry is its method of balancing the two halves of a line, or often two complete lines. This fundamental principle and practice, which is shown alike in the earliest poetry such as the Song of Deborah and David's Lament and in the later poetry of the Psalms, was peculiar not only to Hebrew but also to other ancient poetry such as that of the Egyptians and the Babylonians. It is known as *parallelism* and is in effect a repetition of thought and sometimes even of words, identical or similar. This repetition, or balance, of thought is the essential basis of most Hebrew poetry.

There are several forms of this parallelism, the most frequent of which I shall attempt to illustrate by concrete examples from familiar passages. The form most commonly used is *synonymous* parallelism. In this form the same thought is expressed in the two half lines, the point evidently being to give added emphasis to the thought itself. Such *synonymous* parallelism is seen in the following verses from the Psalms:

The heavens declare the glory of God; and the firmament showeth his handiwork.

Thou shalt tread upon the lion and adder; the young lion and the dragon shalt thou trample under feet.

The righteous shall flourish like the palm tree; he shall grow like a cedar in Lebanon.

Other outstanding and beautiful examples occur in the ancient Song of Deborah:

They fought from heaven: the stars in their courses fought against Sisera.

Blessed above women shall Jael the wife of Heber the Kenite be: blessed shall she be above women in the tent.

At her feet he bowed, he fell, he lay down: at her feet he bowed, he fell: where he bowed, there he fell down dead.

Why is his chariot so long in coming? why tarry the wheels of his chariots?

Another relatively common form is known, perhaps for want of a better term, as *synthetic* parallelism. Here the second half line, or line, supplements the thought of the first by giving the consequence or result of the first, or by exemplifying the first, and in this way synthesizing or joining the thoughts of each. The order of this form is often variable, the consequence, result, or exemplification frequently occurring in the first line. The following examples from the Psalms illustrate *synthetic* parallelism:

I cried unto the Lord with my voice, and he heard me out of his holy hill.

I will call upon the Lord, who is worthy to be praised: so shall I be saved from mine enemies.

When I consider thy heavens, the work of thy fingers, the moon and the stars which thou hast ordained;
What is man, that thou art mindful of him? and the son of man that thou visitest him?

Because thou hast made the Lord, which is my refuge, even the Most High, thy habitation;
There shall no evil befall thee, neither shall any plague come nigh thy dwelling.

Yea, though I walk through the valley of the shadow of death, I will fear no evil: for thou art with me; thy rod and thy staff they comfort me.

Synonymous and *synthetic* parallelism often occur in the same verses, the repetition of the thought and its result being skillfully combined to give added emphasis. This combination is beautifully illustrated in the following verses from the 27th Psalm:

The Lord is my light and my salvation; whom shall I fear?
The Lord is the strength of my life; of whom shall I be afraid?

And in the famous quotation from David's Lament in the 1st chapter of II Samuel:

Tell it not in Gath, publish it not in the streets of Askelon; lest the daughters of the Philistines rejoice, lest the daughters of the uncircumcised triumph.

A third form of parallelism, not so common as *synonymous* and *synthetic* and yet often used in Hebrew poetry, is *anti-*

thetical parallelism. Here the second half, or full, line contrasts with the first by a directly opposite thought as in the following examples, again from the Psalms:

A thousand shall fall at thy side, and ten thousand at thy right hand; but it shall not come nigh thee.

Weeping may endure for a night, but joy cometh in the morning.

All the workers of iniquity shall be scattered.
But my horn shalt thou exalt like the horn of a unicorn.

Another excellent example of *antithetical* parallelism is found in the last verse of the Song of Deborah:

So let all thine enemies perish, O Lord; but let them that love him be as the sun when he goeth forth in his might.

Still a fourth form of parallelism is known as *climactic* parallelism. This is far less common than the other forms illustrated, and yet its use is not infrequent. It is sometimes called "stair-like" parallelism to signify the building up of the thought and its expression to a climax. In Psalm 29 such parallelism occurs:

Give unto the Lord, O ye mighty, give unto the Lord glory and strength.
Give unto the Lord the glory due unto his name.

Or again in the following verses:

The voice of the Lord divideth flames of fire.
The voice of the Lord shaketh the wilderness;
The voice of the Lord maketh the hinds to calve, and discovereth the forests.

And in the Song of Deborah this same kind of parallelism is found together with the other forms:

Curse ye Meroz, said the angel of the Lord, curse ye bitterly the inhabitants thereof.

78

I am quite aware as I conclude this brief presentation of the most important and frequent forms of Hebrew parallelism that I have left unmentioned other less common and more intricate forms and that I have given but the briefest description of other less outstanding traits of Hebrew poetry; yet I have proceeded on the assumption that to understand clearly the most important aspects of a large subject is far better for the common reader than to be confused by a mass of material not only difficult of comprehension but actually not entirely clear to scholars themselves. It must be remembered always not only that we are dependent upon a translation for our study of biblical poetry, but also that the great translators themselves could not always discover or ascertain the original poetic form of many of the books with which they were dealing. Their work was remarkable in that it managed to preserve in English so much which was characteristic and innate in Hebrew. It must be remembered, too, that the verse division of the Bible with which we are so familiar was not the form in which it was originally written. Moreover, it is hard at best to distinguish always between Hebrew poetry and prose, as the poetry depended not upon the careful division into so many syllables to a metrical foot as in most English poetry, but rather upon the beat of the accented words, the stress of the rhythm and the sound. In other words, in Hebrew poetry the number of syllables is nothing; the accented words are everything. They alone supply the rhythm, and they alone give the effect. And more, I think, than in any other poetry they suggest the accents of the human voice as expressive of human emotions at their height and depth.[2]

[2] For those who are interested in studying further the forms of Hebrew poetry I would recommend the article on this subject in Hastings' *Dictionary of the Bible*. The general reader, however, who is more intent upon the beauty and the meaning of the poetry itself will, I believe, find that I have given sufficient for his needs in this brief description.

PART II

THE OLD TESTAMENT

I

The Earliest Stories of the Hebrews

1

LEGENDS OF THE CREATION

One of the first things that readers of the Bible must understand clearly is that the initial books contained within its covers are not necessarily the oldest in terms of literary composition. Since the Bible wisely begins with the story of God's creation of land and sea, sun, moon, and stars, of trees, animals and creeping things, with the making of man and woman and with their first tragic sin, it is easy to assume that these ancient tales were the first composed, or collected, by the many Hebrew writers who together gave us our Bible. This is not true. The myths and legends of the book of Genesis were compiled and written over a period of several centuries and by several different men whose names are quite unknown to us. For example, the first chapter of Genesis, by all standards the most beautiful of that book in its simplicity, its vividness, and in the loveliness of its language, was probably written about 500 B.C., whereas much of the other material in Genesis, Exodus, and in the other three books which comprise the so-called Pentateuch, or the Five Books of Moses, was written two or three centuries earlier. In other words, the five books of the Pentateuch are a really extraordinary compilation of material, some early, some relatively late, made over a long period of years and finally issued as one collection of books, much as we have it today, around the year

400 B.C. In age very few parts of it are so old as certain of the historical and biographical narratives of Saul and David which were written much earlier.

It seems best in my book to discard actual chronology of composition, or at least not to be hampered by it, to begin this study of the great literature of the Bible with those stories of the beginning of things, and to continue by relating our subjects as nearly as possible to the progress of Hebrew life and thought, regardless of when the material which we shall consider was actually written. Following this plan, then, the first biblical literature to engage our attention will naturally be the legends which begin the book of Genesis.

The authors of these stories need not long concern us here, although we shall learn more about one of them in the second part of this chapter. The man who wrote the incomparable first chapter of Genesis is known to scholars as P, because he was undoubtedly a Jewish priest, who lived following the Return to Jerusalem, and because his writings throughout the Pentateuch bear a distinctly religious flavour. The three other chief authors of the Pentateuch are called by scholars J, E, and D: J, because this unknown and brilliant author, who lived probably about 850 B.C., used the Hebrew word Yahveh, or Jehovah, for God; E, because this also unknown author, writing perhaps one hundred years later, used in his earliest stories the name Elohim for God; and D, because this initial letter serves to identify the author, or compiler, of much of the book of Deuteronomy together with other portions of the Pentateuch. These authors, now one, now another, are responsible for much of the material also in the books of Joshua, Judges, and the books known as Samuel. Still another writer, or compiler, known as H, because his work, written about 570 B.C., is called the Holiness Code, compiled certain chapters of the now seldom read book of Leviticus.

It would be impossible, useless, and inexpressibly dull to attempt to distinguish here all the various chapters written, or compiled from more ancient material, by these alphabetized authors. What concerns us is the stories themselves and only those stories which have become memorable to countless millions of people over many centuries. In other words, we want to become aware of the value of the stories as literature, of the reasons why they have endured in the minds and affections alike of people lost in dim ages and of people living today.

The stories of the creation of the world, of the sin of man, of Noah and the flood are not essentially Hebrew in all their details. The tale of a great flood, for instance, is common to many ancient peoples and doubtless arose originally from some crude notions of the geological formation of the earth and sea, of the mysterious age of the world and of human life thereon. Similarly there have been lost Paradises and "Towers of Babel" in the ancient literature of other races, although no lost paradise has entered into theological thought or caused such speculation and such searchings of soul as the lost paradise of Eden. And yet in no literature have ancient myths such as these been told with such surpassing power, with such knowledge of human nature, and with such understanding of the mystery of human destiny and of the questioning which has been the lot of man from his birth.

No person who wants to read the Bible with greater intelligence and appreciation can do better than to study with care the first chapter of Genesis. He will note at the start the complete, almost stark, simplicity of the style, the absence of adjectives, and the surprising use of monosyllables. Apparently to its author the event in itself was so breathtaking and colossal that it needed no elaboration for its effect. The very first phrase, "in the beginning," is in itself startling in its appeal to the imagination, an appeal of which the author of the Gospel of St. John was aware when centuries later he began his book with the same stirring words.

The author of this first chapter understood, too, the impression to be gained by the device of repetition. *And the evening and the morning were the first day,* he writes, and marks the dramatic progress of God's creation with the same clause throughout his description. *And God saw that it was good. . . . And it was so* are two other examples of the same repetition until these repeated clauses become almost like poetic refrains and his account in prose a poem.

There is something very appealing also in this author's picture of God Himself, in the almost childlike suggestion that God thoroughly enjoyed His power to make "two great lights; the greater light to rule the day, and the lesser light to rule the night," to frame the stars in their courses, and to create great whales; something charming and even humorous in God's blessing of the whales and saying to them: *Be fruitful and multiply and fill the waters in the seas.* This first picture of God does not portray Him in His later roles as a God of thunder or of awful majesty on the top of high mountains. He is here the Creator who has pride and pleasure in His work, and who even Himself seems a bit surprised by it all.

When after the 3rd verse of chapter 2 another author takes up the account of the creation with the making of man and of woman, he, too, continues the simple, almost naive account of the beginning of things. God to him is a very human sort of Being, who plants His own garden and walks in it "in the cool of the day," and who even seems to be planning new things as He continues with His work, learning from experience as a man might learn. He is also apparently much moved by human emotions. The disobedience of His first children not only angers Him, but it grieves Him "at his heart" that those whom He has made and loved should set about making such great trouble for themselves. He may punish them, but He also makes coats for them out of skins before He sadly sends them forth out of the garden He has made for them.

The second author of these earliest stories of life on the earth is not perhaps a finer artist than the first, and yet in many ways he is a greater dramatist. His dialogue between Eve and the

86

serpent and between God and Adam and Eve is terse and vivid. And, if one reads him carefully, one can gather through these dramatic conversations that he was a man of long and puzzling thoughts and of consuming interest in humanity and its future. He is perplexed and saddened by the reasons for human suffering, by the fact that knowledge of good and of evil both opens man's eyes and makes him as a god and yet causes him suffering and sorrow, by the judgment upon woman that she must suffer more than man and that she must need love more than man will need it. In other words, he is aware not merely of the tragedy of Adam and Eve, but of the universal tragedy of human life, unbounded by any time or place. There is, in fact, in these early stories of the man called J a sense of mystery akin to that felt by P, the writer of the first chapter, when he says simply that "the spirit of God moved upon the face of the waters."

We must remember, in reading these legends of the creation and of those to follow later concerning Noah, the patriarch Abraham and his descendants, that they were chosen and in some cases re-edited out of a vast body of material. Hebrew editors and scholars worked for slow centuries in preserving them and in finally choosing those which had been written down by several authors and which, in the judgment of these editors, should at last, together with much other material, form the first books of the Bible. Perhaps, indeed, the Pentateuch is the greatest single work of compilation and of editing in literary or in religious history. In making it the scholars had much to consider: they must satisfy the people by preserving for them the old J and E stories, which, edited about 650 B.C., had become a kind of national epic as dear to the Hebrew people as the *Iliad* and the *Odyssey* were to the Greeks; they must omit nothing of the social, political, or religious history of the nation; they must include, above all else, those documents which codified and interpreted the Jewish Law, or Torah, to them the Law of God for His people. For the Old Testament is from first to last the preservation in words of the spiritual life of the Hebrew people. From its earliest legends to the utterances of prophets and poets and from its first half-historical records to those well-authenticated accounts of the last bitter years of a small, yet great, nation, this fact stands forth. Its literature is great and lasting because the Spirit of God, moving first "upon the face of the waters," never ceased to quicken the souls of those who wrote it for their own and succeeding generations.

2

THE JACOB-JOSEPH SAGA

Many persons, although they may be unfamiliar with much of the rich content of the Old Testament and may know little of it as a connected account of the fortunes and the fate of the Hebrew race and nation, remember vaguely, or clearly, certain of its stories. And many of these familiar stories, which they have known from their childhood, are parts of one of the most remarkable epics, or sagas, in any literature, ancient, medieval, or modern: the story of Esau's selling of his birthright to Jacob; of Jacob's toiling seven years for Leah whom he hated and seven more to pay for Rachel whom he loved; of Joseph's coat of many colours and of the pit into which he was cast; of Potiphar's wife; and of the silver cup in the sack of grain. This great saga occupies twenty-four chapters of the book of Genesis, beginning with Chapter 27 and ending with Chapter 50.[1] It is preceded by Chapters 12 to 26, which tell the story of Abraham, the patriarch of Israel and legendary father of the Hebrew race, chapters in comparison far less interesting and less vivid than those which actually comprise the Jacob-Joseph Saga. The saga itself can be helpfully divided into two distinct parts: Chapters 27 to 35 inclusive, which form the story of Jacob; Chapters 39

[1] Chapter 36 is one of genealogy and may well be omitted, as may also Chapter 38, which is an isolated incident of Judah, one of the sons of Leah.

to 50, which form the story of Joseph. Chapter 37, with its brilliant characterization of young Joseph, is an interlude between the two parts.

Some scholars prefer to call this story, together with its preface and long sequel, an epic, since they see in it not only the dawn of a nation, from its dim beginnings in the beginning of time itself to its triumph in the throne and empire of David, but also the life histories of the great heroes of Israel. They compare it to other epics like those of the relatively contemporary *Iliad* and *Odyssey* of Homer and that of the much later *Aeneid* of Vergil. They stress the patriotic fervour which breathes through all epics, the national glory of its conquests, the pride in its race. They recall its legendary heroes, the ageless stories clustered about them by the tenacity of tradition, heroes and hero tales which are an integral part of all epics. And surely the complete story is epical both in style and in subject, both in atmosphere and impression.

But, since we are dealing here with only one portion of the narrative, the story of Jacob and of Joseph, the greatest of his twelve sons, and since, to me at least, the story of the Israelitish race is never separated from the Israelitish family and especially from the twelve families, or tribes, bound together by those strong family ties essentially Hebrew, I like better to think of the story as a saga and to call it by that name. For almost more important than the passionate religious zeal and the national fervour which runs through and holds together this dramatic story of Hebrew life and destiny, are the family relationships and fortunes which make it one of the most human documents ever written in any language.

The author, at least in greatest part, of the Jacob-Joseph saga is the man known to us as the Yahvist, or as J. It was he, we remember, who began his story with the 2nd chapter of Genesis. His conclusion of it is not agreed upon by scholars. Whether he closed it with the exploits of the judges, or with the anointing of Saul as king in I Samuel, or even with the beginning of the story of David, we do not know, since so much material by other hands was interspersed with his. We do know, however, that no portion of his great work ranks with the Jacob-Joseph saga in interest, appeal, and literary excellence, that this saga is, in fact, one of the masterpieces of the Old Testament. Let us begin, then, with the first part of the saga, Chapters 27 to 35 of the book of Genesis, and try to see which of its qualities as a story of human beings and of their lot in life bear out this perhaps superlative statement.

We are aware at once when we begin with the scene of the blessing of Isaac that its author is a dramatist of the first rank. The resourcefulness and quick thinking of Rebekah, who will not see her favourite son Jacob deprived of the birthright, the vivid details and the concentrated incidents through which her schemes unfold, the suspicion of Isaac allayed by her cleverness, the nervousness of Jacob, the bitter cry of Esau when he realizes upon his return from hunting that he has been outwitted and set aside, his hatred of his brother and his designs upon Jacob's life once their father is safely dead, the panic of Rebekah when she knows of the fury of Esau—these are the stuff from which great dramas are made. Throughout this first part, the story of Jacob, this sharp sense of dramatic situation is ever present, in literally every chapter. Jacob in his flight from Esau's revenge sleeps and dreams of a ladder reaching even to heaven, with "angels of God ascending and descending on it"; his premonition of his love for Laban's daughter Rachel is so strong that he tries to rid himself of the shepherds at the well in order that he may meet her alone as she draws near with her sheep; the scene of the wedding night when Laban deceives Jacob by substituting the sore-eyed Leah for Rachel is unsurpassed in its vivid suggestion of tragic fury; the scene between the jealous Leah, who has already borne her husband four sons, and the desperate Rachel, who has borne none, over the mandrakes that Reuben has gathered is bitter in its ironic conclusion of yet another son to Leah; Jacob's shrewd increase of his flocks and herds by the white-streaked rods (a fine use of the belief in primitive magic for pre-natal influence) and its effect upon Laban is high comedy, as is the picture of Rachel sitting calmly upon the household gods which she has stolen. The fear of the meeting with Esau on the way and the preparations made for safety and appeasement; the wrestling with the angel at Peniel; the tragedy of Dinah, the only daughter of Jacob, and the awful revenge of her brothers upon the young man, who sincerely loves her, and upon his city; the pathos of Rachel's death in childbirth in the wilderness, so near to Ephrath and yet so far: these, too, are among the great dramatic situations in literature as they surely were in that ancient life which they depict.

It is, for the most part, through the vividness of his dialogue that the author of the Jacob story makes his characters stand out in all their reality, for Hebrew writers rarely give details of human appearance. We know only that Rachel is beautiful and well-favoured and that Leah has "tender," or *sore* eyes, that Esau is hairy and Jacob smooth of skin, that the countenance of Laban is unfriendly—all details necessary and relevant to the given situation rather than existing for themselves. But details are actually unnecessary for our knowledge of the characters. They speak, and we know them. *Bless me, even me also, O my father,* cries Esau, with "a great and exceeding bitter cry." *Surely the Lord is in this place; and I knew it not,* says Jacob in his wonder. *How dreadful is this place! This is none other but the house of God, and this is the gate of heaven.* Leah storms at Rachel over the mandrakes: *Is it a small matter that thou hast taken my husband? And wouldest thou take away my son's mandrakes also?* The grasping Laban describes himself when he begs Jacob to stay at Padanaram: *I pray thee, if I have found favour in thine eyes, tarry: for I have learned by ex-perience that the Lord hath blessed me for thy sake.* And Jacob shows his disgust over his sons' impulsive and cruel deceit when he says: *Ye have troubled me to make me to stink among the inhabitants of the land.*

91

In the portrayal of places, in spite of little actual description, rarely used by Hebrew writers, the author shows his sensitiveness to them and to their atmosphere. If we read carefully, we are aware of Bethel, that "certain place" where Jacob had his dream, the darkness of the night, and the stone beneath his head, upon which stone in the early morning he pours oil to mark the "house of God." We can see the well in the field with the three flocks of sheep lying by it and the great stone upon its mouth; the sacred oak tree under which Rebekah's old nurse is buried; the pillar upon Rachel's grave "in the way to Ephrath." The unknown J. had evidently a special fondness for women drawing water from wells. Four times he portrays such a scene. He is sensitive, too, to times of day, using always, in common with other Hebrew writers, the custom of describing the time by the occupation usually connected with it. In a chapter preceding the opening of his saga, Genesis 24, he says of the servant of Abraham: *And he made his camels to kneel down without the city by a well of water at the time of the evening, even the time that women go out to draw water.*

All these qualities continue throughout the second part of the saga, the Joseph story. This portion is, according to most scholars, partly, if not largely, the work of the other unknown author called E, although J's work is discernible in many parts just as in portions of the Jacob story E doubtless had a lesser hand. Again we are not particularly interested in assigning the respective portions to either of these ancient writers. What we are interested in is the literature itself and the brilliant power of its composition.

The Joseph story, or Joseph in Egypt, is prefaced by Chapter 37, which forms a kind of interlude between the two parts and which is worthy of special note because of its realistic picture of Joseph as a boy in relation to his brothers, the sons of the jealous Leah and of Jacob's two concubines, Bilhah and Zilpah, handmaids to Leah and Rachel. The author is peculiarly honest in his portrait of Joseph. Although he is to play the main role in the

92

second part of the saga and exhibit in that role generosity and understanding, in the interlude he is anything but an attractive youth. He is a tale-bearer, a petted child, a boaster, and a supercilious dreamer, who pompously relates to his brothers the dreams in which they are subservient to him. He is apparently idle, well-dressed, and bumptious; and one has sympathy with his hard-working brothers who cannot "speak peaceably unto him." It is apparent that the sons of Leah, Judah and Reuben, are better disposed toward him than the sons of the concubines. They at least do not wish to slay him. Reuben suggests the pit in the wilderness in the thought that he may later be able to save his brother for his father's sake; but Judah proposes that he be sold to the Ishmaelites who are on their way to Egypt. All apparently connive in the deception of their father by which he shall believe that an evil beast has devoured the first-born of Rachel, whom Jacob loved. This interlude is one of the most graphic of all the incidents in the complete story because of its vivid concreteness of action and of dialogue and its wealth of human emotions, delineated without praise or blame. Perhaps, indeed, it has become one of the most familiar of Old Testament stories because of the manner of its telling as well as for its fascinating material.

In addition to those fine qualities of drama, of characterization, and of atmosphere, which we have seen in the story of Jacob and which continue through that of Joseph, there are other interesting elements in the Joseph story which we should not fail to note. Chief among these is the use of material common to various forms of early literature, such as, for instance, the ballad and the romance, material which has its source in the long past of every people. We have already seen in the Jacob story the prevalence of popular superstitions, by no means entirely dead in the life and literature even of today, concerning pre-natal influences and the efficacy of mandrakes. We recall, too, that Jacob served seven years for Leah and for Rachel, a time of service which occurs again and again in popular tales of many races. The Joseph story opens with the familiar tale of Potiphar's wife, clearly here an Egyptian source and reminiscent of other much later and yet old tales such as *Sir Gawain and the Green Knight*, in which a man preserves his chastity in spite of the wiles of a designing woman. Such a theme recurs again and again in the literature of all peoples and in all languages. The dreams of the butler and the baker and of Pharaoh's kine and ears of corn recall the popularity elsewhere of the dream *motif*. The lavish giving of gifts, which Jacob prepared for Esau, is echoed not only in the changes of raiment, the pieces of silver, and the twenty asses laden with food in the Joseph story but in similar giving of presents in countless other ancient tales, such as, for example, those told by Homer in the *Iliad* and *Odyssey*. And the revelation of Joseph's identity to his brothers after he has concocted various schemes to bewilder and to try them is as old as literature itself.

The human interest continues throughout the second part of the saga, that knowledge and quick perception of human emotions which mark all Hebrew literature. An excellent example of this at its best occurs upon the return home of the brothers to their father after they have been forced to leave Simeon as a hostage in the hands of Joseph, whose identity they do not yet know. The telling of their story in chapter 42 is touching in its detail and simplicity and in its concern for the old man, their father. Judah's sense of responsibility for Benjamin in chapter 43 is equally memorable. The scene of the dinner in Egypt with Joseph's questions concerning their father is drawn with simplicity and charm; and one does not soon forget the selfless pathos in Judah's pleading words to Joseph when the brothers' fear for Benjamin is strong upon them: *We have a father, an old man, and a child of his old age, a little one; and his brother is dead, and he alone is left of his mother, and his father loveth him. . . . How shall I go up to my father, and the lad be not with me?* Nor should one fail to appreciate the account in chapter 48 of the blessing of Joseph's children by their grandfather, the almost petulant insistence by Jacob upon his position as head of the family to the end, and in chapter 49 his shrewd use of metaphor and of unrelenting frankness to describe his twelve sons who are to succeed him in the making of a nation.

Lastly, one should become conscious in the Jacob-Joseph saga of the absence of war, soon to play such a part in the narratives of the Hebrew writers, or even of struggle after a land in which to settle and to dwell. Whatever problems there are in this ancient, homely story are those of family relationships, of the need for life, of the search for food for men and for animals, of the final reconciliation of brothers estranged and lost. Its pastoral atmosphere, on the whole, is one of peace, and over it hovers that dreamy haze which one connects with the golden age of legend. The pattern of its movement is fluid and continuous with no clearly defined beginning or end; and we are not so conscious of change as we are of an odd permanence as though we were back in the beginning of things where nothing can confuse us. In this ancient setting the passage of time means little or nothing; days, months, and years blend together imperceptibly; and we are not surprised to learn that the years of Jacob were one hundred and forty-seven and that those apportioned to Joseph were five score and ten.

The unknown author J, with E who assisted him, composed his saga out of stories which had so long circulated among his people that their actual beginnings had become lost in the mist of centuries and their characters symbolic of common life and destiny rather than actual persons. His contribution lay in the remarkable arrangement of his material, in his feeling for time and atmosphere, and in the style with which he wrote, a style made strong and vivid by his intense devotion to his race and to its boundless and mythical past. Combining his ardent patriotism with his inviolable sense of a peculiar religious destiny, he became in his saga and elsewhere one of the creators of Hebrew identity and individualism. The charm of his single stories

95

should not blind one to their place within the structure as a whole or the pleasure given by themselves obscure the zealous conviction of the author that he is both preserving the rich heritage of a nation and through that preservation prophesying its matchless future as the people of God.

2

The Great Leaders of Ancient Israel

1

MOSES

We have already become somewhat acquainted with the figure of Moses in the chapter on the history of the Hebrew people and recall him now as the deliverer of his kindred from the Land of Goshen in Egypt, as the framer of their early laws under the inspiration and revelation of God, as the welder, even the founder of their national unity, and, above all else, as the spiritual leader who redeemed their rudimentary and incomplete monotheism and made of it an established and inviolable religious faith. Israel under Moses became one people, the people of God, their destiny inseparable from Him, their patriotism firmly rooted in Him. All Jewish law, social, ethical, ecclesiastical, originated with Moses, at least in theory; for many centuries he was believed to have been the inspired author of the Pentateuch, the name of which was the Five Books of Moses. He was, then, after God, the rock upon which the national and religious unity of Israel was firmly built.

When we consider what Moses actually meant in the history and religion of the Hebrews, when we know that his contribution to his race was the greatest sole contribution recorded in the Old Testament, it seems strange and not a little disappointing that the story of him and of his work as given in the books of Exodus, Leviticus, Numbers, and Deuteronomy lacks much of the interest and appeal of the Jacob-Joseph saga. There are,

I think, more or less obvious reasons for this generally accepted fact. In the first place, the story of Moses lacks the concentration and, therefore, the vividness of the saga. It is scattered throughout four books; it is interspersed with material having little to do with Moses; it is interrupted by endless chapters of Jewish laws, rites, and observances, of little or no meaning to the modern reader. And, in the second place, the several narrators of the story, for the men known as J, E, D, and P all had a hand in writing it, were so deeply impressed by the part played by God in the life of Moses, and hence in the life of their race, that they are inclined always to give the major role of the story to God and not to him. In other words, God so constantly overshadows him that unless we read selectively and with care we are apt to miss the great figure and personality of Moses himself.

I have come to the conclusion, therefore, that the best way in which we may understand and appreciate his really astonishing nature and character is to abandon any attempt to read his story as a whole and, instead, to select certain chapters of it which will reveal him to us in all his manifold and, in a sense, contradictory traits. For no man who could, and did, more than three thousand years ago stamp upon a few thousand Hebrews the pattern of a nation and a religion should fail to interest us today merely because he is either half buried beneath a mass of comparatively uninteresting material or overshadowed by the awfulness and majesty of God.

In beginning the story of Moses we must bear in mind that quite naturally a mass of tradition grew up through the centuries around his name. Many of the tales concerning him are unquestionably legends with little or no basis in sober history. He may or may not have been hidden among the bulrushes of the Nile by his frightened mother and adopted by the daughter of Pharaoh, although it seems relatively certain that his name was Egyptian and that he was not entirely unknown to the ruling house of Egypt. He presumably could not bring water out of a rock by striking it with his rod, or make that same rod into a serpent at will. The plagues which God is said to have visited upon Pharaoh in such a terrible succession of frogs, lice, flies, boils, hail, and locusts doubtless had their source in a series of national calamities of one sort or another and can hardly be literally taken as told by their authors.

Yet, since we are attempting to reconstruct the personality of Moses, the intrinsic truth of these marvels does not matter. The fact remains that he was a man about whom legends arose because he possessed such memorable qualities that lesser men must needs interpret his greatness in terms of the miraculous. Perhaps, indeed, he himself to them was more incredible than the stories which, in an attempt to explain him, they told concerning him.

If we select those incidents in his life which best portray him as a national figure, setting aside the question of their actuality, we shall easily discover wherein lay his extraordinary genius. That he was impetuous and hot-headed by nature is made clear both in the story given in Exodus 2 of his slaying of the Egyptian taskmaster who was beating the Hebrew labourer and in the later story in Exodus 32 which shows him beset by such consuming fury that he broke the sacred tables of the Law, ground the golden calf to powder, mixed the powder with water, and made the idolatrous children of Israel drink of it. That he was humble, which is the real meaning of the adjective *meek* attributed to him in Numbers 12, is apparent from his questioning of his own powers before the commands of God in Exodus 4. *O my Lord, I am not eloquent, neither heretofore, nor since thou hast spoken unto thy servant; but I am slow of speech and of a slow tongue.*[1] That he felt as his own the sorrows and hardships of other men and was not content until he had intervened in their behalf is proved, not so much by the rather sen-

---

[1] In his fine book, *A History of Hebrew Civilization*, p. 225, Alfred Bertholet warns us, however, that we should not take too seriously the many instances in the Old Testament of self-depreciation, which, he claims, meant to the Oriental simply a polite way of expression.

tentious narrative of the plagues in which Pharaoh and God consume most of the conversation and action, but instead by his actual initiative and heroism in accomplishing the flight of his oppressed people.

The most revealing of the incidents in Moses' life, however, are those which describe his relation with God. Intermixed as these are with legendary material, they nevertheless prove beyond a doubt that he was a man set apart from other men by a consuming sense of the presence and the reality of God; and this aspect of him becomes all the more significant when we remember that he was a man among men in his assumption of responsibility, in his powers of leadership and organization, and in his care for all those practical details made necessary through a precarious life among his people in the wilderness of Kadesh. In the words of the Epistle of St. James, he was both a *doer* and a *hearer*, a man both of fervent action and of equally fervent contemplation.

There are certain chapters in the long story of Moses which depict this relationship with God and which we may well discover and rescue from the immense bulk of priestly material threatening to engulf them. Among these are Exodus 3, in which God first appears to him in the bush which burns with fire but is not consumed; Exodus 4, in which Moses' lack of faith is restored; Exodus 32, in which Moses boldly argues with God on Mount Sinai and wins repentance for his people, and Numbers 11, in which he more boldly reproves God for the burdens laid upon him; Deuteronomy 32, which gives in the so-called Song of Moses, a song actually written centuries after Moses' day, the affirmation of his faith in God and in the survival of the Israelitish nation; and, finally, the last chapter of Deuteronomy, which depicts the death of Moses on Mount Nebo and his burial by the hand of God Himself.

It is in these chapters that the spiritual gifts of Moses are made manifest, gifts rare in any day but almost unaccountably so in those primitive times in which he lived. He was, in Spinoza's words, a "God-intoxicated" man and through that intoxication confirmed, one might better say *created,* in the Hebrew race that religious faith which was to endure after their life as a nation had died and to which we owe the religion of Christianity. And it is significant in these chapters that Moses' spiritual gifts, like Job's in a much later day, were not limited to wonder and awe at the awful presence of God in the thunder and lightning on Mount Sinai. Wonder and awe are there, but there is also clearly suggested such an intimacy with God, such an understanding of His innermost being, that Moses dares not only to intercede for his people but actually to reprove God for His anger against them. In such narratives as these God appears in a far less favourable light than does Moses! Indeed, one is convinced through them that it is Moses' faith in his people, not God's, which is to redeem them from destruction.

This understanding of two seemingly incompatible traits in the nature of Israel's God, His anger and His boundless compassion, this intimacy in which Moses retains his own sense of justice and actually upbraids God for His unreasonable anger, form together, I think, the most complete conception of the great leader of Israel which it is possible to gain from the relatively undistinguished literary material written concerning him and his imperishable gifts to his race. The prophets to come five hundred years after his day were to look upon God after the manner of Moses, inspiring a fear of Him in His people and yet within that fear teaching them assurance of His mercy and compassion. This was the inheritance bequeathed to them by Moses, an inheritance the power of which was to be made manifest in their own and in the following centuries.

2

JOSHUA

The book in the Old Testament known as Joshua contains the largely legendary story of that warrior, whose name like that of

Jesus, another form of the same word, means *deliverer.* Joshua's idea of deliverance, however, bears little resemblance to that held by the later possessor of his name! He has come down to us as the most revengeful character in the Bible, great warrior though he unquestionably was; and his book is most certainly a chronicle of blood and cruelty.

Although this book, which narrates his wars for the conquest of Canaan, was originally thought to have been written by himself, we now know that it is a compilation of material made over a space of many centuries and written by various hands. J, E, P, and D played their several parts in its composition, although it is impossible now to discover the portions originally composed by each nor has the exact form in which they were written been preserved. The book is an interesting, if somewhat horrible, narrative largely because it contains, with all its bloodshed and indiscriminate slaughter, a few excellent and vivid stories and one ancient and beautiful song.

As a matter of fact, we have very little information that can be termed dependable about Joshua himself. In the long cycle of stories concerning Moses, most of which we have found to be largely traditional, Joshua appears several times. He is commissioned by Moses to choose out fighting men whom he is to lead against the Amalekites; he is chosen to accompany Moses as his "minister" when he goes up into Mount Sinai, the mountain of God; Moses upon one occasion leaves him in charge of the sacred tabernacle in which the Ark of God was housed; and at the approach of his death Moses, under the command of God, gives to Joshua the leadership of the Israelites with the injunction that he is to bring them into the promised land of Canaan. These stories are without doubt largely traditional also, and yet within them there are surely more than grains of truth.

Joshua is by no means an attractive figure. The days are fortunately past when he was extolled as a mighty and saintly hero in Sunday-school lessons. And if he himself is unattractive, the God whom he served and fanatically obeyed is even less appealing. Joshua, unlike Moses, stresses nowhere the compassion of God. His God is a God of war, revenge, and bloodshed, who hates the enemies of Israel with merciless and bitter hatred. At one moment, He uses the tactics of cruel men, slaying with great slaughter the hosts of the five wretched kings encamped before Gibeon, in chapter 10, and even "chasing" along the way what remains of their armies; at another, He makes use of His heavenly power and casts down hail-stones upon them. He is apparently pleased with Joshua's disposal of the five kings themselves, who, after being confined by force in a cave, lose their heads and are hanged on trees "until the evening." He swears, in fact, in chapter 7 that He will not be with His people any more unless those who have seized the spoil of battle be immediately slain, stoned with stones, and burned with fire. After the ceremonious circling for seven days of the walls of Jericho in chapter 6, in which Joshua's God is careful that religious rites be observed, He commands that the city be accursed and that all the inhabitants of Jericho "both man and woman, young and old, ox, and sheep, and ass" be destroyed by the edge of the sword. This is primitive religion at its worst, and the best that can be said either for Joshua or for his God is that their ferocious methods doubtless seemed necessary for the task they had set out to accomplish, the conquest of Canaan.

In the midst of these chapters of carnage and cruelty the story given in chapter 2 of Rahab, the harlot, is memorable partly because of its relative freedom from horror, partly because of its lively description of Rahab herself: her clever deceiving of the king of Jericho, her ingenuity in hiding the spies under her stalks of flax, her scarlet cord by which she let them down from her window and which later she bound in the window as the signal of her safety. Likewise there is fine and ironic narrative in chapter 9, which recounts the ruse attempted by the wily inhabitants of Gibeon, condemned in payment for their desperate trickery to become "hewers of wood and drawers of water."

And lastly, for a moment's poetic relief in so much gruesome realism there is in verse 12 of chapter 10 an ancient song attributed to Joshua and yet composed long before his book was compiled or even written. It belongs among those earliest Hebrew writings of which we have record and which were preserved in ancient collections now lost. The names, however, of two of such early collections we know: the *Book of the Wars of Yahveh* and the *Book of Yashar, or the Upright*. This song attributed to Joshua belongs within the ancient poetic material preserved in these collections, originally made probably around 1000 B.C., and was itself included, as the author of the chapter evidently recognized, in the *Book of Yashar*. It may well be of older origin, since it was doubtless part of that folklore and tradition which clustered around the name of Joshua and the conquest of Canaan. It is beautiful in its sharp rhythm, in its simple language, and in its use of old place names:

Sun, stand thou still upon Gibeon; and thou, Moon, in the valley of Ajalon.

It is difficult to think of Joshua paying much heed to the sun or to the moon, even in order to give commands to them. But the poem, considered quite apart from its bloody context, is worth remembering both for itself and for its ancient heritage. Perhaps, indeed, it is the best that we can salvage from Joshua or from his book.

3

DEBORAH

We owe to Deborah the greatest single masterpiece of Hebrew poetry and one of the finest odes ever written in any language. Although she was not herself its author, she provided the stirring occasion for its composition by her flaming patriotism with which she incited Barak to lead the Israelitish armies against

Sisera, captain of the king of Canaan and possessor of "nine hundred chariots of iron."

As to Deborah herself we know little. She is described in Judges 4 as a prophetess who dwelt under a palm tree, known as the tree of Deborah. A location such as this belongs doubtless among those many sacred places designated throughout the Old Testament as special shrines of God. Holy trees like Deborah's palm are numerous. Gideon is called to his mission by an angel under an oak tree; Moses sees God in a burning bush; Saul and Jonathan are buried under a tree in Jabesh; and Elijah is visited by an angel as he sleeps under a juniper tree. Such references as these prove the persistence of ancient place superstitions, probably originating in Canaanitish cult practices and invading the monotheism of the Hebrews. Deborah's palm tree was without doubt looked upon as a sacred place where God gave her counsel as He had given counsel under other trees to other leaders of Israel. Aside from her tree, the information that she was a judge of Israel, and the thrilling story of the power which her faith gave to Barak, all contained in the 4th chapter of Judges, we know nothing of her. And yet because of her mysterious existence in the Hebrew world of her day, we shall forevermore be the possessors of a great and noble poem.

This Song of Deborah, written by an unknown poet, was doubtless composed immediately after the victory over Sisera, who, we recall, had headed a league of the Canaanitish tribes in a furious attempt to oust the encroaching Israelites from the lands which they had seized. The date of this victory, upon which so much of the future of the Hebrew nation hung, is given by scholars as about 1150–1100 B.C. This ancient date confirms the place of Deborah's song as one of the earliest existing monuments of Hebrew literature. It had tenaciously existed from the time of its composition and was inserted in its rightful place in the Judges narrative when that book was written or when it was given its present form.

No reader of the Bible should neglect a careful study of this famous and brilliant poem both for its total effect and for the manner in which that effect is gained. There is no other poem in Hebrew literature, whether early or late, which displays such seemingly unconscious and spontaneous literary art. The intense patriotic and religious passion of its writer flames in every line, sweeping on and up to the dramatic climax. It is throughout both an ancient *Te Deum* in praise of the God of Israel and a superb account of a mighty contest in which not only kings fought, but the stars of heaven and a river in its divinely swollen course.

The poem will be more clearly understood if its carefully formed divisions are noted. They are three in number, aside from the introductory verses 2 and 3, which call upon all to praise God, and the closing verse 31 with its curse and its blessing.[2] The first of the three parts extends from verse 4 to verse 12 and gives an impressive description of God marching from Sinai to fight for His people, while the earth trembles and the mountains melt before Him. It gives, too, a realistic picture of the conditions prevailing at the time when in fear of the Canaanites villages were left desolate, when war was in the gates, and when, as both rich and poor knew full well, there was no peace or safety for those who went about their accustomed tasks.

Verse 12, with its impassioned appeal to Deborah and Barak to rise in their might, introduces the second part of the ode, which part closes with verse 18. In this second part the rallying of the tribes is described with its terse presentation of each, its praise of the six who responded with all their strength and its bitter reproof to those who, abiding among their sheep folds and on the distant seashore, refused to lend their aid. The ode rises to its most splendid heights in the third part which recounts the mighty battle itself:

[2] The last sentence of verse 31 is obviously an interpolation and was not included in the ode.

The kings came and fought; they took no gain of money.

They fought from heaven; the stars in their courses fought against Sisera.

The river of Kishon swept them away, that ancient river, the river Kishon.

It is in this third part that the poet most truly reveals the magnificent scope of his art. He pictures with equal power the fighting of the stars and of the ancient river, the story of the valiant Jael who will forevermore be blessed above women for her slaying of Sisera, and the pathetic sight of Sisera's mother looking from her window for the return of her son. His concrete detail in Jael's welcome of Sisera to her tent, in her giving him milk which has soured to butter in the best of her dishes, is equalled in dramatic effect by his use of irony in the account of Sisera's mother, asking desperately of her ladies why his chariot is so long in coming, and yet allaying her premonitions of disaster by her dependence upon their explanation that he is delayed only because of the spoils of battle to be allotted to him. These verses in part 3 have the directness and simplicity of an old English or Scottish ballad together with the ballad's use of understatement and economy in portraying a tragic situation.

The poem throughout is rich in all the forms of Hebrew parallelism, already illustrated in a previous chapter. The separate scenes, each with its own abrupt and superb climax, are thrilling in themselves, in the ever-increasing breadth which they lend to one's imagination; and the manner in which they are woven into one dramatic whole bears witness to the genius of their author. Nothing is finer in the annals of war of any literature than this, nor has it been excelled in imagination or in expression by any of the later war poems of Israel.

GIDEON

The story of Gideon, which is given in the 6th, 7th, and 8th chapters of Judges, is one of the most graphic narratives of the Old Testament, lively in its movement and in its details, rich in its variety of incidents, and revealing in its many-sided picture of Gideon himself. Because of these qualities there is little wonder that it has endured in the affections of all manner of persons and especially in the imaginations of the young, who (if they are so fortunate in these latter days as to know it at all) like it because of its rapidity and excitement and because of its kinship in many ways to the modern thrillers of the screen.

As a piece of literature, the story in its present form is composite, the work doubtless of the authors J and E with, very possibly, changes made in their original narratives by later authors or editors. Much of it is surely reminiscent of J with its drama, its sense of detail, and its knowledge of human nature. Since scholars, however, find it difficult to distinguish clearly between the work of these two men or of later additions, we need not here go into that intricate problem, but rather consider the story itself as one salvaged from oral and perhaps even from earlier written forms and preserved as an extremely interesting account of a desperate situation.

This situation, which was instilling terror into the Israelites in the Land of Canaan probably around the year 1100 B.C., was caused by a people known as Midianites. They were Bedouin tribes who began at about this time to swarm in from the deserts east of the Jordan, bent on pillage, plunder, and destruction. They were seeking no settlement or permanent home, but only whatever they might seize of material value and make away with. Few stories in the Old Testament begin with such graphic and arresting words as those which describe these unwelcome hordes of ravaging invaders:

And the hand of Midian prevailed against Israel: and because of the Midianites the children of Israel made them the dens which are in the mountains, and caves, and strongholds.

And so it was, when Israel had sown, that the Midianites came up, and the Amalekites, and the children of the east, even they came up against them;

And they encamped against them, and destroyed the increase of the earth . . . and left no sustenance for Israel, neither sheep, nor ox, nor ass.

For they came up with their cattle and their tents, and they came as grasshoppers for multitude; for both they and their camels were without number; and they entered the land to destroy it.

And Israel was greatly impoverished, because of the Midianites; and the children of Israel cried unto the Lord.

It was at this frightful crisis that an angel of the Lord appeared beneath an oak tree and held conversation with a young man named Gideon, the son of Joash. Gideon, because of his terror of the Midianites, was at that moment laboriously threshing wheat by hand near his own wine-press instead of on the summit of a hill where it might be trampled out by horses or oxen and where the wind would conveniently carry away the chaff. Such a usual process had perforce been abandoned in these perilous days, for from the hill summit the work would be spied by the Midianites encamped in the vicinity. The angel proceeded, in the face of Gideon's humility before him, to proclaim him a mighty man of valour. Moreover, distressed by Gideon's voluble scepticism and by his resentment of God's desertion of His people in time of danger, the angel, after the manner of angels in those days, gave proof of his own identity by setting on fire some cakes and broth which he had ordered Gideon to place in the hollows of a nearby rock.

This canny shrewdness of Gideon, his desire not to be taken in merely by signs and wonders, does not vanish at once as the story proceeds and serves delightfully in the presentation of his character. To be sure, he obeys the command of God to destroy the altar which his father Joash has set up to the Canaanitish god Baal, going out by night to do this for fear of his father's household. But his very human doubt returns when God summons him to meet "the Midianites, the Amalekites, and the children of the east" in open battle in the valley of Jezreel. He is not yet thoroughly convinced, and, since he is taking no chances on divine help which has seemingly failed him in the past, he conceives the idea of trying God with a fleece of wool. Nor is he convinced by one trial only; he must have two.

God, also, who in this story is the War God of Joshua, though somewhat less revengeful and destructive, looks out for His own laurels. If there are too many Israelites to fight against the Midianites, He reasons, they will assume that their own hands and not His have saved them. God, therefore, in the naive story of the lappers of the water in Judges 7, designs a clever ruse by which He will both impress Gideon and save His own reputation.

In these narratives one discerns, of course, material savouring of primitive folklore and ancient popular traditions. But, as in many of the legends told of Moses, they not only lend atmosphere to the story but serve also as excellent methods of characterization. Whether true or not, they obviously suggest the esteem in which the characters were held by the people of their own day.

Gideon is the most brilliant military strategist of whom we have ancient record. He seems never at a loss for an idea. His use of the night as a cloak for his outwitting of the Midianites adds excitement to the story and proof of his clever daring. Creeping into the Midianite camp where they and their camels lay "as the sand by the seaside for multitude," he overhears a man telling a dream to the fellow lying near him and in this dream of the destructive cake of barley bread wisely sees himself. His ingenuity in the conception of the empty pitchers with the lamps inside them follows close upon the faith-renewing dream and magnificently accomplishes his purpose. His treatment of the men of Succoth, for whom he designs the original, if hideous, punishment of tearing them with thorns and briers, is reminiscent of Joshua; nor does he hesitate, with greater justice, to take bitter revenge upon the two Midianite kings for their slaying of his brothers.

Yet although Gideon belongs with Joshua in representing the War God idea in the religious development of Israel and lacks entirely any of those higher conceptions of God so discernible in Moses' attitude toward Him, we do not remember him primarily for his religious significance. His story is rather that of a distinctly human person who rises to an acute and dangerous situation in a remarkably praiseworthy manner. With all his heroism for his people he is not without his personal vanities, the possession of which makes him all the more real to us. His collecting of the ear-rings, the ornaments and the purple raiment from the battle spoils, his childish and even idolatrous making of the ephod, or image, his contented life, after his successful campaigns, in his own house with his many wives and his seventy sons—all these add to the vividness and reality of his portrait. According to the narrative, he dies before he can know of the conspiracy of Abimelech and the tragic slaughter of his many sons.

That he consistently refuses to accept the kingship over his people, fearing lest they look toward an earthly king rather than to God, redounds to his credit as does his apparent inoculation of his one surviving son Jotham with the same wholesome point of view. The fable of the trees spoken by Jotham in Judges 9 is, in fact, a fitting close to his story, even without the bloody tale of the treacherous Abimelech. This fable probably was inserted by one of the authors of Gideon's story who knew it as a part of the vast store of folklore in circulation among the people of his day. Scholars date it among the earliest existing specimens of Hebrew literature; and for that reason it is worth

111

study as well as for its fanciful imagination, the simple and poetic charm of its lines, and the common sense and vision of its teaching. Placed in the midst of the horrible story of Abimelech, his wicked plotting and his disgraceful end, it is a refreshing conclusion to the story of Gideon, who had within him, as perhaps his primary characteristic, that sense of abounding life so cherished by his people and who, one remembers, himself met the angel of the Lord beneath a tree.

5

JEPHTHAH

The brief and tragic story of Jephthah, given in chapter 11 of the book of Judges, is not his alone but also that of his daughter, and perhaps more hers than his. A girl who is accorded no name, she has yet been referred to again and again in the prose and the poetry of many languages. One especially recalls her as the source of Charles Lamb's apt figure in "Mackery End in Hertfordshire" and as the subject of Shakespeare's dialogue between Hamlet and Polonius. She and her ironic fate are perennial and immortal, and her story is memorable not only because of itself but because of its probably mythical background which connects it with other tragic stories of human sacrifice such as that of Iphigenia, the daughter of Agamemnon.

In the short space of one chapter this double tragedy forms one of the most dramatic and beautifully told stories of the Old Testament. It should be read with the imagination as well as with eyes and ears, for its appreciation depends largely upon the skill with which the reader supplements for himself the details which are so briefly suggested.

The tragedy is introduced by the simple statement that Jephthah was the son of a harlot, "a strange woman," and that, because of the cruel fate of his birth, he was deprived of his inheritance by his half-brothers and obliged to flee from his father's house. We are told that he went from his home in

112

Gilead to dwell in the land of Tob, an unknown country whose name, ironically enough, means the land of Goodness. That he was, however, remembered for his qualities as a man and as a potential leader is apparent, for when the Ammonites made war against Israel during its slow conquest of Canaan, the elders of Gilead went out to find and to fetch him that he might be their leader against their enemies. The suffering of banishment and its consequent bitterness are keenly felt in Jephthah's reply to the men of Gilead: *Did not ye hate me and expel me out of my father's house? and why are ye come unto me now when ye are in distress?* His bitterness is even more evident in his ironic speech to the king of the Ammonites and in his sardonic taunting concerning the power of Chemosh, the Ammonite god.

Impressed by the promise of the elders of Gilead that, if he will but lead them against the Ammonites, they will bring him home again, not only to restored respectability but to the leadership of those who have once despised him, Jephthah, fearful of his own strength, makes a rash vow to God. Like many another before and since, so fearful is he of losing what he has longed for that he does not stop to consider the possible consequences of an impetuous promise. In his excitement his first thought is of a sacrifice pleasing to God, no matter what costly or prized animal among his flocks and herds it may prove to be:

Whatsoever cometh forth of the doors of my house to meet me . . . shall surely be the Lord's, and I will offer it up as a burnt offering.

So Jephthah passed over unto the children of Ammon to fight against them; and the Lord delivered them into his hands.

And Jephthah came to Mizpeh unto his house, and, behold, his daughter came out to meet him with timbrels and with dances; and she was his only child; beside her he had neither son nor daughter.

The tragedy of the verses which follow is made more poignant by the continued simplicity of their words and form. No description of the scene is given; that we must supply for ourselves. But the undertones of grief and irony are in every phrase of the brief dialogue between Jephthah who has offered a price and his daughter who is the price itself.

Nor do we, save in our imaginations, know what was the lot of Jephthah, returned in doubtful triumph, during the two months of life granted to his daughter. It is another instance of that weighted expression of the sequence of time which we have already met in the story of the sacrifice of Isaac and by means of which the Hebrew writers gave such simple, yet profound emphasis to their narrative.

The story seems by its conclusion to suggest that it is not so much that of an Israelitish leader or that even of the tragedy of his daughter as it is one written in explanation or in commemoration of an Israelitish custom, observed yearly by the women of the nation and now lost in time. No reliable record, however, of such ceremony has come down to us. But the story of Jephthah and his daughter remains, seemingly, in its suggestion of the caprice of Fate, more Greek than Hebrew and akin to the much later tragedies of the Greek dramatists, who, like the ancient narrators of Israel, utilized the myths of their people for plays no more moving or beautiful than this.

6

SAMUEL

The two books of Samuel, originally a single volume but divided in the sixteenth century, have for many years been the subject of controversy among scholars as to their authorship, their truth as history, the inconsistent statements in which they abound, the various sources from which they were made. These profound and still undecided matters cannot concern us here. What we shall try to discover through the cycle of stories in the first sixteen chapters of I Samuel is Samuel himself, a leader of Israel second only to Moses in Hebrew tradition. Recognizing from the start that fact and fancy are inextricably confused in the narratives concerning him, we shall, first of all, try to see him in relation to his background and, secondly, attempt to evaluate as literature the rich and varied stories connected with his name.

As we already know from the historical sketch of the Hebrews, Samuel lived about the year 1050 B.C. between the last days of the judges and the founding of the kingdom. By this date the land of Canaan had been largely conquered by the Israelites, the marauders from the deserts to the east had been routed and sent homeward, and a gradual amalgamation had taken place between the Canaanites and the Israelites, in which the latter had come off victorious, the Canaanites having been relatively absorbed into the ever-increasing Israelitish population. But no sooner had the Hebrew conquerors become settled in their new land and ready to enjoy its blessings than from the coastal plain of Palestine a more formidable foe arose in the Philistines, that people which occupies so large a part in the stories of Samuel, Saul, and David. In this perilous situation, when a new and even graver danger threatened, the Israelites apparently lacked both military and religious leadership of the character given them by Joshua, Barak, and Gideon; and it was at this juncture that Samuel arose.

It is difficult to discover clearly what manner of person Samuel was: a seer, or clairvoyant, who took money for his oracular utterances; a prophet; a judge; a leader devoted to his people and to their God; a wise or a most unreasonable old man. There are not only great gaps in his life quite unaccounted for, but there are also glaring inconsistencies in the picture that we have of him. After full and lovely stories of his dedicated boyhood, he suddenly drops out of life for some forty years, and we hear nothing of him except that he lived at Ramah and that he "judged Israel," going about in circuit from year to year and from town to town. Then, quite as suddenly, he reappears as an old man to seek out Saul and anoint him as king, to reject him in anger and repent of God's choice of him, to anoint David, the son of Jesse, in Saul's place, and to perform various acts, both just and unjust, both wise and inhuman. That he was a man, however, of outstanding national significance, that he made a deep and lasting impression on his contemporaries, that he had great religious powers and was set apart as the interpreter of the will of God for Israel, and that even as an old man he could rise to a critical situation with great powers of creative invention—these truths seem to be unassailable.

Perhaps, indeed, we should welcome the conflicting stories told about him, the shadow of legend always cast over him from his days as a little boy in the temple at Shiloh to his coming back from the grave at the command of the wise woman of Endor. For there are few stories in the Old Testament more varied in their colouring and atmosphere, more vivid in their many-sided revelations of time and place and human personality than those which cluster about the name of Samuel. We may well leave with the scholars the difficult and doubtless quite insoluble problem of the sober facts to be ascertained concerning him and, for our part, look upon him as the subject or the instigator of certain admirable narratives.

Perhaps the best of these narratives, or short stories, occurs in the opening chapter of I Samuel and is, in fact, not a story of Samuel but of his mother Hannah. In its direct and simple form and in the objective manner of its telling, it reminds one, though in prose, of the method employed by the writers of ballads; yet in those very qualities, plus the realism of its situation, it might be, instead, the most modern of short stories.

The setting is unusual in its details and valuable for the picture which it gives of a simple village home of its time. It is the home of a man named Elkanah, who has two wives, Penninah and Hannah, one with children, the other childless. Penninah is jealous of the greater love which her husband bears for Hannah, and she is not slow to show her jealousy by constantly reminding Hannah of her lack of children. Each year the family

116

goes to the temple at Shiloh, some twenty-five miles distant, for sacrifice and merry-making with friends and neighbours, an event looked forward to throughout the year. The story of Hannah praying for a child and making her vow before God, her reply to the priest Eli who has cruelly misunderstood her tears and her moving lips, the return home and the fulfillment of her desire, the pleasure which she has afterward in remaining behind from the yearly journey in order to have her little boy to herself, her return to the temple with him as her great gift, and her revelation of herself to Eli as the woman whom he had once misjudged—these make a narrative of highest literary excellence and deep emotional appeal.

The sequel to the story is given in chapter 2 in the form of a song sung by Hannah in her joy over having received from God the gift of her son and returned that gift to Him. Although the song is of later composition, probably written around the fourth century B.C. and attributed to Hannah by some later editor because it seemed appropriate to the occasion, it is of great beauty with its various forms of parallelism and its lovely imagery. It is of interest also in its obvious similarity to the *Magnificat* which St. Luke in his first chapter assigns to Mary, the mother of Jesus. *My heart rejoiceth in the Lord,* sings Hannah, and Mary, *My soul doth magnify the Lord,* while both women sing of the hungry filled with bread, the emptiness of the rich, the exalting of those that are low and the debasement of the mighty.

A second and perhaps more familiar story is that told in chapter 3, the story of the child Samuel and his ministering unto God in the temple at Shiloh. The drama of the story with its picture of the boy sleeping in the sacred presence of the Ark and the voice of God sounding in the stillness should for its effectiveness be prefaced by the description given in chapter 2 of the religious situation prevailing at Shiloh, the gross sins of Eli's sons, Hophni and Phinehas, and the effect which such behaviour must have had on the mind of a young boy, perhaps fifteen years old at the time. The conclusion of the story, which really ends with verse

117

18, is a fine climax with its suggestion of Samuel's fear before the high priest as he tells "every whit" of what God has told him concerning the fate of the house of Eli.

In the four verses, 19 to 22, which conclude chapter 4 is a tragic story told with great economy and art, the story of the wretched wife of Phinehas, Eli's son, upon whose wickedness God has pronounced judgment and retribution. As bearers of the Ark of God into battle against the Philistines, Phinehas and his brother are slain. The irony of the disclosure to Eli both that the Ark has been taken by the Philistines and that his sons are dead makes narrative of high order with its culmination in the broken neck of the high priest; but a far finer literary effect is attained in the four verses which narrate so rapidly and simply the tragedy of Phinehas' wife—a woman whose name we do not know, even of whose existence we have not been aware until now. The bitterness of the tidings brought to her in childbirth, her pain physical and spiritual, her refusal to look at her son and her instantaneous, ironic naming of him, together with her heartbroken cry—such a story as this is equalled only by that of the mother of Sisera looking through her lattice for her son who will not return.

Chapters 4, 5, and 6 with their accumulation of legends concerning the Ark, the discomfiture of the Philistines over its possession and their fears aroused by its destruction of their God Dagon, their ancient spells, divinations, and omens, make most interesting and lively reading. They should surely be studied not only for the fascination of the primitive folklore which they preserve, but for the light which they throw upon the Ark itself, the attitude of the Israelites of that age toward it, its awful retaliation even upon men who reverence it. That the Philistines, glad to be rid of so dangerous and awesome a spoil of battle, returned it in relief to the house of a man named Abinadab and not to Shiloh, would suggest that Shiloh and its temple had been destroyed, the truth of which modern archaeology has practically affirmed as happening about the year 1050 B.C. And that this

118

event had a far-reaching influence on the young Samuel, who had been its guardian in the temple there, is suggested in the fact that he seems shortly thereafter to have returned home to Ramah, not to be heard of again save as "judge of Israel" until he is an old man.

The stories of Samuel as an old man throw another light upon him. The first one in chapter 9, in which Saul seeks him out to obtain help in finding his strayed asses, portrays him as a seer, a man gifted in second sight and capable, because of this mysterious power, of assisting people in the most ordinary as well as extraordinary problems of daily existence. The portrait of Samuel in this story is a naive and pleasing one, regardless of its source or authenticity. He has practical as well as visionary foresight here, for, warned of Saul's approach by God, he has been careful to instruct the cook in advance to save some food for him! The homely details of their meeting, the arrangement for payment of the fee, the careful advice of the girls at the well, the announcement of the recovered asses, the parlour, the good dinner, and the long talk at night upon the roof of the house, are quite as delightful as the more solemn anointing of Saul.

The terrible story in chapter 15 strikes a far different note. No longer is Samuel the hospitable host, the friendly seer, or even the prophet who anoints a king. He is instead the voice of the War God who commands the destruction of the Amalekites, "man and woman, infant and suckling, ox and sheep, camel and ass," for an old but never-forgotten score against them dating back to the days of Moses. In this unattractive role, in spite of his high-minded injunction to Saul that "to obey is better than sacrifice," he seems to belong with Joshua among the followers of the God of war and revenge, who relentlessly hates the enemies of His people and who is supposedly gratified when Samuel hews Agag in pieces before Him. The story is horrible in its thirst for blood, which is, in fact, a far stronger motive than is Saul's disobedience; but it is nevertheless superlative in the force and strength of its narrative.

It is pleasant to take leave of Samuel under other and more attractive circumstances. The last story told of him before the simple announcement of his death in Ramah in chapter 25, if we except his appearance as the cruel ghost brought back by the Witch of Endor to torment Saul, is given in the first thirteen verses of chapter 16. This is the familiar tale of the anointing of David to take Saul's place as king of Israel. Usually considered as legend by most scholars, the story is charming in its climactic arrangement of episodes, the seven sons of the surprised Jesse appearing in turn before Samuel only to be rejected as not chosen by God, while the youngest, quite unaware of what is happening in his father's house, keeps his sheep in the fields.

To whatever hand, or hands, we are indebted for these fine pieces of ancient narrative we do not know. Some scholars attribute at least portions of them to J and to E, but no one seems certain of their authorship. Undoubtedly they serve to confuse our picture of Samuel as a single portrait; yet they contribute richly to the content of the Old Testament by their drama, their realism, and their atmosphere, together forming a many-hued preface to their climax in the greater story of Saul.

3

The Folk Tale of Samson

In the middle of the book of Judges, chapters 13 to 16 inclusive, is told one of the most fascinating stories in the Old Testament, the story of Samson. Upon a first reading it cannot fail to have a puzzling, even bewildering effect because it is so obviously a mixture of conflicting and inconsistent themes, a kind of pot-pourri of the holy and the extremely secular, of crude talk and mean tricks, of cajolery and deceit, of incredible tales of physical prowess and of cruelty to animals, of harlots and other designing women, of death by burning, by slaughter, and by falling pillars, of loose behaviour on the one hand and noble patriotism on the other, of a wedding, a heavenly vision, a riddle, and a tragedy—and all these in the brief space of four chapters. The first conclusion drawn from such an odd mass of seemingly unrelated material is that of diversity of origin. The vision of an angel to a barren woman hardly bears much relationship to the slaying of one thousand Philistines with the jaw-bone of an ass. And a child who has been solemnly ordained and dedicated to God from the day of his conception hardly acts in keeping with his high and holy mission in life when he sets the tails of three hundred foxes on fire as a revengeful means of consuming Philistine corn, vineyards, and olive trees!

This conclusion of quite different sources for these interesting, if ill-assorted, tales is a safe one. Although Samson is alleged in two different places in his story to have judged Israel twenty years, he is clearly not to be associated with leaders such as Moses, Joshua, Jephthah, and Gideon. His story belongs, in fact, not among the partly historical narratives of the judges of Israel, but instead to that type of literature common to all peoples and known as the folk tale. The stories concerning him and his chimerical behaviour made up a cycle of such tales which existed perhaps for centuries before they were at last written down and which were told by wandering story-tellers to country people. Nor is Samson an epic hero such as Achilles in the *Iliad,* for instance. Nor does he possess the dignity of Joseph in the Jacob-Joseph saga. In spite of his valiant death, he is not actually of valiant mold, at least until that moment. Instead he is the typical folk hero, brawling and blustering, astonishing simple country people by his amazing feats and delighting them by his quite unrefined manners and his physical freshness and strength. He is, in a word, the Paul Bunyan of the children of Israel in their early days.

Ancient as are these stories incorporated into the book of Judges, the riddle attributed to Samson at his wedding feast is perhaps older yet, its origin like those of most ancient riddles lost in the dim centuries of the long past. It had doubtless long been associated with the Samson cycle of tales and fits well the setting prepared for it by time; for Samson's audacity and quick wit are quite sufficient for him to kill a lion with his bare hands, to discover on his wedding journey that the carcass is filled with honey, and then at the marriage feast to gain the wherewithal to pay for his new marital responsibilities by propounding a riddle to his friends: *Out of the eater came forth meat, and out of the strong came forth sweetness.* Since the stake is thirty sheets and thirty changes of garments, the desperate friends, granted seven days for the solution of the riddle, entice Samson's new wife by threats of burning to find them out the answer through cajolery of her husband. But Samson wins out in the end, for he calmly slays thirty Philistines in Askelon, takes their garments and pays his debt even though he loses his wife through his fury over her trickery of him.

Nor do Samson's relations with women suggest his necessary

stature as a judge of Israel. He is as irresponsible and as undisciplined in matters of love as in matters of quixotic revenge. He is, in fact, a lustful as well as a lusty young adventurer who wants what he wants and means to have it, regardless of the cost; and although he is actually no match for the wiles of women and seems never to have learned his lesson, he sees to it that, until the last ironic episode of his life, he does not come out the loser.

This story of Samson is set amid the wars with the Philistines which, we remember, engaged the Israelites after their successful conquest of Canaan for a century and more until these enemies were at last vanquished under David. In other words, the rescuer of the Samson folk tale proceeded to give it a definite historical setting although originally it had nothing of the sort. Political situations, of course, play small part in folk tales; and although Samson's final author places his story at a given time, this given time is a minor element in the story itself.

In like manner the author has introduced into the original folk tale a religious *motif* which seems not only inconsistent with Samson's character but even absurd. Both the religious and the patriotic theme are especially conspicuous in the beginning where Samson's birth is foretold by the angel to his father and mother and where the angel declares that he shall be a Nazarite, a man set apart from other men because of his religious mission, and that he is ordained to deliver Israel out of the hands of the Philistines. The two themes occur again at the tragic and superlatively written end of the story where Samson pulls down the pillars of the great house at Gaza and goes to his own death with more Philistines even than he has slain in his tempestuous life. In the original tales the Nazarite vow was, of course, absent, nor was there present in them any connection between Samson's heavy hair in which lay his strength and the religious ordinance that his hair should never be cut. The notion that mysterious and extraordinary strength lay in long hair was a common popular fancy quite divorced from the religious significance with which it is here endowed.

The author of the Samson story was without doubt the same J who wrote so much of the Pentateuch and who has already delighted us by his stories of the creation and by his superb Jacob-Joseph saga. This man, as we have seen before, possessed above many other discernible traits both as a person and as a literary artist great religious and patriotic fervour. He was, in fact, by his pen one of the creators of the national spirit of Israel just as Moses by his vision and leadership had created it by his deeds. It was natural, then, that into the crude, rustic folk tale of Samson with its zest and its bravado, its lust and its primitive ethics, its sense of prodigal life in the raw, he should interweave and instil his own ardent patriotism and his consuming faith in God's purpose for Israel against all its enemies. Out of his love for Israel's past and his appreciative understanding of its ancient legends dear to the hearts of its country people, he could not bear that such a folk tale as that of Samson should be lost. Neither could he bear that some patriotic and religious meaning should not be given to it; hence, the story as we have it, marked by his genius in its comedy, its irony, and, at the last, in its bitter and yet glorious tragedy.

Out of that tragedy, as we all know, Milton wrote his poetic drama, *Samson Agonistes*. Like J himself Milton saw more meaning in Samson's death than in his boisterous life as a folk hero, and he used it to construct one of the deathless poems of all literature. His picture of Samson, tricked by the third woman he has wanted and taken, made the prey of her cruel deception after he has "told her all his heart," blinded by the Philistines, brought down to Gaza to "grind in the prison house" and forced to make sport for them, is forever memorable to those who have read *Samson Agonistes*. And although he deals but slightly with the less appealing Samson of the crude pranks and violent behaviour, although he is content to emphasize a part at the expense of the whole, he has been anticipated, in a sense, by the ancient author of the folk tale, who in his last long chapter of Samson's misery and death summons all his literary gifts to construct a final scene unsurpassed among the dramatic narratives of the Old Testament. We may laugh at Samson's quick and careless plans for getting sheets and raiment for his house-keeping and at the picture of him striding toward Hebron with the doors and door-posts of Gaza on his shoulders; we may condone his susceptibility to unworthy women; but we have with his unknown author and with Milton nothing but compassion for him when, blind and helpless, yet still aflame in spirit, he says to the lad that holds him by the hand: *Suffer me that I may feel the pillars whereupon the house standeth.*

4

The Tragedy of Saul

The Hebrew story-tellers, unlike the Greek, did not recognize the power of chance or of fate in the life of man. To them God was the source alike of happiness and of misery, of blessing or of bane, the first, the result of obedience to Him and to His laws, the second, the consequence of disobedience and faithlessness. This orthodox view of life was, to be sure, taken into question by Job in his great argument over the part played by God in the affairs of men and over the apparent necessity of suffering by faithful and faithless alike; but to the more ancient Hebrew writers the problem presented fewer difficulties. Indeed, no other writer of the Old Testament took into question the concern of God over the destiny of His children as did the unknown author of Job. The precepts of the Law, once they were formulated, echoed in large part the earlier conceptions of the Deity, although these earlier conceptions had lost with the years much of their primitiveness. God was all. His mercy and compassion were with those who loved and obeyed Him; His anger and punishment were for those who forsook His ways.

Because of this definite, if difficult and untenable faith, the dark and tragic figure of Saul, the first king of Israel, has found little mercy at the hands of Old Testament historians and even of the prophets. He has been condemned for his weakness and disobedience, for his self-will and his longing for revenge, for his fatal impulses and his bitter jealousy. His story as told in the book of I Samuel is overshadowed by the romantic figure of David, with whom the writers were obviously more in sympathy.

126

His story has suffered, too, from a confusion of sources and from so many later additions by those who apparently wished to use Saul as an object-lesson that only with difficulty can one discover him as he presumably was. And yet, if one reads with imaginative vision and with modern insight the pathetic and bitter account of his life, he emerges actually a nobler personality than David and even a far more appealing one.

The life of Saul is, in fact, at least to modern minds, more easily and more truly interpreted by Greek thought than by Hebrew. This statement does not for a moment mean that Saul in his day or in the hands of his literary creators, some at least of whom were relatively contemporary with him, was looked upon as a tragic figure after the manner in which the later Greek dramatists were to present so many of their characters. He most certainly was not. Instead he was regarded as a man who was called by God and then forsaken by Him, whose misfortunes were richly deserved, and whose sad fate was the result of disobedience, on the one hand, and, on the other, of an evil spirit sent by God to trouble him. Yet, since his story has come to be looked upon as one of the greatest tragedies of any literature, it seems not only wise but necessary for its sympathetic understanding to separate it from the religious dogma which has dimmed its intrinsic greatness and to allow it to stand forth in its full stature. And the suggestion that it is more truly interpreted by Greek thought than by Hebrew means simply that the tragedy of Saul has its counterparts in many of the ancient Greek tragedies written five centuries after his day. Those who are fortunately familiar with the tragedies of Sophocles, the *Ajax* and the *Oedipus Rex*, for example, will understand the comparison, once they have carefully reconstructed the tragic figure of Saul from chapters 9 to 31 in the book of I Samuel.

For Saul from the beginning to the end of his sad story is the prey, first, of chance and, secondly, of his complex and passionate nature which held within itself the seeds of despondency and madness. No character in the Old Testament is more appealing than he when his story opens in chapter 9. He is a "choice young man and a goodly," the son of a prosperous farmer of the tribe of Benjamin. His father's name is Kish, a man described as "a mighty man of power." The village of Gibeah where Saul lived was situated some three miles north of Jerusalem among the hills and must have given a fine view of the surrounding valleys with their flocks and herds. It was among these valleys as a shepherd and farmer that Saul lived his early life, known among his people for his fine stature, his unusual charm, and his power over other men.

To the Hebrew writers of Saul's story, which is, of course, generously mixed with legend, his meeting with Samuel, the seer, is not the result of chance or of accident but, instead, the result of well-laid plans of God. Yet as one reads his story throughout as a work of literature, it is impossible not to see in its first incident that irony which is to follow him to the end. Having gone out to search in vain for the asses of his father, he follows the custom of his day in consulting a clairvoyant as to their whereabouts and is then and there anointed as a king! That this unlooked for and stupendous happening is bewildering and troubling to him is obvious, for he conceals it from his uncle's questions and attempts to hide himself in confusion and embarrassment once Samuel has come to present him to the people. Whether we accept as true the story of the lost asses with its exciting and spectacular sequel or whether we forsake it for the more probable following chapter which accords Saul's kingship to his defeat of the Ammonites, the fact remains that a throne is thrust upon a man who has no desire for it.

There seems no doubt that Saul was an able king who through the force of his personality united his people as David was at first unable to do. Nor was he ever confronted as was David with rebellions against him. Nor is there any question as to his capacities as a leader against the Philistines. But from the beginning of his reign one tragedy follows another because of his impetuous nature, the "fatal flaws" of pride and jealousy on the one hand and of superabundant love on the other. Nor is chance inactive. It is chance again which, through the suggestion of one of his servants, brings David to play upon his harp before the unhappy and anxious king, who straightway loves David and never actually ceases to do so during all their bitter struggles for the leadership of Israel.

Throughout the mounting train of gloomy and fatal incidents which mark the downfall of Saul, one is conscious of the innate bigness of his nature. Headstrong and impulsive though he is, he is, at least before his madness, rarely cruel in an age of cruelty and never personally ambitious. Although he is superstitious and fanatical in temperament and even in mind, he is devoted to God with a single-mindedness which increases the pathos of his rejection by Samuel because of his premature burnt offering at Michmash, and of his bitter cry at Endor: *God is departed from me and answereth me no more.* His disobedience in sparing both the spoil taken from the Amalekites and Agag, their king, presents him actually in a much nobler light than that surrounding the enraged Samuel, who again rejects him in the name of God before he proceeds himself to hew in pieces the wretched Agag. He is quick to acknowledge guilt and to ask forgiveness; to admire bravery in others; and to be ready to sacrifice even his son Jonathan when God casts the lot against him.

Aware at last of his failure to free Israel from the Philistines, rejected by Samuel, estranged from his son, his daughter, and his son-in-law, and forsaken by God, his periods of acute mental depression increase until he is stricken with madness. It is in this irresponsible state, described by his author as the possession of "an evil spirit sent from God," that all the unlovelier traits of his nature are made manifest, his hatred and suspicion of David, his plots for David's death, his fits of uncontrollable anger. Yet even in madness the noble qualities of his nature outnumber the ignoble, and the tragedy of his situation rises above any conception of the justice of his lot. There are few more touching scenes in any literature than that which pictures him in his desperation pursuing David "upon the rocks of the wild goats" and yet saying to him in tears in the cave: *Is this thy voice, my son David? Thou art more righteous than I; for thou hast rewarded me good, whereas I have rewarded thee evil;* or than that in the wilderness of Ziph when he cries: *I have sinned: return, my son David; for I will no more do thee harm . . . behold I have played the fool, and have erred exceedingly.*

Perhaps it was the memory of deeds and words such as these which prompted David to write his generous and beautiful lament when the news was brought to him at Ziklag of Saul's suicide and of Jonathan's death. Perhaps also some inescapable remnant of that same nobility impressed the divining woman of Endor when, in the last tragic scene before his death, Saul came to her house by night and, pathetically forgetful or careless of his own banishment from the land of wizards and those that had familiar spirits, begged her that, as a last hope, she would bring up Samuel from the grave to tell him what to do. At all events, her heart was touched by the sight of the king, fallen to the earth before the cruel prophecy of the disgruntled ghost of Samuel, so that she killed her fat calf and baked bread for him before he rose up and went away into the night.

This last scene at Endor, in fact, culminates the tragedy of Saul. His suicide on Mt. Gilboa is but the inevitable end; nor is it drawn as a scene but rather stated as a naked fact. At Endor, however, in the moving description given in chapter 28 of the meeting between Saul and the woman, all the tragic elements that have marked his life and caused his downfall and death are brought forward. The scene is prepared by his despair in that God will not answer him by dreams, or by lots, or by prophets. There is irony in his very seeking out of the woman, he, the king, who for the sake of his people has banished from Israel all such unwholesome influences; irony in his necessary disgrace as well as in his despair; dramatic irony in the woman's fearful reminder of his act against such as she when he has fallen so low and in his frantic promise that no harm shall befall her. It

130

is she who sees the "gods ascending out of the earth," not the king deprived of his access to divine help. His act of stooping with his face to the ground before the shade of Samuel, whom he cannot see; his pathetic description of his "sore distress" over his loss of God; and the cruel words of the ghost, angry at being brought back from his rest—these close the tragedy of Saul. The last picture of him is that of a child in the hands of the woman of Endor, sitting exhausted and spent upon her bed while she in pity ministers to his need. Into this last scene, which recalls the similar lot of King Lear, himself become again as a child, the author, in spite of the moral and religious judgment of his contemporaries and perhaps of himself, has done justice to what must have been his own sense of tragedy.

For, shorn of all conflicting and confusing material in his story, seen by himself without the brighter portrait of David which dims him, understood as a man of complex and passionate but not of mean or ungenerous nature, Saul surely emerges with all his darkness as one of the finest and strongest figures of Hebrew literature. Hardy recognized his image in Michael Henchard, the mayor of Casterbridge, also "a man of character," doomed alike by mad jealousy and by tempestuous affection to a similar destiny, and used the story of Saul as a theme for his own tragic novel, which itself is built upon the lines of a Greek tragedy.

And although the writer, or writers, of Saul's story may have been ignorant of the effect of their work, the effect is, nevertheless, the same as that described by Aristotle when he defines the nature of tragedy. For *pity* and *fear* must result from a perceptive reading of the life and destiny of the first king of Israel, pity for his human frailties common to all men, for the price they demanded, and for the curse of madness whatever its cause; and fear, because in his passionate and impetuous personality, the prey of love as well as of hatred, we discern ourselves.

5

The Biography of David

Of all Old Testament characters preserved in its literature that of David is given most space and delineated most brilliantly. Reasons for this preeminence are not hard to find. As Moses had brought the Israelites into their first existence as a united people, confirmed and completed their faith in their one God, so David was the founder of the Hebrew nation and state, raising it from insignificance to a place in the world of its day. The dynasty which he established was to endure for four centuries and his house as the House of David centuries longer in the imaginations of succeeding generations of his people. It was he who gave Jerusalem to Israel, a city which was to endure, whatever its earthly fate, as the divine symbol of the spirit of a people, of their achievements in the past and their mystic dreams of the future. To him were attributed all those qualities which go to make the ideal king, the less ideal characteristics becoming blurred and lost to after ages. In the idea of him was born the hope of a Messiah who would come to deliver Israel from its sorrows and raise it again to power and glory.

The sources for our wide knowledge and understanding of David are those given in the two books of Samuel and in the 1st and 2nd chapters of I Kings. Like the sources of Samuel and of Saul they are composite, an earlier and a later source being generally recognized by scholars. It is unnecessary and, indeed, impossible to list as belonging to one or the other source all the scattered material bearing on David; but it can and should be said that for a knowledge of his life and personality the

132

earlier source is the more reliable and of far greater literary value.

The material which best illustrates this earlier source and which forms the most distinguished and unquestionably most accurate portion of it is found in the book of II Samuel and includes chapters 9 to 20 together with the first two chapters of I Kings.[1] As the Song of Deborah holds first place in ancient Hebrew poetry, so the biography of David contained in these chapters deserves to be called the most outstanding work in ancient Hebrew prose. Written some one hundred and fifty years after Deborah's ode, the vividness and clarity of its style, the brilliance of its characterization and its dialogue, the objective approach of its author mark the work as a literary masterpiece.

Who its author was we do not know, but his intimate knowledge of David and of the affairs of his court and household would suggest, if not prove, that he was an eye witness of the happenings which he records and of the persons whom he describes with such psychological insight and power. He was very probably a priest, since at that time priests were generally the only learned men among the Israelites. Some scholars have gone so far as to give him the name of either Abiathar or Ahimaaz, both priests of the king's household. But whoever he was, he was a man of genius; and his thrilling account of David, his sins and his virtues, his sons and their disgraceful behaviour, his ignoble affair with Bathsheba and his more ignoble treatment of Uriah, remains unsurpassed in the annals of history and biography of any date and in any language. We must remember, too, as we admire the charm and strength of his work, that this unknown chronicler of David was the earliest of historians, living in fact five hundred years before Herodotus, who is called the "father of history," and that he had no models as

---

[1] There is also a record of David and his reign given in I Chronicles, chapters 11–29. These chapters, however, are of a much later date and not considered so trustworthy as those in Samuel and I Kings. Nor are they valuable as literature.

guides. Indeed, the writing of history as an art did not exist in his day, and he may well be accorded the honour of creating it in that sense.

It is to this man, who apparently wished above all else to give an honest and unbiased portrait, that we owe our knowledge of the many-sided personality of David. For no personality ever drawn has exhibited more seeming contradictions. Honest and dishonest, naive to the point of childishness and subtle to the point of treachery, magnanimous and cruel, sophisticated and primitive, humble and worldly, generous and selfish, devoted to his people and indulgent to himself, triumphant and broken-hearted, saint and sinner, master and slave, romanticist and realist—these are the conflicting attributes and natures which his biographer, with no personal bias or prejudice, has preserved for us.

The story of David owes much of its richness and variety to the romantic elements which it possesses throughout, and which, legendary though many of them are and as subjects more appealing to the other authors of the books of Samuel than to the writer of II Samuel 9 to 20, have added immeasurably to the sum total of his personality. For just as Saul from the beginning was the prey of fate, so David was seemingly the favoured of fortune. These romantic elements, although they are not lacking in his life as a man, cluster most thickly about his boyhood and youth and recall to us the same current themes in the popular hero stories of other races. His appearance and his gifts are alike romantic. Unlike his brothers he has a fair skin and red hair; he plays upon a harp; he watches sheep on the hillsides around Bethlehem; with his unaided hands he kills lions and bears which threaten his flock; he kills a giant with smooth stones from a brook; he cements a friendship with a king's son which to this day is used to describe complete loyalty and devotion; he is smiled upon by a king, performs feats as mighty as the labours of Hercules, and at last marries a king's daughter. As a young man he flees for his life to the wilderness, lives in caves, gathers about him a band of four hundred discontented men, is magnanimous to his enemy, appeases a hostile Philistine king with treachery, dances in religious frenzy before the Ark of God, and, in other words, plays a dozen roles at once. Whether true or not, these tales are of the very stuff of romance, the material of centuries of minstrelsy and song, and they have added both weight and colour to the composite portrait of their possessor.

But it is in the realistic details of David's life that the truer picture is drawn, now dark, now light, pleasing and displeasing in turn; and it is in giving these details that his great biographer has distinguished himself as well as painted an immortal portrait of his king. It is difficult to choose among his superb chapters those that deserve most careful reading and study, those that characterize most clearly their subject. Perhaps none is better and few so good as the ironic story, given in chapter 11 of II Samuel, of Bathsheba and of David's guilty love for her and its moving sequel in chapter 12.

The biographer of David throughout this story keeps himself behind the scenes. He makes no comment; the story is his business, and he employs all his powers in telling it. Like other writers of lesser note he expects us to fill in the gaps between his terse and dramatic succession of events: the king's sight of Bathsheba as she bathes on the roof of her house, his lust for her, her discovery that she is to bear his child, his swift sending for her husband Uriah. The device employed throughout the story and its sequel is that of irony, and seldom has it been better used. The irony of Uriah's disturbing piety in the face of David's dishonesty and distress is exceeded only by the king's letter to Joab which plans for Uriah's death and which Uriah himself, all unsuspecting, delivers to Joab. This is great narrative. The shrewd Joab knows his king and in his charge to the messenger characterizes himself as well. And in the following chapter the author, still in the background, by means of Nathan and his apt, ironic story reveals another and more generous side to David's nature.

In the sordid confusion of the king's court and household at Jerusalem, its intrigues and its crimes, David's biographer found ample material for his talents. For although David was strong as a king, he was lamentably weak as a father. There are few uglier stories than the behaviour of Amnon toward his sister Tamar given in chapter 13 and few more bitter ones than that in the chapters following of the revenge of Absalom and of his revolt against his father. Here again the author remains out of sight with neither praise nor blame. He can at one moment repel us with David's weak indulgence and at the next arouse our pity by his picture of the weeping king going barefoot up the ascent of Mt. Olivet and by his heartbroken cry when he is told of Absalom's ironic and degrading death. In the same manner he spares us nothing of the unloveliness of the king's last days when he is "old and stricken in years" and when his sons, Adonijah and Solomon, together with Solomon's mother, Bathsheba, connive and plot over the succession and over the possession of the girl Abishag.

It would be unfair to the author of these superb narratives not to mention traces within his work which suggest a new and unusual religious outlook for his day. Strictly objective and impartial though he is, free from moralizing reflections, he yet shows both in the story of Bathsheba and in its sequel an attitude toward ethical and moral conduct in the sight of God which is far in advance of the conceptions of his age. The old idea of God as the relentless champion of Israel and as primarily a God of war prevailed at the time of his writing and is clearly evident in David's own primitive conceptions of religion. It is, therefore, significant that so ancient an author should, two centuries in advance of the earliest prophets, at least foreshadow in his work a new and finer perception of human behaviour and of God's hatred of cruelty and sin.

Although none of the many other stories told of David in I and II Samuel equals in literary excellence those in II Samuel, 9–20 and in I Kings 1–2, there is little doubt that the same author wrote at least some of them. Chief among these not contained in the unexcelled narrative of the court and household are those which have to do with David's life as an outlaw, with his flight to Achish, king of Gath, and his later dishonourable dealings with that Philistine ruler. One such story, told with great liveliness and picturesque detail in chapter 25 of I Samuel, relates David's adventure with a rich shepherd called Nabal, whose name means a *fool,* and with Nabal's generous wife Abigail, who later, by a rather happy accident ascribed to God, is freed from her stingy husband to become one of the several wives of David. The chapter immediately following narrates in an equally picturesque manner an incident in the wilderness of Ziph, already referred to in our study of Saul, where David stealthily makes off with Saul's spear and water pitcher while he sleeps, and then taunts the king from the top of a hill on his coming forth to "hunt a partridge in the mountains." Another story, descriptive of his undeserved luck in ridding himself of the embarrassment of the Philistines of whom he has made shrewd use, is told in chapters 27 and 29, a story which, although it does not redound to David's credit, unmistakably depicts him as a soldier of fortune, destined to make all things serve his ends.

Still other stories in the earlier chapters of I Samuel, written by other hands and of not so high a literary value, record the love of Saul's son Jonathan for David and of that of Michal, Saul's daughter, to whom David was later to be so unjust. These stories attest the remarkable loyalty which David was able to instill in others, the prices they would pay and the sacrifices they would make because of their devotion to him. That his charm as a man was undeniable and his personal magnetism unequalled seem to have been true from the beginning to the end of his life. Nor must one overlook the numberless instances of his generosity, which, although they may well have brought him their rewards, constantly redound to his credit and in large part explain the devotion of later ages to his name.

It is small wonder that legends grew up about him, among them that of such passionate love for God that he composed numberless Psalms in praise of Him. His devotion to God was intense, to be sure; there is no hint throughout his long story that he ever countenanced other worship; and yet within it were the superstitious and primitive traits inherent in the religion of his day. The Psalms, attributed to him through the tradition of his genius as a musician and poet and by the glamour which succeeding generations lent to his name, were practically all written centuries after his time. But that he was a poet of highest excellence is shown in the lament which he composed in praise of Saul and Jonathan.

This lament, which is included in chapter 1 of II Samuel, may well close the portrait of him as a man and as a king. With the exception of his brief elegy over Abner, the captain of Saul's army, given in chapter 3 of II Samuel, it is the only poem unquestionably his which has come down to us; and as we read its moving and beautiful lines, we can regret deeply that this is true. Written shortly before the year 1000 B.C. when he ascended the throne of Israel and doubtless immediately following the deaths of Saul and Jonathan on Mt. Gilboa, it remains like the Song of Deborah one of the earliest treasures of Hebrew poetry.

The poem is an expression of deep and genuine sorrow. In no sense religious but rather a poem of personal and national grief, it belongs among the great elegies of all literature. Its total lack of sentimentalism and even of bitterness, its classical restraint, simplicity, and universal appeal, its note of generous forgetfulness of all past enmity reveal the best and highest self of its author. The beauty of its language, the use of ancient imagery, the repetition of suggestive words, the haunting, sombre refrain, and the musical and rhythmic stress of the naturally accented words give to it a solemnity and a dignity which cannot be too highly valued. It should be memorized by all lovers of poetry and cherished as a permanent possession:

The beauty of Israel is slain upon thy high places: how are the mighty fallen!

Tell it not in Gath, publish it not in the streets of Askelon; lest the daughters of the Philistines rejoice, lest the daughters of the uncircumcised triumph.

Ye mountains of Gilboa, let there be no dew, neither let there be rain, upon you, nor fields of offerings: for there the shield of the mighty is vilely cast away, the shield of Saul, as though he had not been anointed with oil.

From the blood of the slain, from the fat of the mighty, the bow of Jonathan turned not back, and the sword of Saul returned not empty.

Saul and Jonathan were lovely and pleasant in their lives, and in their death they were not divided: they were swifter than eagles, they were stronger than lions.

Ye daughters of Israel, weep over Saul, who clothed you in scarlet, with other delights; who put on ornaments of gold upon your apparel.

How are the mighty fallen in the midst of the battle! O Jonathan, thou wast slain in thine high places.

I am distressed for thee, my brother Jonathan: very pleasant hast thou been unto me: thy love to me was wonderful, passing the love of women.

How are the mighty fallen, and the weapons of war perished!

6

Elijah and Elisha and Their Stormy Times

When I was a child, I was given as a reward for memory work in Sunday-school a series of ten pictures of Elijah. They were in crude colours on cheap pasteboard, and from an artistic point of view I am sure nothing could have been more hideous. Nevertheless, they gave me an idea of Elijah which has stayed with me for many years and which is, I believe, substantially correct. Each pictured the ancient prophet in the same guise, that of a bearded man with wild eyes and flowing hair, dressed in scanty skins of wild beasts, and always in a state of intense physical and mental activity. Their titles bore out this notion of him: *Elijah Runs Faster than Horses, Elijah Confounds the Prophets of Baal, Elijah Threatens the Wicked Jezebel, Elijah Smites the Waters, Elijah Goes to Heaven in a Whirlwind.*

Elijah was himself a whirlwind only somewhat less devastating than his follower and disciple, Elisha. These supermen were actual historical characters, who confounded, and irritated, the northern kingdom of Israel about 850 B.C., nearly a century after the Division under Rehoboam, the son of Solomon. They dart in and out of the narratives of the two books of Kings like flames of fire, and that is evidently precisely what they were. Since we have, aside from these incomplete stories, no record of writings left by them, they are often called "speaking prophets." Perhaps, indeed, they wrote nothing. They surely seem always in too great a state of agitation to keep still long enough to write anything at all!

The stories about Elijah did not originally belong to the book of the Kings, which was at first one volume and issued about the year 600 B.C. They were written about two centuries earlier and inserted, only in part, in a later edition of the book. They are, therefore, incomplete, the original beginning and end being lost. Regardless of that fact, however, the remainder preserved to us is so vivid, lively, and picturesque that the figure of Elijah does not suffer overmuch; indeed, the beginning which we have in I Kings, chapter 17, by its very suddenness conveys a memorable impression of the completely unpredictable appearances and vanishings of the prophet. For Elijah was, above all other characteristics, *sudden!*

This ancient fragment of Elijah's biography is contained in chapters 17, 18, 19, and 21 of the book of I Kings and continues with material purely legendary in chapters 1 and 2 of II Kings. Wholly different from the chapters surrounding them, which are political accounts of Israelitish history and written by chroniclers of the day, the Elijah stories reflect instead a popular point of view. They obviously had their origin in the admiration of the common people for the strange prophet and may be considered largely legendary, whereas the surrounding narrative is factual and objective. The unknown editor who inserted them in the historical annals of Israel was evidently a great admirer of Elijah, and felt that at least a portion of his biography should be preserved. For this common sense and loyalty we can be forever grateful, as the Elijah stories, traditional or not, are among the most brilliant and charming in Hebrew literature and their author an unsurpassed teller of tales.

Moreover, these narratives of Elijah throw no small light on the conditions, social and political, existing in the northern kingdom at the time and give vivid supplement to the less interesting accounts of the various kings. We recall from our historical sketch that the northern kingdom of Israel lacked the firmly established dynasty of the house of David possessed by the southern kingdom of Judah, that it had arisen through the rebellion of Jeroboam, that it was far less secure in its position because of its nearness to enemy country, and that there was within it a far larger proportion of foreign blood. This last situation resulted in a more mixed race than that of the south and naturally in the importation of foreign religions.

When Elijah, who was called the Tishbite apparently from the name of some obscure village east of the Jordan, suddenly appeared before Ahab, king of Israel, there was a dreadful famine in the land, an event well authenticated by history. To Elijah, however, this famine of bread was far less important than the famine of religion. For under Ahab's wife Jezebel, a princess of Tyre, the worship of her god Melkart had risen to such prominence and even power that those loyal to the God of Israel were in despair. They were in despair, too, over the infiltration of strange, non-Israelitish customs, the new luxury of the court, the increasing social inequality and injustice—all conditions against which a century later Amos was to cry out in fury.

But Elijah could not wait for Amos. His life, which had evidently been spent in the desert regions east of the Jordan, had given him time to think over the sorry state of affairs; and when he appeared before Ahab, it was with purpose in his eyes. Ahab, according to most scholars, was not himself a Baal worshiper or probably so black a figure as we gather from the outbursts of Elijah, whose very fanaticism invited exaggeration; and yet that grave injustice did exist in Israel and that there was widespread apostasy from the worship of its one God seem unquestionably true. At all events, from the fine story of Naboth's vineyard it is clear that Elijah was concerned with oppression of the poor by the rich and that he saw in God not alone the one and only deity to be worshiped, but also a God who stood for justice and righteousness against injustice and sin —surely an advance from the earlier conceptions of God as a God of mountain thunder and as a War God of revenge and anger.

All of the few stories left us of Elijah should be read, as there are no more vivid single narratives than they in the Old Testament. They begin in I Kings 17 with a picture of the famine as a judgment of God against Baal worship. Journeying seventy miles from Gilead to the brook Kerith, Elijah sojourns in the wilderness, fed by ravens on bread and meat until the waters of the brook dry before the drought, when he goes to the Sidonian village of Zarephath to lodge there with a widow, whom God has commanded to sustain him. The story of her cruse of oil which fails not under the presence of the prophet and of her son whom Elijah restores to life is beautifully told with moving simplicity of style and with fine dialogue. One remembers that it is referred to in chapter 4 of St. Luke's Gospel where Jesus commends the ancient prophet for his kindness and breadth of vision in thus ministering not to an Israelite but to a foreigner.

Chapter 18 which follows, especially from verse 17 to its close, is certainly one of the most brilliantly written incidents in the Old Testament. In its picture of the religious contest between the worshipers of Baal and of God, in its sharp dialogue and equally sharp drama, and in its extraordinary use of irony in the taunting of the prophets of Baal by the mocking Elijah, it portrays an immortal scene. *Cry aloud*, he calls to them, after they have implored Baal from morning until noon to set fire to the wood beneath the sacrifice, *cry aloud: for he is a god; either he is talking, or he is pursuing, or he is in a journey, or peradventure he sleepeth, and must be awaked*. The extra detail of the barrels of water poured into the trench not only adds to the drama of the situation but serves as a means of postponing and strengthening the triumphant climax.

Behind the story, lending an atmosphere not described for us but understood by the people of its day and later, is the setting: the wooded headland of Mt. Carmel rising high above the blue Mediterranean; the solitary prophet standing on its height and crying to the hundreds of people below him: *How long halt ye between two opinions? if the Lord be God, follow him: but if Baal, then follow him*; the servant of Elijah climbing still higher

143

seven times to look at the reaches of the sea; the little cloud "like a man's hand" rising from the water; the growing blackness of the sky with clouds and wind; and at last the driving rain.

The remorseless slaying of the prophets of Baal in the brook Kishon contains within it traits of primitive religion, which we are not surprised to find continuing in Elijah's time and mingled with his more gracious sense of God. Another survival of it is shown in chapter 18 which records his mighty journey of two hundred miles on foot to Horeb, one of the primitive sites of the home of the mountain God. And yet here, in the sensitive picture of God in the still, small voice rather than in the wind, or the earthquake, or the fire, one glimpses quite another aspect of His presence.

Since we must regard as legend the spectacular accounts in II Kings 1 and 2 of Elijah's calling down fire from God to consume King Ahaziah's soldiers and of his ascent to heaven in a chariot of fire drawn by flaming steeds, the last more reliable story of Elijah is the famous one of Naboth and his vineyard. Here in the sulking of Ahab over Naboth's refusal to sell his land and in the wicked scheming of Jezebel, we are given a clear picture of the king and queen, the weakness of the one, the vigorous wickedness of the other. After the queen's perfidy has been rewarded by the stoning of Naboth and the possession of his vineyard, Elijah appears with his customary suddenness before the frightened and guilty Ahab and pronounces his awful prophecy of the cutting off of Ahab's sons and of the dogs that shall eat the wicked queen.

It is in this story that one discerns Elijah's sense of social justice and of his conception that God's "still, small voice" demands righteousness in one man's relation with another. With his prophecy of doom against the house of Ahab the prophet disappears from sight, having already chosen Elisha, the sturdy farmer with the twelve yoke of oxen, to carry on his work for Israel. Whatever has been lost from his original biography we do not know, but enough has been saved to preserve him as one of the arresting and memorable figures of early Israel. Even the legends that surround him enhance through their rich colours and the strength of their primitive outlines the truth of his reality and his power. One is not surprised to read in chapter 17 of St. Matthew's gospel that of the two men who appeared to Jesus on the Mount of Transfiguration and were seen by Peter, James, and John one was Moses and the other Elijah.

The cycle of Elisha stories, contained for the most part in the first nine chapters of II Kings, was written somewhat later than those of Elijah. As literature they fail to attain the reality and the dramatic power of the former stories. They form together not so connected an account as do those of Elijah, but are rather a series of narratives very loosely held together. Moreover, they are even more filled with the miraculous and the legendary, although the miracles accorded to Elisha are less spectacular. Nevertheless, Elisha was just as unquestionably an historical personage as was Elijah, although he lacked the titanic stature of his great predecessor.

Unlike Elijah, who was more concerned with religion than with politics, Elisha took almost too active a part in the political affairs of his turbulent times. Committed by Elijah to accomplish the downfall of Ahab's family, he instigated a reign of terror by anointing as king of Israel a ruthless army officer named Jehu, who has become known to us not only as a furious and reckless driver of chariots but as a wholesale murderer. This high-handed act of Elisha, although it resulted in the welcome death of the wicked Jezebel, hardly brought strength to the northern kingdom, which experienced under Jehu even darker days than under Ahab and his sons. It serves to prove, however, Elisha's influence in affairs of state. We are told, moreover, in the various narratives of II Kings how succeeding rulers of the unhappy northern kingdom came to lean upon the prophet for advice and counsel which seem often to have been anything but wise. At Elisha's death, described in the 13th chapter of II Kings,

Joash, king of Israel, was with him, the prey of his last out-burst of anger and of his last prophecy concerning the war with Syria.

Scattered throughout these accounts of wars and rumours of wars, with the Moabites, the Syrians, and between factions of Israel itself, in which Elisha played the part of counsellor, or instigator, or prophet, are many incidents of his activity as a friend and helper of all manner of persons. It is hard, indeed, to reconcile his concern with political affairs and his even greater concern with the rank and file of people about him; for he is more interesting and attractive as a friend to numberless human beings than as a meddlesome and erratic associate with inglorious kings. Unlike Elijah, who is always appearing suddenly and mysteriously and whose whereabouts are seldom known, Elisha seems omnipresent. *This is a holy man of God, that passeth by us continually,* says the Shunamite woman of him, and it is an apt description.

Humorous in many ways as is the picture of the fanatical prophet (for there is humour in the very variety and multi-plicity of his favours as well as in the fact that he was always about) there is also an appealing simplicity in his constant help-fulness. At one moment he is promising the Shunamite woman a son; at the next he is restoring a borrowed axe-head to a poor man. He provides food for the hungry, emulates Elijah in bring-ing back a child to life, heals one man of leprosy and confers the same disease in righteous anger upon another, increases a pot of oil to tremendous proportions, and cleanses the impure water supply of Jericho with salt.

Elisha apparently possessed the amazing physical vitality of Elijah. Not only is he always moving about in all manner of places, but in the lovely legendary story in chapter 2 of II Kings he is quite able to run by the side of Elijah from Gilgal to Bethel, from Bethel to Jericho, and from Jericho to the banks of Jordan. The picture of the two ecstatic prophets running side by side for a distance of some forty miles has its humorous aspects as well as its holy and must have amused as well as impressed those who saw them tearing along the country roads.

The writer, or writers, who wished to preserve Elisha's life and personality did not possess outstanding literary gifts. As single stories only one of those relating to him holds the artistic qualities of the Elijah narratives. That occurs in chapter 5 of II Kings and is the familiar story of Naaman, captain of the Syrian armies. A unit in itself, this story does not suffer from the confusion characteristic of so much of the Elisha cycle. The picture of the little girl of Israel, maid to Naaman's wife, and her concern over her master's illness, of Naaman's letter to the king, of Elisha's characteristic behaviour and Naaman's injured pride, of the washing seven times in Jordan, and of the high price paid by Gehazi for his covetousness—these incidents following rapidly upon one another with their graphic dialogue make together a fine literary achievement.

There is nowhere evidence throughout the stories that Elisha had the developed ethical sense of Elijah or that he stood on any high plane of religious thought. It must be admitted that, in spite of his kind deeds to divers and sundry men, women, and children, his ideas both in the realm of ethics and of religion were decidedly primitive. He cursed the ill-bred children who called him "bald-head" and apparently summoned two bears from the wood which "tare forty and two of them." He was without doubt responsible for Jehu's savage extermination of the sons of Ahab. And although the conception of God as a God of war and revenge is perhaps less objectionable in his story than in that of Joshua, for instance, it is surely not disputed or even relieved by any higher idea.

Yet, both in fact and in fiction he is a dramatic and waylaying figure, more than a trifle mad perhaps, and he introduces into the confusing and often dull annals of the kings of Israel a great deal of liveliness and not a little amusement. Much as we dislike his ideas, we can enjoy his prodigious vitality and his perennial ability to rise to any occasion whatsoever. And if the truly noble mantle of Elijah rests less well upon his shoulders, his somewhat uncouth wearing of it only serves to heighten in our imaginations and memories the stature of the greater man, the forerunner in a real sense of the mighty prophets of Israel.

7

The Great Prophets of Israel

1

AMOS

Among ancient peoples the Hebrews were unique in the possession of prophets and in the reverence accorded them. Just as Greece revered her philosophers and her poets and as Rome honoured her statesmen and military leaders, so Israel extolled her prophets. In the stories of the Pentateuch and of the books of Samuel and Kings the word *prophet* has, however, a different meaning and connotation from its later use. The term *seer* was the original term for prophet. It is often used in those books to describe those who were apparently endowed with peculiar and mysterious insight and contains within its original meaning powers of divination and of the foretelling of events. These earlier prophets, or seers, were evidently men, or groups of men as they seem to have been in the story of Saul and in the Elijah and Elisha stories, susceptible to mystical or prophetic states, who wandered about the country foretelling events, practising clairvoyance as Samuel did in the case of Saul's strayed asses, and arousing religious or perhaps patriotic fervour. In other words, such men in the early history of Israel were religious enthusiasts or even fanatics, given to emotional states of one sort or another. It was not until the reign of King Ahab in the middle of the ninth century that they became articulate in any powerful sense as did Elijah as a champion of God; and not until a hundred years later did they increase their mental and

149

spiritual stature as persons and enter into the prophetic literature of Israel.

Around the year 750 B.C., however, a new element came into
Hebrew thought and Hebrew writing in the startling figure of
Amos, the first of the "writing prophets." He it was who, like
many of those to follow him during the next three centuries,
introduced into the life of his day both the necessity for reformation in human behaviour and a new and wider conception of
God. He gave Israel, too, through his impassioned thought and
language some of the noblest of her poetry.

The time of Amos marked a critical period in the history of
the northern kingdom of Israel. In the half century between
the death of Elisha and the coming of Amos the growing empire
of Assyria had increased in power and lay like a dark, threatening shadow on the horizon. The people of Israel, however, had
had more immediate trouble with Syria, which bordered their
land on the north. In the books of the Kings we read of raids
by the Syrians against Israel and of cities taken by them. By the
time of Amos these raids had temporarily ceased, largely because
Syria was having her anxieties over Assyria; and a generation
had grown up in Israel which had not known war. The threatening presence of Assyria was forgotten for the moment in a
brief interlude of dangerous prosperity. The towns and cities
of Israel had become wealthy under days of peace, and many of
the former holders of land, small farmers and shepherds, had
moved to the towns to take up mercantile pursuits. The conditions under Elijah and Elisha were, in fact, primitive and
simple so far as social and economic life were concerned as compared with those of the days of Amos.

If we read carefully the nine chapters which comprise the
book of Amos, we shall gain a picture of this sudden prosperity
and of the evil and injustice in its train. The prophet has much
to say about the luxury among the rich, their winter and their
summer houses, their beds inlaid with ivory, the good foods,
meat and wine and oil, which they enjoyed, the music which

they cultivated, the drunkenness which they encouraged. He has more to say of the influence of such luxury upon the poor, the crooked business dealings from which they suffered, their difficulties in obtaining legal justice, the fact that they have been "sold for a pair of shoes."

Although Amos prophesied at the shrine of Bethel in Israel, he was a Judean from the region of Tekoa, some twelve miles east of Jerusalem. Tekoa was situated on a high plateau bounded on the north, west, and south by mountains and eastward sloping downward toward the Dead, or Salt, Sea. It was largely a wilderness, growing less and less fertile as it sloped toward sea and desert. A sparsely settled region, it was a place where a man could spend long days of solitude as he watched his sheep and where one given to thinking would have not only ample opportunity but ample encouragement in the stillness about him.

As one notes in the poetry of Amos the imagery drawn from the wilderness and the countryside, one recognizes that he must have been a thoughtful, sensitive man who brooded for solitary hours not only over the life of his day but over the meaning and nature of God. He was not unfamiliar with the life of towns, for he apparently journeyed at intervals twenty-five miles to Bethel to sell the wool from his sheep and he had observed the conditions there from the ancient shrine where religious festivals were held and from the talk in the market-places. When at last, convinced of a mission to his people, he decided to write and to speak, he burst like a whirlwind upon those gathered at Bethel for their business pursuits and for religious observances. He must have seemed to them in their easy prosperity the unwelcome voice of doom. To himself he was assuredly the mouthpiece of God.

The book of Amos is an objective book. In its pages one learns very little about Amos himself, his past, his family, his life in Tekoa. When Amaziah, the priest of Bethel, complains of him to the king of Israel as a conspirator against the crown and as a speaker of words which "the land is not able to bear,"

Amos discredits his lineage as a prophet, saying only that he is a herdsman and a gatherer of sycamore fruit whom God has called as he followed his flock of sheep. And yet, though he gives no more details than these, his vigorous mind and enlightened spirit show us what manner of man he was.

His book, which with the exception of a few doubtful passages is unquestionably his own, is divided into three well-defined parts: the first section, chapters 1 and 2, consists of a series of short oracles against seven nations and of a longer oracle against Israel; the second, chapters 3, 4, 5, and 6, forms a collection of outspoken and even violent denunciations against the social and religious sins of the kingdom; the last two chapters are descriptions of visions granted to Amos by God and sounding the doom of Israel.

From reading his oracles against the nations one gathers at the outset of his book that Amos is preaching a strange and even revolutionary conception of God and of his dealings with humanity; in fact, he marks through them a new era in the history of religious thought. Before his day the religion of Israel had been a national religion which before all else emphasized the limitation of God to Israel, its people and its land. With Amos God's interest and power are extended throughout the world. In the impassioned words of his oracles God is to punish other nations for their sins just as in the last chapter He is represented as having given home lands to other peoples as well as to Israel and as having led other nations in the past.

Are ye not as children of the Ethiopians unto me, O children of Israel? saith the Lord. Have I not brought up Israel out of the land of Egypt? and the Philistines from Caphtor, and the Syrians from Kir?

If, indeed, in the thought of Amos God has chosen Israel for a peculiar destiny, it is only because He means to enforce upon the Israelites and to exact from them a higher standard of conduct. To Amos God is God without discrimination of races and nations.

In this conception of God Amos, so far as we know, had no forerunners. Elijah's idea of God as One who demanded justice and righteousness, fine as it was, held nothing of the thought that He was the God of all nations. And it is obvious from chapter 7 that Amaziah, who must have been a religious leader of intelligence, had never before heard any such surprising teachings and regarded them as dangerous, if not seditious.

Because of this all-embracing idea of God we are not surprised to find in the denunciatory addresses of Amos, which form the second section of his book, his anger over the attitude of the people toward religious rites and ceremonies, their extreme devotion to the outward forms of religion. To him religion consists in righteous living, not in ritual, in justice toward the poor, not in meticulous oblations. He, therefore, pronounces doom upon Israel for substituting mere forms of piety for inward honesty and for service to others less fortunate.

I hate, I despise your feast days, he cries in the name of God. *Seek good and not evil that ye may live.*

Forasmuch therefore as your treading is upon the poor, and ye take from him burdens of wheat: ye have built houses of hewn stone, but ye shall not dwell in them; ye have planted pleasant vineyards, but ye shall not drink wine of them.

These addresses of Amos are scornful and bitter in their condemnation of the sins of Israel. There is no vanity or injustice that he leaves untouched in his prophecy of punishment and doom. Lust and wealth, bribery and oppression, feast days and images, drunkenness and frivolity, ease and trust in material possessions—all take their turn. In chapter 4 he inveighs with awful irony against the fashionable women of the city of Samaria who beg drink of their husbands. They are not only cows, but they are the sleek, well-fed cows of the fertile fields of Bashan. These things God will not tolerate, and the day of calamity and doom is certain. The armies of Israel in which they have so much pride will be as nothing in the day when they are surrounded by mightier armies and conquered because of their decadence and their spiritual ruin as a people.

In the last section of his book the prophet recounts a series of visions which God has vouchsafed him. By his intercession with God during the visions of the locusts and the fire, the dangers that threaten have been averted; but in the visions of the plumbline, the basket of fruit, and the destruction of a temple, ruin has again become certain and inescapable.

And it shall come to pass in that day, saith the Lord God, that I will turn your feasts into mourning, and all your songs into lamentation; and I will bring up sackcloth upon all loins, and baldness upon every head; and I will make it as the mourning of an only son, and the end thereof as a bitter day.

The greatness of Amos as a religious thinker and as a man of selfless devotion to his country is equalled by his remarkable ability as a writer. His book is beautifully and logically arranged; he knows the value of the principle of emphasis in the placing of his material as is especially well shown by his saving until last the denunciation of Israel in the series of oracles. He is familiar, too, with impressive rhetorical devices such as the repetition of words as an ominous refrain: *For three transgressions of Edom, and for four, I will not turn away the punishment thereof. For three transgressions of Israel, and for four, I will not turn away the punishment thereof.*

Amos knows also how to use imagery with fine and strong effect. In his apt comparisons and use of concrete objects one reconstructs something of his life in the wilderness of Tekoa, of his sensitiveness to the inner meaning of the simplicity and ruggedness of that life. *As the shepherd taketh out of the mouth of the lion two legs, or a piece of an ear; so shall the children of Israel be taken out. Can a bird fall in a snare upon the earth, where no gin is for him? Behold, I am pressed under you, as a cart is pressed that is full of sheaves.*

Amos has been perhaps justly called the prophet of doom, and it is true that he sounds little of the promise of hope. He is vigorous and rugged, cynical and ironic, severe, even castigating in his torrents of language. He does not know the meaning of patience and forbearance; he will not minimize or condone sinful behaviour. But although his message is a dark one, except for his new vision of the all-embracing nature of God, it vibrates with force and strength; and the admiration which one feels alike for his power as a literary artist and for his wisdom and breadth of mind should not be diminished by the mere fact that he had unpleasant things to say. So had Jesus to the money-changers in the Temple. So had Martin Luther before the Diet at Worms. So had Savonarola at the Duomo in Florence.

2

HOSEA

Whatever Amos lacks in sympathy and in tenderness both in thought and in its expression is supplied by the prophet Hosea, the second of the great prophets of Israel, who probably wrote his book or at least made his addresses a few years later than did Amos. Hosea was a northern Israelite and, unlike Amos, a man of the town rather than of the desert. The social and economic conditions prevailing in the Israel of his day were substantially those which engrossed the concern of Amos, although the emphases which Hosea placed upon them differ somewhat from those of Amos. Political problems were more acute in Hosea's day, for Assyria was encroaching more closely, and the rulers and people of Israel had become more aware of the danger which threatened them from that great empire.

The book of Hosea is divided into two parts: the first, which includes chapters 1, 2, and 3, records a rather obscure bit of biography; the second, chapters 4 to 14, contains in a somewhat disorganized and rambling form Hosea's addresses to his people. Scholars differ widely as to the interpretation of the first three chapters of Hosea's book, several claiming that they are only an allegory or a parable, more, that they record a genuine personal experience. It is impossible here to go into the various arguments to which they have given rise and sufficient to say that they seem to refer to a domestic tragedy in Hosea's life, a tragedy caused by the faithlessness to him of his wife Gomer. This faithlessness was, however, forgiven by Hosea both in pity for her waywardness and in understanding that God Himself was suffering a similar faithlessness in Israel's lack of love for Him. The best proof of the story as an actual or at least similar experience in Hosea's life would seem to me to lie in the tone of the following chapters; for underlying all his addresses is the obvious note of personal suffering, of tenderness, of pathos, and of extraordinary understanding and compassion.

The note of unfaithfulness runs throughout Hosea's book like a minor tone of sadness. Israel has played the part of a harlot with God who loves her. She has been unfaithful to Him, first, in her worship of other gods "upon the tops of the mountains, under oaks and poplars and elms," and even when her people have nominally worshiped Him in these "high places," they have forgotten that He demands loyalty and not sacrifice. In the second place, Israel, or Ephraim (a word often used by Hosea for Israel), has played the harlot morally both in revolting Canaanitish religious practices and also in the sins of adultery, robbery, and lying. And, thirdly, she is again a harlot, disloyal to God, because of her political and diplomatic intrigues with other nations, her seeking after foreign alliances with Egypt and Assyria in order to secure a doubtful peace instead of depending upon God's might for her safety. In judgment upon such conduct as this God will become the enemy of Israel, as the wild animals are to her flocks and as the moths are in her homes, and she shall be desolate.

Although Hosea in his addresses inveighs against the sins of swearing, dishonesty, murder, and adultery among the inhabitants of Israel, he is not primarily interested in the larger aspects of social inequalities and injustice. Nor does he look upon God as did Amos as the God of all nations and peoples. It is to Israel alone that he feels himself sent, and he is concerned only with her return to her God, with her conversion as a nation. The most outstanding contribution which he makes to Hebrew prophecy is through his original metaphor of the marriage relation between God and His people. To Hosea religion is an inward and emotional experience. He does not, like Amos, sound the note of doom, but rather the note of the love of God for His inconstant and erring children. Throughout his broken and restless sentences one is made conscious both of his own grief over Israel and of God's sorrow; and, even although he is forced to recognize the inevitable punishment of his people, one realizes that he does so in anguish rather than in anger and that God Himself shares that bitter pain.

It is difficult to gather from Hosea's book the orderly arrangement of thought which is so clear in that of Amos. Instead, Hosea speaks, or writes, impulsively and passes from subject to subject without any clear transition. It is as though his heart and mind are so full that he cannot take time to develop one thought before another comes pressing upon him. Thus divergent and even contradictory emotions follow fast upon one another, now anger and indignation, now an almost heart-breaking tenderness.

For I will be unto Ephraim as a lion, and as a young lion to the house of Judah: I, even I, will tear and go away; I will take away, and none shall rescue him.

O Ephraim, what shall I do unto thee? O Judah, what shall I do unto thee? for your goodness is as a morning cloud, and as the early dew it goeth away.

This style and diction throughout Hosea's prophecy reflect his deeply emotional and sensitive nature. His sentences are filled with cadences of grief and compassion. Bitterness is conquered by pathos, and practically all his lines have a distinctly subjective way of falling at their close in sharp contrast to the strong objectivity of the style of Amos. He is also far more simple in his manner of expression, his sentences, for the most part, short and poignant, suggestive of a pleading voice.

157

Come, and let us return unto the Lord: for he hath torn, and he will heal us; he hath smitten, and he will bind us up.

I taught Ephraim also to go, taking them by their arms; but they knew not that I healed them.

In contrast to such lines and words as these, which make one think of the muted notes of a flute, the plangent, ringing words and lines of Amos are like sonorous organ music. Perhaps, indeed, Hosea is the most appealing of all the prophets because of the deep tenderness of his emotions and the touching quality of his style.

As a poet Hosea is unexcelled in his beautiful use of similes. Comparisons seemingly came quickly to him, and he uses them lavishly throughout his book. They are taken from all manner of sources, and they show his wide and acute powers of observation and his familiarity with many sides of life both in town and country. The back-sliding of Israel is "like a back-sliding heifer"; the wicked in Samaria are "hot as an oven"; Ephraim is "like a silly dove without heart"; the sinners in Israel are "as the chaff that is driven with the whirlwind out of the floor, and as the smoke out of the chimney"; the king of Samaria is cut off "as the foam upon the water"; the people of Israel "have sown the wind, and they shall reap the whirlwind."

It is perhaps, indeed, more as a poet than as a prophet that we shall remember Hosea. For his thoughts share the poetic quality of his language. His use of an actual or imaginary experience in his own life is basically poetic as is his continued use of the metaphor of marriage between God and His people. In his belief that this relationship is fundamentally one of love, that God yearns over Israel, and that in the knowledge of Him is life, he continues his poetic and emotional appeal. And in his wide and beautiful use of similes as in the melodious quality of his language he is unsurpassed by any of the other poets of Israel.

THE GREAT ISAIAH

It is safe to say that the name of the prophet Isaiah is more familiar to most readers than that of any other Hebrew prophet. There is a lofty connotation about it, a sense of dignity, majesty, and power which is felt even by those who know little about Isaiah himself. We know that he is quoted again and again in the New Testament as chief among the prophets; we remember that his book was read by Jesus in the synagogue at Nazareth and that Jesus Himself was constantly allied with him in popular imagination.

Much of this admiration and even reverence for Isaiah is more than justified. He was actually in many ways the noblest among the prophets. Not only in the surpassing beauty of his language does he stand supreme, but also in many of his religious conceptions which were to illuminate his dark age and to survive in the pages and the precepts of the New Testament. Throughout a ministry of some forty years he was not only a poet, a prophet, and the inspired leader of a desperate nation, but he was also a statesman of great importance and influence. More clearly than any other man in Judah he saw the evils of his time and the destruction that faced his country. He laboured with kings inferior to him to avert impending disaster, protested against foreign negotiations and alliances, thundered against secret plots, attacked the social evils of his day which rulers were doing little to correct, and saw in the Assyrian menace the downfall of Israel and the humiliating vassalage of his own land of Judah. He must, therefore, be regarded as a statesman as well as a prophet, as a man of political affairs as well as a contemplative, a reformer as well as a poet—in fact, with the possible sole exception of Jeremiah, the most many-sided and influential among all the prophets of Israel.

Moreover, again with the sole exception of Jeremiah, his work extended over a long period of time. He did not, like Amos, dash in fury from the wilderness to utter stormy words and then return to his flock, or like Hosea utter almost plaintive words of appeal and of hope and then become lost in darkness. We know, in fact, a great deal about him and about the long years in which he laboured in Jerusalem, his cherished city.

He was apparently born there, some time between 770–760 B.C., and died not long after 700 B.C. So far as we know, he did not minister elsewhere. It is significant in his writings, both in his prose and poetry, that his imagery is derived from city scenes, from the Temple and its ritual, from the brook Shiloah which supplied water for Jerusalem, from the orchards and the vineyards just outside the city walls. Seldom does he make any references to the country or to the wilderness. But he sees with quick eyes the fashionable women of the town, the daughters of Zion, with their well-set hair, their rings, their bonnets, their tinkling anklets, their nose jewels, the scarlet clothes of the men, the houses of brick and stone, the sycamores in the gardens and on the hills. Tradition has assigned him an aristocratic birth and breeding, and it is very probable that he was of an excellent family, for he seems to have had early access to the court and during his long life to have been the uneasy and even unwelcome companion of several kings of Judah. He must have been married about the year 740 or shortly after because in 735 he had a little son who went with his father to meet King Ahaz "at the end of the conduit of the upper pool" in Jerusalem. We know nothing of his wife except that Isaiah refers to her as "the prophetess," a term which apparently does not in any way characterize her as a person but which means simply that she was the wife of a prophet. We can imagine, however, that, wedded to such a husband, she did not lead the most calm or uneventful of lives; and we may well wonder what she thought of the symbolic names which Isaiah fastened upon their two sons. For he called the first *Shear-jashub* meaning "a remnant will return," and gave to the second the ominous and somewhat weighty name of *Maher-shalal-hash-baz,* or "Swift is the spoil, speedy is the prey."

Before beginning to read the book of Isaiah we must become familiar with certain facts about the book, which in our Bible comprises sixty-six chapters. For many centuries it was assumed that Isaiah was the author of all these many chapters even although the most cursory study will prove that such could not have been the case. As a matter of fact, the book is a compilation of various prophetic writings, some by Isaiah, others by authors of later dates. The mistake, uncorrected for so many centuries, was without doubt caused in the beginning by the copying on scrolls of papyrus of this really unrelated material in order to utilize the papyrus—an early instance of saving paper! In this way prophecies never uttered by Isaiah and containing completely different historical backgrounds and theological thought came to be assigned to him.

It is necessary, therefore, to understand clearly what portions of the book called by his name were written or spoken by him. His own work is contained within chapters 1 to 39, and yet we cannot be at all sure that he is the sole author even of these chapters. Obvious differences in the style of several of them, or of parts of them, make it exceedingly unlikely that Isaiah is their author. It has been, in fact, generally concluded by the best scholars that Isaiah 1–39 is a collection or an anthology of oracles and prophecies by various now forgotten authors and that Isaiah's own work is scattered here and there within the collection. The authorship of the second half of the book, chapters 40–66, will be considered later; but for purposes of distinction we are conferring upon the writer of much of the first half the name of the Great Isaiah.

The difficulty of distinguishing Isaiah's work from that of other writers is increased by the fact that, unlike Jeremiah, Isaiah obviously did not prepare a book of his prophecies. He was probably far too involved in too many affairs for such concentrated occupation. Instead he merely wrote down from time to time some of his experiences, or thoughts, or addresses, a poem here, a prose passage there. His style and material, however, are so unique and characteristic that scholars are, for the most part, agreed as to parts undeniably by him; and it is these great and incomparable passages which will now engage our attention.

Readers of Isaiah should begin the book, not with chapter 1 but with chapter 6, for it is in this memorable and beautiful story of his vision in the Temple about the year 740 B.C. that Isaiah's great literary and religious work begins. There is no chapter in the Bible more effective and affecting than this one in its account of an overwhelming religious experience granted to a young man, who, probably from habit, has gone into the Temple for prayer or for some daily service held there. The account of the vision is majestic with its rising, lofty style and its wealth of dramatic detail:

In the year that king Uzziah died I saw also the Lord sitting upon a throne, high and lifted up, and his train filled the temple.

Above it stood the seraphim: each one had six wings; with twain he covered his face, and with twain he covered his feet, and with twain he did fly.

And one cried unto another, and said, Holy, holy, holy, is the Lord of hosts: the whole earth is full of his glory.

And the posts of the door moved at the voice of him that cried, and the house was filled with smoke.

Then said I, Woe is me! for I am undone; because I am a man of unclean lips, and I dwell in the midst of a people of unclean lips: for mine eyes have seen the King, the Lord of hosts.

Then flew one of the seraphim unto me, having a live coal in his hand, which he had taken with the tongs from off the altar:

And he laid it upon my mouth, and said, Lo, this hath touched thy lips; and thine iniquity is taken away, and thy sin purged.

Also I heard the voice of the Lord, saying, Whom shall I send, and who will go for us? Then said I, Here am I; send me.

Such writing as this is rare in any literature, and equally rare

162

is the effect of the mighty happening upon the mind and imagination of the beholder of the vision. To the young Isaiah God is exalted in His holiness above all human and earthly limitations and yet fills the whole earth with His glory. Before such glory he becomes sorrowfully conscious of his own littleness and his own inadequacy and yet so moved that from henceforth all his life must be seen and lived in the light of this vision of God.

After reading and rereading this chapter of chapters in which Isaiah's prose becomes so "impassioned," in De Quincey's word, that in its exalted quality it is actually poetry, we cannot do better, I think, for a relatively clear understanding of Isaiah as a man and as a literary artist than to consider his work under its three-fold aspect: as prophecy, as poetry, and as a distinct and peculiar contribution to the conception of God, which became a heritage both to Jewish and to Christian thought.

The prophetic addresses of Isaiah deal very largely with outcries, similar in material to those of Amos, against the shortcomings and the sins of the people of Judah; and yet in the style of Isaiah one sees at once a combination of the rugged vigour of Amos with the appealing tenderness of Hosea. His first prophecy, one of his country's destruction for her evil doing, is given in chapter 1, verses 2 to 8 inclusive; and in its verses one can easily discern the variety and the richness of Isaiah's style and language:

Ah sinful nation, a people laden with iniquity, a seed of evildoers, children that are corrupters: they have forsaken the Lord, they have provoked the Holy One of Israel unto anger.

Your country is desolate, your cities are burned with fire: your land, strangers devour it in your presence, and it is desolate, as overthrown by strangers.

And the daughter of Zion is left as a cottage in a vineyard, as a lodge in a garden of cucumbers, as a besieged city.

The women of Jerusalem deserve and receive stinging censure in Isaiah's sardonic picture of them in chapter 3. This prophecy is almost a tirade in its sharp, short sentences and in the almost hissing, spitting quality of his speech. Disgrace and ruin are the portion of these women, and one can imagine the angry shame with which they must have listened to the prophet's exhaustive catalogue of their vanities.

In verse 7 of chapter 5, where Isaiah is inveighing against the oppression meted out to the poor, one hears in the fall of his language the accents of his own grief and pity: *For the vineyard of the Lord of hosts is the house of Israel, and the men of Judah his pleasant plant: and he looked for judgment, but behold oppression; for righteousness, but behold a cry.*

. . It is often difficult in Isaiah's work to distinguish clearly the poetry from the prose, for, as in chapter 6, the rhythm of the prose is often so distinct and its language so poetic that it is, to all intents and purposes, itself poetry. There are, however, many passages of pure poetry with its characteristic parallelism, its musical stress, and its wealth of imagery. Always reserving chapter 6 as Isaiah at his best, we find in the first six verses of chapter 5 his famous song of God's vineyard, in which God sings a song to the inhabitants of Jerusalem and the men of Judah. There is in its verses a distinct melody almost suggesting that Isaiah sang it to the accompaniment of some ancient stringed instrument; and throughout its cadences one is reminded again of the qualities of Hosea's style and emotional approach.

In direct contrast to this song is Isaiah's poem on the armies of Assyria, given in the last five verses of the same chapter. These dark, hurrying lines with their terrible pictures of war and tumult, their sound and their fury, show the poet's power in quite another mood: *And in that day they shall roar against them like the roaring of the sea: and if one look unto the land, behold darkness and sorrow; and the light is darkened in the heavens thereof.*

It would be a pity to omit in this appreciation of Isaiah's poetry verse 2 of chapter 9, which is a poem in itself, as perfect as a fragment of Sappho or as a single quatrain of Housman. It is a poem of hope prefacing one of Isaiah's Messianic prophecies in which he is looking forward to the coming of peace and of righteousness through some wise and beneficent prince of the House of David, a prince who shall, unlike so many of his forefathers, walk in the ways of God. In each of its two parallel lines it rises both by the nature of its vowel sounds and by the placing of its clauses. No single verse in the Bible is more beautiful or more sure both in its choice of words and in its manner of using them; and it should be memorized and cherished as exemplifying the Great Isaiah at his best:

The people that walked in darkness have seen a great light: they that dwell in the land of the shadow of death, upon them hath the light shined.

With all due admiration for Isaiah's power as a thinker of his day, one should assign him, I think, higher praise as a poet. Although he had much of value and beauty to add to the religious conceptions of his time, he was not the equal of Amos, who transformed the God of Israel into the God of all nations and peoples. In his religious thinking Isaiah was far less radical and revolutionary than Amos. Nowhere in his work do we find him similarly international in outlook. Instead, his attitude toward Judah and especially toward Jerusalem would surely suggest little interest in foreign peoples for their own sake as other human beings. And yet he was more immediately constructive than Amos in seeing, not doom alone in God's judgment upon Israel and Judah, but the possible dawn of a better day in the future; and his teaching of the remnant to be saved, which runs throughout his prophecies, is characteristic of him and individual with him.

It was really Isaiah's great poetic genius and insight which in him as in Hosea largely accounts, I think, for the two most distinctive and most beautiful features of his religious thinking. The first of these is the emphasis laid throughout his work on the holiness and the majesty of God, His transcendence and yet His all-pervading presence. More than any other Old Testament writer he lays stress upon this conception, which is apparent in his very names for God, the Lord of Hosts, the Holy One of

Israel. God to him is above time and space and yet within them. In Isaiah for the first time in the religion of the Old Testament the Reality of God exists for itself rather than for tangible gifts and gains; and the song of the seraphim before the throne, *Holy, holy, holy, is the Lord of Hosts,* has come to be perhaps the purest and the highest form of worship.

And, lastly, in his mystical conception of Jerusalem as the Holy City, the sacramental dwelling-place of God, he becomes the unconscious forerunner of Plato's City of God, of St. John's New Jerusalem coming down out of heaven, of the great Latin hymns of the Middle Ages written by the saints of Cluny and of Clairvaux, and even of William Blake's ecstatic vision of the building of Jerusalem "in England's green and pleasant land." To this apocalyptical and visionary idea and ideal the poetry and the religious devotion alike of future ages owes more than can be described or estimated in words:

And the Lord will create upon every dwelling place of Mount Zion . . . a cloud and smoke by day, and the shining of a flaming fire by night: for upon all the glory shall be a defense.

And there shall be a tabernacle for a shadow in the daytime from the heat, and for a place of refuge, and for a covert from storm and from rain.

4

JEREMIAH

Before we begin to study the selfless and devoted work of the prophet Jeremiah for his country and to read certain of his poems, we must, first of all, rid ourselves of a prevailing misconception concerning him. As Job has been popularly extolled for his *patience,* so Jeremiah has been popularly known for his pessimism and sadness. He has been, and still is, called the "weeping prophet," and expressions of unrelieved despair are even today know as *jeremiads.* Actually, in spite of the contention of St. James in his epistle, Job was the most triumphantly impatient of men, unwilling to accept for a moment the sententious orthodoxy of his stupid and tiresome friends; and Jeremiah was, in point of fact, anything but the weeping willow of popular conception. Without doubt the mistaken attribution to him of the book of Lamentations, which he did not write, has added to this quite erroneous idea of him. Once we have learned of him, of his times, and of his untiring labour for his distressed country, we shall be far more ready to see in him the "iron pillar," the "defense city," and the "brazen walls," by which terms God characterized him when he was called to his long and disappointing ministry.

The days of Jeremiah were the darkest and most desperate days in the history of the kingdom of Judah. There is small wonder that his heart should "make a noise in him," that he could not hold his peace, and that a note of anguish and of bitter distress should be in most of his writings. But no amount of anguish or of distress could lessen the strength of his ministry or obscure the force of his indignation and anger on the one hand and of his unquenchable faith on the other. He could curse as well as weep, forsake the life of solitude and prayer for which he was fitted and for which he longed, in order to give unwelcome and despised advice to half a dozen kings. Among all the prophets there is none who gave so freely of himself to his country, who had so much in himself to give, or who endured so much of physical and mental suffering for his people and for his faith.

Jeremiah's prophetic service was a long one and perhaps the most eventful and indefatigable of any described in the Old Testament. He was born in the village of Anathoth near Jerusalem about 645 B.C. and came of a priestly family apparently of wealth and standing. In the year 626 B.C. he was called by God to his ministry when, in his own words, he was but a child, and warned that the kings whom he should advise and counsel would hate him and fight against him. His untiring battling against them continued throughout his life until he was carried away into Egypt where he presumably died shortly after 586, the date of the second and chief exile of the Israelites to Babylon.

From the many characterizations of himself expressed and implied which he gives in his long book, he seems to have been of a sensitive, introspective, even timid nature, reserved and solitary, loving the country more than the city, and having no taste and apparently, in his own estimation at least, few gifts for the life demanded of him. That he conquered his innate reserve and fear, that he became able to defy the world of his day, and that he kept his faith impregnable is in itself a record of triumph even greater than the inspiration of his poetry and the profound religious influence which he exerted upon his own and future centuries.

It was granted to him, or perhaps rather exacted from him, to live in times of even more complete disillusionment than those of Isaiah and under the nearer shadow of impending and inevitable disaster. His public ministry in Jerusalem covered forty years which were both epoch-making and shattering in the political history of Judah. The northern kingdom of Israel had already in 722 B.C. been overrun by Assyria and annexed to that Empire. When Jeremiah entered upon his work, the kingdom of Judah had long been a vassal state, which under the peaceful reign of Manasseh had paid for its absence of war by a cringing subservience to its Assyrian overlords and by the adoption of Assyrian religious practices which had made their unwholesome inroads upon the minds and lives of the people. At the beginning of his ministry Jeremiah found added cause for distress in the threatened invasion of Scythians from the north, who between 630 and 624 B.C. overran the Mediterranean coast and who had already impaired the power of Assyria. *The lion is come up from his thicket . . . to make thy land desolate,* cries Jeremiah of these advancing hordes. Once that tide had ebbed from Judah, the swift disintegration of Assyria before the rising power of Babylonia foretold more confusion. A brief period of Judean independence under the religious and national reforms of Josiah, the son of Manasseh, made possible by the downfall of Assyria, lasted little more than a decade and was doomed to destruction, for Josiah met his death in attempting to battle against Egypt, who, herself terrified, had come to the aid of Assyria. From the death of Josiah in 609 to the final siege of Jerusalem by Nebuchadnezzar, king of Babylon, in 597, three miserable kings of Judah, for whom Jeremiah had nothing but contempt, played inglorious roles of bribery, barter, and treachery.

Jeremiah throughout these confusing years became the enemy both of kings and people. Unlike Amos, Hosea, and Isaiah he did not in his addresses deal so specifically with the social sins of his people. He was more concerned with their religious apostasy, with their hardness of heart, and with their spiritual blindness. His prophecies are more general than theirs and far more repetitious in their one note of consuming sorrow. But like them he made the mistake of believing that he could make his way of thought and prayer the basis of any national life or national aspiration. Like them he was actuated by a spiritual vision and idealism unattainable and even undesired by those whom he tried to teach. His exalted conception of religion like that of St. Francis nearly two thousand years later fell upon ears more deaf than hearing. He was considered a traitor because he saw in Nebuchadnezzar's conquest the one hope of reconstruction for his people and because he recognized even in the brief period of Jewish independence under Josiah and the codification of the Jewish Law, only a life regulated by observances and not by the spirit. He was humiliated publicly, put in the stocks and in prison, and for seven years, in order to escape death at the hands of King Jehoiakim, forced to live in seclusion if not in hiding. It was out of a life such as this that he wrote his prophecies, condemning foreign religious practices, denouncing the vain hope of blind kings, preaching the ruin even of the Temple, and reiterating his conviction that only in the spiritual salvation of the individual lay the salvation of a people.

169

The long book of Jeremiah is divided into three parts: chapters 1 to 25 inclusive record his addresses and exhortations, his laments and his own confessions, his denunciation of kings and his dark warnings; chapters 26 to 45 form the so-called biography of Jeremiah supposedly dictated to Baruch, his companion and secretary; chapters 46 to 51 comprise various oracles against foreign nations.[1] For purposes of our knowledge and appreciation of Jeremiah as a prophet and a poet, the first part of his book is of greater importance than the rest, although Baruch's biography gives us, together with the details of Jeremiah's life, many of his addresses and one of his most memorable poems. Those contained in the first part, however, are, with this one exception, of a much higher literary quality, since the biography is largely in prose and seldom prose of a very high order. When the reader compares its chapters with those of Part I, he is tempted to see in the most of them more of Baruch's work than of Jeremiah's.

Yet even in Part I, where the best of Jeremiah as a writer is to be found, there is a great discrepancy at times between the beauty of his thought and language and the dull and repetitious addresses which he not infrequently makes. The originality and distinction of certain passages too often give way to mere rhetoric and to quite uninspired utterances. Perhaps the best explanation of the unevenness of the work is the assumption that, in preparing a complete edition of the book, Baruch combined Jeremiah's writing with his own, even rewriting many of his master's addresses with none too happy a result. Nevertheless, even in the midst of much that is monotonous and dull, there is more that is beautiful; and if we read carefully the best of Part I, we shall gain a deep appreciation of Jeremiah as a great lyric poet.

Jeremiah's manner of expression is more like that of Hosea than like that of any other prophet, and one can but assume

[1] Chapter 52 is a kind of historical appendix to the book of little importance to the whole, and really quoted from II Kings.

that he was deeply influenced by the former poet. He possessed the same emotional approach to life and to poetry as did Hosea, felt the same sorrow over his people, and echoes in his language much of the same subjective cadence of the earlier prophet. He is almost never objective like Amos and rarely exalted like the Great Isaiah. The pain of his own life enters everywhere into his words as does that of Hosea and endows his poetry with a deep personal significance. Like Hosea, too, he possessed a keen interest in the daily affairs of life, watched the potters, the grinders, and the smiths at their work, and used his observations of them to give point and vividness to his messages.

Although he was compelled to live in Jerusalem, he was apparently always homesick for the country, for in his poetry is a feeling for nature even stronger than that of Amos or Hosea and seen only in Job and in the Psalms, upon which latter book he exerted great influence. He describes lions emerging from their hiding-places; he knows the leopards and the wolves of the plains; he is distressed when wild animals, the hinds and the asses, have to forsake their young in the fields because of drought and when their eyes fail for want of grass; he watches the mysterious emigrations of the stork and the turtle-dove, the crane and the swallow, and contrasts their knowledge and wisdom with the ignorance and foolishness of men who know not God. He knows the snows of Lebanon and the "cold, flowing waters" of other mountains and hills; the partridge that sitteth on her eggs, the trees that spread out their roots by the rivers. His own heritage he compares in his despondency to that of a speckled bird against which the other birds assemble and his portion in life to a vineyard which men have destroyed. He speaks often of the high places, of bare hills, of dreary wastes of land, perhaps in thought of the wild barren hills near Anathoth, his birthplace, and sees in these the future desolation of Jerusalem.

More than any other of the prophets he excels in the description of terror, the terror of evil and disaster appearing out of the north, the terrors of darkness and of the paths that are lost.

Even God is a wayfaring man who must seek shelter against the night. For the first time in literature death in his poetry is called the reaper and his victims "the handful after the harvest-man." The figure of mourning runs through his verses. He writes a dirge for the women of Jerusalem to sing, and he hears the lament of mountain and of pastures:

A voice was heard in Ramah, lamentation, and bitter weeping; Rachel weeping for her children refused to be comforted for her children, because they were not.

He repeats again and again the pathos of sudden silence where once was activity and life, "the voice of mirth, the voice of gladness, the voice of the bridegroom, the voice of the bride," which cease in the streets of Jerusalem and in the cities of Judah, and "the light of the candle" which must go out. Such figures and images as these have without doubt strengthened the conception of him as a weeping prophet, but they must rather be taken as characteristic of his poetry and not suggestive of any lack of strength in him as a man. Moreover, though they give to his lyrics a note of melancholy and of darkness, they also add a beauty of their own, much as the so-called cynicism of Housman lends its own peculiar grace and understanding to his work. For surely the beauty of poetry is in no sense dependent upon its power to enliven the human mind or even to assuage human suffering.

Chapters 15 to 20 inclusive are perhaps the most significant chapters in Jeremiah's book, for they constitute what may be called his personal confessions. In these passages, which are partly in prose and partly in poetry, he analyzes his mind, discovers his fears, even resents God's calling of him, deplores his isolation and the rejection of him by his people, and like Job curses the day that he was born. And yet also throughout them is interwoven a theme, even a psalm, of conviction, of security and trust. *But the Lord is with me as a mighty, terrible one. Sing unto the Lord, praise ye the Lord.*

The importance of these confessions is not primarily perhaps a literary one, beautiful as are many of their verses. Their deep significance lies in the fact that they mark the beginning of a new type of poetry which rises to its height in the Psalms. This poetry is devotional, even mystical, in character, and has for its subject all the varied emotions of the human soul, remorse, anguish, fear, peace, joy in the nearness of God, distress in the sense of His absence, and, above all else, the conviction of His Reality even although those who know that Reality may experience no deliverance from their sufferings. It has been said that Jeremiah especially in these confessional chapters is not only the forerunner but the creator of the Psalms, many of which, not only in subject but in actual language, echo his words and emotions.

Within the confessions and in other chapters of Part I are certain units of literary expression which may well be studied as the best examples of Jeremiah as a poet. Perhaps the first such unit occurs in chapter 4, verses 23 to 27, in which Jeremiah is foretelling the threatened invasion of the wild Scythian hordes:

I beheld, and, lo, there was no man, and all the birds of the heavens were fled.

The poem is marked by the obvious device of repetition which both lends the sense of astonishment on the part of the poet and binds his poem together with dramatic effect. It is characterized also as is practically all the poetry of Jeremiah by a falling of the final lines of each verse after the manner of Hosea.

In chapter 8, verses 18 to the close, is a short poem of personal grief and disillusionment over the waywardness of the people of Judah. The simple statement with which the poem begins, *When I would comfort myself against sorrow, my heart is faint in me,* strikes the note of directness which runs throughout; and the haunting questions of the last verse are as characteristic of Jeremiah as are any of his personal revelations. There are, in fact, few sadder, more beautiful questions in literature than the familiar two which all readers of Jeremiah always connect

173

with his name: *Is there no balm in Gilead? is there no physician there?*

There is a series of dirges in Jeremiah which in the opinion of critics are among the finest of that type of literature. These occupy the greater part of chapter 9, beginning with the 10th verse. The first lament is over his country, the second over his people, and the last and most moving of all is that over death by destruction from forces without:

For death is come up into our windows, and is entered into our palaces, to cut off the children from without, and the young men from the streets.

Even the carcasses of men shall fall as dung upon the open field, and as the handful after the harvestman, and none shall gather them.

These dirges are remarkable for their quick changes in style, now exclamatory, now interrogative, now imperative, for their wealth of imagery from mountain and wilderness and field, and for their note throughout of irretrievable pain. Verse after verse closes with Jeremiah's characteristic falling note, with a trailing phrase, or, as in verse 10, with the simple statement, "they are gone."

Within the chapters of confession and subjective analysis are two curses, one against his life and another against his birth. These are, of course, reminiscent of Job, who also curses the night in which he was conceived and the day wherein he was born. The first and shorter begins the confessions of Jeremiah in verse 10, chapter 15, when his mother is upbraided in that she has borne him "a man of strife and a man of contention to the whole earth"; the second and longer closes the confessions with verse 14 of chapter 20. In reading the latter with its phraseology so similar to that of Job one feels convinced that the author of Job, who was without doubt one of the most learned men of his day, may well have known the work of Jeremiah.

The prevailing darkness and sorrow of Jeremiah's poetry is not entirely unrelieved by light. In chapter 31 of the portion

174

of his book usually assigned to Baruch there is a lyrical and beautiful poem on the return of the exiles to Jerusalem and of the New Covenant which God will make with His people of Israel and Judah. In the midst of so many chapters of dull and undistinguished prose it stands forth as an expression of hope and even of ecstasy. In its melodious and exalted lines Jeremiah restores in prophecy all those goodly and pleasant things which formerly he has described as lost: wheat and wine and oil, vineyards and watered gardens, dancing and song. And above all these material blessings is the new life of the spirit, when all men from the least to the greatest shall know the ways of God, and when the old law of rites and ceremonies shall be superseded by the new law written only in the heart of every man. This poem is, in fact, the final oracle of Jeremiah, a spiritual testament of the prophet in which he bequeaths to his people that assurance and faith in the possibility of an intimate knowledge of God, which has made his own life unique and his suffering glorious:

At the same time, saith the Lord, will I be the God of all the families of Israel, and they shall be my people.

Thus saith the Lord, The people which were left of the sword found grace in the wilderness; even Israel, when I went to cause him to rest.

The Lord hath appeared of old unto me, saying, Yea, I have loved thee with an everlasting love: therefore with loving kindness have I drawn thee.

Again I will build thee, and thou shalt be built, O virgin of Israel: thou shalt again be adorned with thy tabrets, and shalt go forth in the dances of them that make merry.

Thou shalt yet plant vines upon the mountains of Samaria: the planters shall plant, and shall eat them as common things.

For there shall be a day, that the watchmen upon the mount Ephraim shall cry, Arise ye, and let us go up to Zion unto the Lord our God.

For thus saith the Lord; Sing with gladness for Jacob, and shout among the chief of the nations: publish ye, praise ye, and say, O Lord, save thy people, the remnant of Israel.

Behold, I will bring them from the north country, and gather them from the coasts of the earth, and with them the blind and the lame, the woman with child and her that travaileth with child together: a great company shall return thither.

They shall come with weeping, and with supplications will I lead them: I will cause them to walk by the rivers of waters in a straight way, wherein they shall not stumble: for I am a father to Israel, and Ephraim is my firstborn.

Hear the word of the Lord, O ye nations, and declare it in the isles afar off, and say, He that scattered Israel will gather him, and keep him, as a shepherd doth his flock.

Such poetry as this has its echo only in the ecstatic, infectious outpourings of the Second Isaiah, and one is quite as comforted in the hope which it must have given to Jeremiah himself as to his exiled and miserable people.

Jeremiah bears the distinction of the first among the prophets to record his innermost experiences and as the first also to express the possible heights and depths of intimate communion with God. In the midst of days of darkness and chaos, of despair, dejection, and failure, of mental anguish, and even of anger against the life demanded of him, he was able to preserve a tenacious and even an exultant faith. He was an ancient St. John of the Cross, who never doubted there was light even though it was invisible and who, in the days when his doomed world was falling about him, foreshadowed in moments of agony as well as of illumination the dawning of a brighter day.

5

NAHUM

Nahum, who is numbered among the twelve minor prophets of the Old Testament, was not, in fact, a prophet at all. He was instead a great poet of war, second only to the unknown creator of the Song of Deborah. He was numbered among the prophets only because the original title of his martial song was *The Book of the Vision of Nahum, the Elkoshite*, which title with its prophetic word *vision* gave him an entirely undeserved place and recognition. Place he surely deserves and the highest of recognition, but as a poet and not as a prophet.

Nahum was a contemporary of Jeremiah, and it is easy to be quite accurate in the dating of his poem since the subject of it is the destruction of Nineveh, the capital city of the Assyrian Empire. Nineveh was destroyed by the Babylonian and Median armies in the summer of 612 B.C. The intense nationalism which breathes through Nahum's poem would suggest that he wrote it either during the short period of Judean independence from Assyria around 620 B.C., when King Josiah began his reforms, or just after 614 when Nineveh experienced its first assault.

Most of the first chapter of the three which comprise the book of Nahum is not by him at all. Some editor, who lived about the year 300 B.C., prefaced Nahum's ode with a psalm of his own time in precisely the same way that other editors inserted a psalm in the mouth of Jonah and a hymn of praise in that of Hannah, the mother of Samuel. Except for perhaps a few verses, the first chapter has nothing to do with the ode itself, which begins its stirring lines with chapter 2 and ends with the close of Nahum's book.

Nahum was not only a great poet; he was a great patriot. A complete and confirmed nationalist, he hated the "bloody city" of Nineveh, "full of lies and robbery." His fury against that "well-favored harlot, the mistress of witchcrafts that selleth nations through her whoredom," inspired his triumphant lines which together form an ode of great literary power. It is a poem of bloodshed and horror, of vengeance and destruction, with little to relieve its savagery and violence; but it must be admired for the sheer power and force of its expression and for its awful, but brilliant, imagery.

The poem is carefully formed. There are two main divisions, each consisting of three parts. The first division includes the whole of chapter 2; the second comprises chapter 3 to verse 18, which closes the ode with a dirge over the fallen city. Each of the divisions deals with the same material although the order is somewhat different: the attack on Nineveh, the crimes of the city, its capture and complete destruction.

Nahum excels in superb word-pictures and in the atmosphere of noise and tumult: the scarlet tunics of the fighting men, the flaming of the justling chariots, the noise of cracking whips and of prancing horses, the corpses piled in heaps, the shaking of the fir trees. He is masterly, too, in the haste of his lines which speed on with the speed of the battle itself. *Keep the munitions, watch the way, make thy loins strong, fortify thy power mightily. . . . The chariots shall rage in the streets, they shall justle one against another in the broad ways: they shall seem like torches, they shall run like the lightnings.* His figures are apt and brilliant: the strongholds of Nineveh shall be like fig trees with the first ripe and falling figs; the devouring fire shall eat like the cankerworm and the locusts; the kings and captains of Nineveh are like grasshoppers before the hot sun. Now he questions: *Where is the dwelling of the lions?* Now he commands: *Take ye the spoil of silver, take the spoil of gold;* now he bursts into lurid prophecy: *Behold, I am against thee, saith the Lord of hosts, and I will burn her chariots in the smoke . . . and I will cast abominable filth upon thee, and make thee vile;* now he mocks and taunts: *Behold, thy people in the midst of thee are women!*

Much as we may dislike the furious vengeance of Nahum, who seems to have little pity for children dashed in pieces or for the wholesale slaughter of the honourable with the dishonourable, we cannot fail to admire his consummate literary art. And when his fury has at last ceased with the destruction of Nineveh, we can perhaps admire most of all the quiet, almost still, lines and words of his epitaph in verse 18:

Thy shepherds slumber, O king of Assyria: thy nobles shall dwell in the dust: thy people is scattered upon the mountains, and no man gathereth them.

I, for one, could wish that he had seen fit to close his poem with the moving silence of this beautiful verse rather than with the joyful shout and the clapping of hands with which the nations who have suffered greet the triumphant downfall of Assyria's great city on the Tigris.

6

DEUTERO-ISAIAH

With the exception of the Psalms no part of the poetry of the Old Testament is so well known and so equally well loved as that portion of it included in the book of Isaiah, chapters 40 to 55 inclusive. I have already explained in the treatment of the Great Isaiah how much of the material in the book accorded to him came to be attached to his own work, unrelated as it was; and I have also in the historical sketch given in chapter III of Part I of my book, introduced briefly the author of Isaiah 40–55 as a man known to us as Deutero- or Second Isaiah. Now in this section of the chapter on the great prophets of Israel I shall attempt to write more fully about this poet and prophet whose ringing and ecstatic words are so familiar, at least in part, to all readers of the Bible. My presentation of him will be far more brief than I could wish, for the full appreciation of his poetry and the understanding of his great gifts to three great religions of the world, Judaism, Islam, and Christianity, would require a complete and even a long book.

Deutero-Isaiah, we recall, lived two centuries after the first, or Great Isaiah, and in Babylon with the exiled Israelites. Beyond these facts we know nothing further concerning him except for those conclusions which we are able to draw from his poetry and his thought. One assumes, perhaps with small basis, that when he wrote his matchless poems of comfort and of hope, he

179

was a young man, for the vitality and buoyancy of youth seem to be in his infectious outpourings, his effervescent spirits, and his vaulting dreams. This assumption, however, is a mere conjecture. We recall, too, that in the last years of the captivity in Babylon he saw in the rise of Cyrus of Anzan not only the deliverer of exiled Israel, but the shepherd raised up by God to bring about the return to Jerusalem and the rebuilding of the city and the Temple. From at least the year 546 B.C., when Cyrus was completing his conquests, Deutero-Isaiah may be thought of as proclaiming through his prophetic poetry deliverance and restoration to his people.

His book, written almost entirely in poetry, is a collection of poems placed in no clear sequence and often so overlapping one another that a close connection between their material and their thought is sometimes hard to grasp. Moreover, the outstanding characteristics of Deutero-Isaiah are not those of an Amos, whose arrangement of his book shows such a sense of order and of logic. This poet of the exile is far too full of things to say to pause for a logical arrangement. His feelings and thoughts run too fast even for his hurrying words. He leaps from one to another, springs out of one mood into the next; he mounts up with wings like the eagles of which he writes, bursts out with freshness like his fountains in the midst of his valleys. The understanding of his book is deepened and its beauty and value increased if several of his best poems are separated from their context and read by themselves. This method we shall follow in our study of him, first as a poet, and second as a thinker, for he was these more than he was actually a prophet.

What then are the qualities of his poetry? First and foremost is the quality of song, or perhaps more literally that of singing. His style is the exultant, rapturous manner of one singing a rhapsodic hymn:

O Zion, that bringest good tidings, get thee up into the high mountain; O Jerusalem, that bringest good tidings, lift up thy voice with strength; lift it up, be not afraid; say unto the cities of Judah, Behold your God!

Break forth into joy, sing together, ye waste places of Jerusalem: for the Lord hath comforted his people, he hath redeemed Jerusalem.

This singing style is heightened in its effect by the great number of musical images which he constantly employs. Not only are the waste places of Jerusalem commanded to sing together but "the isles and the inhabitants thereof," the heavens, the earth, mountains and forest and wilderness, the watchmen on the gates, childless women, and the redeemed of Israel. It is only the daughter of Babylon who must sit in silence and in darkness.

The Second Isaiah is intoxicated also by figures of speech. Single words, beautiful as they are in his highly imaginative use of them, are not enough. He must personify and compare. Jerusalem has drunk the cup of the fury of the Lord; she must arise and put on her beautiful garments; Babylon must sit in the dust, for she is no more "the lady of kingdoms"; God shall feed His flock like a shepherd and gather the lambs with His arm; the trees of the field shall clap their hands; God is the husband of Zion, of her that has been a grieved and forsaken woman, but is now a bride to be surrounded by many children. All flesh is as grass or as the flower of the field; the inhabitants of the earth are as grasshoppers; God stretcheth out the heavens as a curtain or as a tent; the moths and the worm shall eat the enemies of Israel like a woolen garment; Israel shall grow up before God like a tender plant; the word of God shall be as the rain and the snow which come down from heaven to make the earth bring forth seed and provide bread for those who are hungry.

His fancy is unchecked in his poetry and ranges from his pictures of the blessings to be conferred upon the poor and the sorrowing to that of the New Jerusalem with its foundations of sapphires, its windows of agates, and its borders of pleasant stones. He loves to use this fancy in a hundred different visions of restoration and of joy.

Every valley shall be exalted, and every mountain and hill shall be made low: and the crooked shall be made straight, and the rough places plain . . .

I will open rivers in high places, and fountains in the midst of the valleys: I will make the wilderness a pool of water, and the dry land springs of water . . .

Instead of the thorn shall come up the fir tree, and instead of the brier shall come up the myrtle tree . . .

I will bring the blind by a way that they knew not: I will make darkness light before them, and crooked things straight.

He loves to break forth into ecstatic commands which raise one's thoughts to his own exalted imagination and vision: *Comfort ye, comfort ye my people, saith your God,* he cries in the beginning of his message to his people in Babylon. *Keep silence before me, O islands . . . Listen, O isles, unto me; and hearken, ye people, from far. . . . Sing, O heavens; and be joyful, O earth. . . . Awake, awake, O Zion; put on thy beautiful garments, O Jerusalem, the holy city. . . . Ho, everyone that thirsteth, come ye to the waters, and he that hath no money; come ye, buy, and eat.* And in the same ardent, glowing enthusiasm he bursts again and again into rhetorical questions: *To whom then will ye liken God? or with what likeness will ye compare unto him? . . . Have ye not known? have ye not heard? hath it not been told you from the beginning? . . . Who hath believed our report? and to whom is the arm of the Lord revealed?*

In addition to the singing quality of his style, it has also a way of mounting higher and higher as he builds up phrases and clauses to a final climax both in form and in thought. This quality, shown in literally every chapter of his book, lends a sense both of haste and of height to his poetry and gives the same effect as that obvious in the ecstatic lyrics of Shelley, with whom, in fact, he has much in common as a poet. We noted this trait in the famous 6th chapter of the Great Isaiah where he describes his vision in the Temple; but the effect is even more marked in the later poet. The first Isaiah belongs among the classical poets of Israel and, exalted as is his poetry, he is more restrained in expression; the second Isaiah, writing two hundred years later, is close to the romantic age of Hebrew literature and is far nearer the poetry of the Psalms and of that of Job. This rising quality is best shown in the last verses of chapter 40, which begins his collection of poems and which of all chapters is perhaps throughout not only most characteristic of him but most beautiful.

Hast thou not known? hast thou not heard, that the ever-lasting God, the Lord, the Creator of the ends of the earth, fainteth not, neither is weary? there is no searching of his understanding.

He giveth power to the faint; and to them that have no might he increaseth strength.

Even the youths shall faint and be weary, and the young men shall utterly fall:

But they that wait upon the Lord shall renew their strength; they shall mount up with wings as eagles; they shall run, and not be weary; and they shall walk, and not faint.

In the same chapter 40 and prefacing the poem on the allness of God, which begins with verse 18 and ends with the passage just quoted, is a poem on the greatness of God, the mystery of His creation, and the majesty of His power and wisdom. This shorter poem is included between verses 12 and 18. Each of these poems on the nature of God and on the wonder of His works inevitably recalls both the thought and the expression of the book of Job. Did Job know the poetry of Deutero-Isaiah or did the latter know that of Job? This is a question argued by scholars but seemingly, to most of them at least, unanswerable, because the date of Job has never been securely established as is that of Deutero-Isaiah.

Chapter 55 complete gives us yet another unit of Deutero-

183

Isaiah's poetry. Here again are all the familiar means by which he gains the combined effects of exultant song, of ever-increasing height and climax, of beautiful imagery, and of the personification of various aspects of nature. One is carried on by it as by a wind and swept by it as with beams and shafts of sunlight. For Deutero-Isaiah dealt little in darkness. Only Babylon sits in darkness and Israel in the relatively infrequent memories of her apostasy from God. By far the greater portion of these chapters is bathed in a kind of incandescent glow, and in reading them one dwells in a place of light and new life, of hope and of expectation. It is not the depressing present in which Deutero-Isaiah lives, but in the glorious and magnificent future when the blind shall see, the deaf hear, when the faint shall receive power, when the crooked shall be made straight, the waste places a garden, and the rough places plain.

The poem given in chapter 53 is one of the most moving and even tender of all those by Deutero-Isaiah. It is also one which has played a great part in Christian thought and teaching. For many centuries it was believed to be a so-called Messianic poem, foretelling the coming of Jesus and recounting through prophecy His sufferings in atonement for the sins of the world. Such an interpretation is untenable; and yet in recognizing this fact one in no way minimizes the beauty and value of the poem, which is one of a group known as the Servant poems. Others of the same type and message, although not so high in literary quality as chapter 53, are found in chapters 42: 1–4, 49: 1–6, and 50: 4–9. They have been variously interpreted as to their common subject and as to their meaning. Some scholars have seen in the suffering Servant of God a past figure in Israelitish history, possibly Jeremiah; others have believed the Servant to be Deutero-Isaiah himself; still others the promised Messiah. The most reasonable explanation and that held by the best scholars assigns the part of the suffering Servant to no individual, but rather to Israel herself, who for her forgetting of God is now in exile, but who through her suffering will actually bring about the purpose of God not only for herself but for the world. Thus as her suffering has been in accordance with God's plan, so her restoration will be doubly glorious.

The poem is without doubt idealized. The apostasy of Israel is minimized and even overlooked; her patience in exile is hardly true; and the thought of vicarious suffering for the sins of many had surely never before been stressed. Yet, as we read the appealing lines with their tenderness and compassion, we realize that the poet, as always, was writing in the terms of the ideal and not of the real. He wanted to arouse his discouraged people, the handful of a dispersed nation, by instilling them with the thought that their suffering in Babylon had a world-wide significance, for through it they had themselves become the means of intercession and of hope for many.

Both the poetry and the teaching of Deutero-Isaiah comprise a kind of spiritual epic, an epic which not only aroused and influenced the faith of Israel, but actually surpassed all other writings of the Old Testament in its widespread influence upon Christian thought. No other of its passages are so close in their hope of redemption and of final joy to the precepts and the doctrines of the New Testament. Deutero-Isaiah, as I have said, was a thinker and a poet rather than a prophet in the actual sense of the word. Unlike the earlier prophets he did not, except in infrequent and brief passages, deal in reproof or in dire warnings. In his tender solicitude for suffering, in his perception of human dignity and worth, in his wisdom and understanding, and in his sense of joy through faith in God, he could move the hearts of people as could no other Old Testament writer.

The conception of God, which he revealed not only to his people but to later ages, was as hopeful and even as beneficent as were his words. God is, to him, first and foremost, a God of love. He will and must punish for sin, but He will likewise bind and heal. His powers of redemption and of forgiveness are vaster than those of punishment and suffering. Having chosen Israel as His people and given His pledge to her, He will keep

185

it forevermore. His loyalty endures and His love is everlasting:

For a small moment have I forsaken thee; but with great mercies will I gather thee. In a little wrath I hid my face from thee for a moment: but with everlasting kindness will I have mercy on thee, saith the Lord thy Redeemer. . . .

Therefore, the redeemed of the Lord shall return, and come with singing unto Zion; and everlasting joy shall be upon their head: they shall obtain gladness and joy; and sorrow and mourning shall flee away.

Nor was Deutero-Isaiah's conception of God limited to His justice and mercy toward Israel. No one, in fact, contributed more than he toward the transformation of the national religion of Israel into a religion for all men and nations. Except for Amos, the former prophets had limited God's care to that people whom He had chosen; Deutero-Isaiah saw that care and solicitude in a world-wide vision. To him, although only Israel is in possession of the true religion, that religion cannot and must not be hers alone. There is no God but God, and through Israel He must be made known to all the earth:

Thus saith the Lord, the King of Israel, and his Redeemer, the Lord of hosts; I am the first and I am the last; and besides me there is no God.

I am the Lord; that is my name: and my glory I will not give to another.

Passage after passage reiterates this faith and often in almost identical words. It is as though Deutero-Isaiah cannot impress too forcibly upon his people this truth which shall make them and all men free, and which, although he could not know it, was destined to become the corner-stone, not only of later Judaism, but of Islam and of Christianity.

And, finally, Deutero-Isaiah everywhere emphasizes the wonder and glory of God as "the Creator of the ends of the earth," who "fainteth not, neither is weary" and the comprehension of whom is forever lost in mystery. He, like Job, reiterates the insignificance of man and even of nations before the might of

God, "that bringeth the princes to nothing and maketh the judges of the earth as vanity," that "taketh up the isles as a very little thing." Like Job, too, he stresses, together with the might of God, His knowledge and His wisdom:

For my thoughts are not your thoughts, neither are your ways my ways, saith the Lord.

For as the heavens are higher than the earth, so are my ways higher than your ways, and my thoughts than your thoughts.

There are few readers who are not deeply affected by the thought and the poetry of the Second Isaiah, and especially in these present days of bewilderment and fear both for our own grievous time and for the dark and uncertain days to come. There is still need for his faith in the atoning effectiveness of suffering and death, for his infectious confidence in the future, and for his vision of the dawning of a Golden Age, in which all men, without distinction of race, may from the least to the greatest "go out with joy and be led forth with peace."

7

TRITO-ISAIAH

Before closing this chapter on the great prophets of Israel, at least a few words should be said concerning the poetry of that man known to us as the Third Isaiah, or as Trito-Isaiah. We shall recall that his time is that of the Return to Jerusalem, a time of distress and disillusionment to those Babylonian exiles who had in such courage and hope marched across the deserts on their long way home. It was largely to dispel that disillusionment that Trito-Isaiah in the last chapters of the book of Isaiah wrote his poems. Like his master Deutero-Isaiah he, too, dealt with the future although he has also much to say concerning the ethical and moral aspects of the religion of his day. Some scholars attribute all of chapters 56 to 66 to him; others will accord to him only portions of 59 to 66; still others see in these last chapters of Isaiah a compilation of the work of several writers. There is, however, such a similarity of thought and expression in many of the chapters and such an obvious dependence upon Deutero-Isaiah in tone and in expression that it is safe to believe that one man is the author of at least a major portion of them.

Most of the chapters preceding chapter 60, where the best of Trito-Isaiah's poetry begins, deal with the religious conditions necessary to be fulfilled in order that the returned exiles may become heirs to the glorious promises of God. These chapters, except for a few isolated passages, are not of so high a literary excellence as those beginning with 60. They deal with the necessary attitudes of the Jews of Jerusalem toward the strangers whom they have found in their old home, with the need of a temple not made with hands but with contrite and humble hearts, and with the relative merits of pious observances and of righteous living. As literature they do not need to concern us overlong.

It is with chapter 60 that our study and appreciation of Trito-Isaiah's poetry and message should begin, or perhaps even better with 61 where he describes in some of the most beautiful words of the Bible his acceptance and understanding of his mission to his people:

The Spirit of the Lord God is upon me; because the Lord hath anointed me to preach good tidings unto the meek; he hath sent me to bind up the broken-hearted, to proclaim liberty to the captives, and the opening of the prison to them that are bound;

To proclaim the acceptable year of the Lord, and the day of vengeance of our God; to comfort all that mourn;

To appoint unto them that mourn in Zion, to give them beauty for ashes, the oil of joy for mourning, the garment of praise for the spirit of heaviness.

In such lines and words as these one hears the lilting, singing style of Deutero-Isaiah, the underlying tenderness, the sense alike of solicitude and of hope. One is aware also of the figurative language and the use of moving and appealing single words.

In chapter 60 occur those familiar passages which have been used again and again in the hymns and anthems of the Christian Church and which again repeat the atmosphere of light, not only in their long vowel sounds but in their rising, exalted style:

Arise, shine; for thy light is come, and the glory of the Lord is risen upon thee.

For, behold the darkness shall cover the earth, and gross darkness the people: but the Lord shall arise upon thee, and his glory shall be seen upon thee.

And the Gentiles shall come to thy light, and kings to the brightness of thy rising.

Like Deutero-Isaiah, the Third Isaiah is concerned, as I have said, not so much with the disheartening present as with the glorious and triumphant future. He was sent to a discouraged people whose dreams had not come true, whose cities were in ruins, and whose homes in Jerusalem faced broken walls and gates. His mission is to arouse them to hope by his pictures of the days to come when prosperity shall return, when violence shall no more be heard in their land nor destruction within their borders, but when, instead, foreign kings shall come to see the greatness of Jerusalem and when Salvation and Praise shall be the names of her walls and of her gates:

The multitude of camels shall cover thee, the dromedaries of Midian and Ephah; all they from Sheba shall come: they shall bring gold and incense; and they shall show forth the praises of the Lord.

Thy gates shall be open continually; they shall not be shut day nor night; that men may bring unto thee the forces of the Gentiles, and that their kings may be brought.

These are the passages of Trito-Isaiah's work which we like best to remember. In some of the other chapters, which may or may not in their entirety be his, there is more concern with the outward aspects of religion and far more nationalism and even pessimism than in Deutero-Isaiah's poetry. On the whole, the disciple was much inferior to his master both in thought, to which he contributes relatively little, and in expression. And yet so often does he capture the spirit of his model and so deeply have certain of his poems become ingrained in the memories and imaginations of many that no study of the greatest of the prophets of Israel is complete without him.

8

The Fiction of the Bible

There is, of course, fiction throughout the Old Testament in those stories obviously legendary, in folk tales with but a slender basis of fact, if any, and in many of the narratives given as history which are at least partly, if not wholly, fictional. We distinguish these, however, from the conscious writing of fiction as fiction, that is, as a type of literature. In the Old Testament is found this type of literature in as pure a form as we find it in the short stories and novels of today; and we shall in this chapter proceed to consider the short stories of Ruth and of Jonah and the short novel of Esther.

1

RUTH

The book of Ruth is one of the most graceful and charming of short stories not only in ancient literature but of any time and in any language, and well deserves the high place accorded it by critics of various countries and ages. Goethe, among many others of its admirers, calls it the most beautiful of all idylls.

The story was written about the year 450 B.C. or some one hundred years after the Return to Jerusalem from Babylon. Its unknown author, however, sets it some seven hundred years earlier, for he begins it well and directly with the words: *Now in the days when the judges ruled, there was a famine in the land.* There has always been a controversy among students and admirers of his story over whether he had a purpose in telling it

191

beyond simply the writing of a pleasant tale, as to whether he was an ancient propagandist or merely an ancient artist. Artist he certainly was, too good a one to append a moral to his tale. But when one considers the date of its composition, the time from which it came, it is difficult not to believe that he was a liberal of his day with strong ideas of his own at variance with those dominant ones about him.

If we recall for a moment some of the conditions which met the Jews upon their disillusioning return from Babylon, we shall remember that among the vexatious and anxious problems awaiting and besetting them on all sides was the problem of mixed marriages. Their prophets of the Return had inveighed against this deplorable custom which began to spread even among the former exiles themselves; and Nehemiah had enforced the prohibition of such marriages by ruthless measures. This situation, coupled with the fact that some practical purpose usually lay behind most of the Hebrew writings, leads me, in common with many others, to feel that the author of Ruth had something definite to say in relation to his time and that he used his story as a lovely means to a good and wise end.

Although he places it in the wild, rough times of the judges, around 1100 B.C., the impression we have throughout is one of idyllic, even idealized surroundings. After the generous decision of Ruth, her husband Mahlon having died, to return to Bethlehem with Naomi from her native country of Moab, the scene is largely set in the fields of Boaz, the kinsman of Naomi, at the beginning of the barley harvest. The picture of Ruth, the Moabitess, working with the reapers and receiving her portion of food at noon-day from the hospitable hands of Boaz, of the seemly behaviour of his young men toward her, of her gleaning until evening, has a pleasing, pastoral quality which reminds one of other ancient settings of Arcadian simplicity, drawn by Theocritus or by Vergil.

This idyllic atmosphere extends also to the characters. The author has drawn them with no sense of the uncertainties of human psychology such as the writer of the story of Jonah was to show so brilliantly a century or two later. Not one of them is in the least complex; the natures of all are open and simple. Naomi, it is true, may show some shrewdness in her foresight in planning for her daughter-in-law's future happiness at the hands of Boaz; nevertheless, her act is not so much designing on her part as it is in accordance with the Hebrew custom of reminding a kinsman of his duty. The characters are as idealized, in fact, as is the setting and atmosphere. Boaz is the ideal land-owner and overseer, friendly and fatherly toward those who work for him. Naomi is as thoughtful of her foreign daughter-in-law as though she were of her own kindred, not failing, for instance, at night, in a homely touch of the author, to save supper for her after her day's work in the fields. Ruth herself, in the words of Boaz, is blessed by God in spite of her Moabitish inheritance in that she has eyes for no young men "whether poor or rich." And even the neighbours are capable of honest rejoicing with Naomi when her grandson is born and of saying that this foreign daughter-in-law of hers has proved better to her than seven sons.

A charming air of courtesy runs throughout the story. Everyone is on his best behaviour from start to finish. Everyone has gentle manners and is extremely gracious and considerate toward everyone else. All address one another in formal, courteous salutations; each appreciates openly the good qualities of each; the young men are chivalrous; even the kinsman, faced by the alternative offered him by Boaz, is frank and friendly.

The use of tradition and custom add their age and, therefore, their richness of atmosphere. The approach of Ruth to Boaz by night, the redeeming of the inheritance, the "manner in former time in Israel" of plucking off the shoe as a testimony—these add atmosphere and charm. The same values are gained by the blessing of Ruth and Boaz by the people, who compare her to Rachel and Leah, the two women held in reverence by them all as builders of the house and lineage of Jacob.

Throughout his short, and even slight idyllic story the style and language of the author heighten the effect which he wishes to gain and hold. His simple and direct prose has from first to last an undertone of poetry. There is obvious rhythm in Ruth's well-remembered words to Naomi: *Entreat me not to leave thee or to return from following after thee: for whither thou goest, I will go; and where thou lodgest, I will lodge: thy people shall be my people, and thy God my God.* This same poetic effect is easily apparent in Naomi's words: *I went out full, and the Lord hath brought me home again empty,* and in those of Boaz to Ruth when he prays that a full reward may be given her from the God of Israel "under whose wings thou art come to trust." It is apparent, too, in the manner of the narrative itself quite apart from dialogue: *For she had heard in the country of Moab how that the Lord had visited his people in giving them bread. So they two went until they came to Bethlehem.* And in the simple, suggestive description of the earliest dawn: *And she rose up before one could know another.*

As a story, Ruth is undeniably slight in its emotional appeal, perhaps sentimental, even a bit "pretty" when one compares it with the stronger and far richer story of Jonah with its wealth of human emotions and with the ironic approach of its author. Yet we must not demand of the writer of Ruth that he do something of which he had no intention. Within his narrowly prescribed limits he has beautifully done what he obviously set out to do: to suggest by means of a lovely and idyllic story the truth of which he was himself convinced, that God is no respecter of persons, that human love is able to bridge the shallow differences of nationality, and that true religion is a matter of the heart and not of race.

Nor is he devoid of humour. He must have taken especial delight in the climax to his story, in the nice touch of Naomi's neighbours deciding upon the baby's name, and finally in his quiet announcement that this child, born of a marriage between Israel and Moab, became no other than the grandfather of the exalted David!

194

JONAH

Cursory readers of the Bible or those who do not read it at all not infrequently criticise its lack of humour. They claim that it is a most sombre work, even a dismally pious one, quite wanting in any light or even cheerful touch which might relieve its high seriousness. Such comments as these prove conclusively that their makers do not know well what they are so glibly talking about. The Bible, since it deals with most serious matters, is naturally a serious book (though the adjective is both inept and incomplete) and yet it is not lacking in humour; or in irony; or in mockery; or even in farce, buffoonery, and horseplay. These critics, as an introduction to the humour of the Bible, might well begin by reading those four short chapters in the Old Testament which comprise the inimitable book of Jonah.

Jonah was written perhaps a hundred, perhaps two hundred, years after the book of Ruth and also by an unknown author. It purports to be a story about an ancient prophet named Jonah, who supposedly lived and prophesied about 750 B.C., but none of whose prophecies has come down to us, and who was the son of an unknown man named Amittai. Its author evidently shared the views of the author of Ruth, for his ironic narrative has obviously the purpose of proving that the compassion of God is not restricted to the Jews but extends even to the heathen. Through it he is clearly protesting against the religious arrogance of his people, against their hope, even expectation, that God will annihilate these heathen for their own benefit and well-being; yet, like the author of Ruth, he is too good an artist to append a moral to his tale. Instead he allows Jonah and God to discuss an uncomfortable situation with sullen fury on Jonah's part and with keen enjoyment over Jonah's predicament on the part of God.

In this story of Jonah we are reminded of the many-sided humour often seen in the old miracle plays. Nor is the parallel, I think, a bad one, for the story itself is dramatically constructed in three clearly-defined acts: the disastrous flight of Jonah which ends by his being swallowed by the fish; his final arrival in Nineveh and his bitter humiliation there; and God's triumph over his recalcitrant and still sulky servant. Moreover, as in many of the old plays we find in the story a mingling of all manner of material, credible and incredible, serious and almost slapstick.[1]

In spite of the simplicity of the author's narration, perhaps indeed because of it, Jonah emerges from the story as one of the most complex characterizations in the Old Testament. Although he takes at least the name of a prophet, he is, first of all, an egotist, who does not want God interfering with his life. When he hears God telling him to go to Nineveh and cry against its wickedness, he makes up his mind that he will do nothing of the sort. Instead he determines to escape from God by going on a Mediterranean cruise to Tarshish, presumably the ancient name for the port of Cadiz in Spain. He is also something of a braggart or at least a most voluble and indiscreet soul, for we are informed that he has already told the sailors that he is fleeing from God. He has, however, like most romanticists, a strong sense of justice in his nature, for, once the storm becomes disastrous and he is conscious that the lot cast by the sailors has fallen to him as its cause, he begs them to throw him into the sea lest he be the means of their death. We actually know nothing of him during his three days and three nights in the fish's belly; for the pious psalm accorded to him, in chapter 2, verses 2-9, as he languished there was added by a later editor, who may have thought the original author a bit too jocose and lighthearted and interpolated the psalm to put a better face on things. From the author himself we know only that Jonah in the fish's

[1] So far as I have been able to discover from a study of lists of miracle plays there is no evidence that one was written upon Jonah.

196

belly prayed to God and was straightway "vomited out" upon dry land. Deciding wisely to take no more chances, he proceeds to Nineveh when the second call comes from God, and, again loudly asserting himself, enters the city, dramatically informing the people of Nineveh that their days are numbered. He is, of course, entirely unprepared for their immediate repentance and conversion and quite obviously not only incensed but humiliated in that his effectiveness as a terrorizer has been so suddenly pricked and that his mission has proved fruitless. After furiously informing God that God's foolish leniency and not the honest repentance of the people of Nineveh has brought him to this embarrassing fix, he begs God to take his life, for he cannot bear the awkward and ridiculous position in which he has been placed. Infuriated further by the taunting question of God, he escapes from the now triumphant Nineveh and sulks by the roadside under the shadow of a booth which he has made. And so far as we know from the story he emerges from the sulks only to be exceedingly rude to God by a saucy and belligerent answer to God's repeated question.

The author of the story again shows his ironic gift for characterization in his portrait of God. And here again the comparison to certain of the old miracle plays is, I think, an apt one, for God displays many of those distinctive human attributes which the medieval plays often assigned to him. The God who commands Jonah to go to Nineveh and cry out against that wicked city is a God who is clearly not going to stand any flouting of His commands. Nor is He above using every measure He can conceive in order to humiliate Jonah and to make him a laughing-stock. He creates a mighty tempest in the sea; He prepares a great fish to swallow Jonah and to house him for three miserable days and nights; He decides to teach Jonah a lesson even at a sacrifice of His own dignity; and at length He even descends to a kind of practical joking in first preparing a gourd to cover Jonah from the heat, then in creating a worm to eat the gourd, and finally in raising up "a vehement east wind" to make Jonah sick, and weary of his wretched existence. All of these acts, though they serve as object lessons to Jonah, are too quixotic not to be taken humorously, and it seems to me very evident that the author meant them to be so taken. The almost impertinent sparring between God and Jonah in the last chapter, God's climaxing concern over the 120,000 infants in Nineveh, so young that they cannot tell their right hands from their left and over the "much cattle" there, and throughout the story both His apparent pleasure in Jonah's discomfiture and His ingenuity in devising means of increasing it must have given great delight to the author who conceived them.

I am sure that the scholars and the theologians are right when they see in the story of Jonah an object lesson for the rigid, law-ridden Jews of the time in which it was written and when they characterize its author as a man of vision and tolerance, impatient before the narrow exclusiveness of many of his race and universal in his conception of the limitless compassion of God. I think, however, that too few of them give him his due as an artist who effectively used his gifts of irony and of imagination in the charming conception and construction of his story. I even think that he may have been daring enough to use the name of a prophet in this same way and to have pictured the distinctly human, even fun-loving attributes of God in the same spirit as a means of making more vivid his protest against the narrow, nationalistic tendencies of his day.

That he enjoyed telling his story is evident in every line of his sharp, eager narrative; and that he loved fiction for itself is shown by his use of the material doubtless current at the beginning of the Greek period in which he probably lived. Big fishes like that of Lucian and of the author of the Book of Tobit play a part in many ancient tales; gulling and baiting an embarrassed victim is as old as mankind though few might have the temerity to make God employ such means; and the odd description of the beasts of Nineveh repenting in sackcloth has an echo in the story of Herodotus, who describes in one of his vivid tales how horses and oxen were shaved of their hair at a season of mourning.

At all events, whether one is uplifted by Jonah's message or delighted by its fun, here is his story. Moreover, uplift and delight do not, I think, need to be mutually exclusive emotions!

3

ESTHER

The unknown author of the book of Esther was an architect, rivaling even Thomas Hardy in his innate sense of form. The arrangement of incidents in his short historical novel has rarely been surpassed. Its perfect symmetry will be obvious to all who read it, as will be the causes of that symmetry: the skillful placing and the ironic unfolding of those episodes which foresee the outcome and motivate the plot, the proportion in space accorded to each, and the almost exact length of the rising and the falling action. When we have finished the book, we are conscious of the neat figure of an isosceles triangle.

Having given the author of Esther his due in these important respects and complimented him on the vigour of his prose and on his remarkable use of irony, it is difficult to give him much else. For his book is as sadly disappointing in the narrowness of its purpose as it is in the characters whom he has drawn with such vividness. Not one of them, except Vashti, who possessed the courage of good convictions, is worth preservation. All are self-seeking, designing, revengeful, and even cruel. Each, after carefully looking out for himself and his own future, has no concern left for the rights of others except in so far as the doubtful patriotism of Esther and of Mordecai plans for the preservation of their people by means of the slaughter of an incredible number of their non-Jewish enemies. As in the book of Ruth everyone delighted us by his courtesy and compassion, so in Esther everyone revolts us by his intolerance, his hatred, and his ruthlessness.

Few persons upon reading Esther can fail to ask why it was included among the so-called canonical books of the Bible. For, in addition to the unattractiveness of its characters, it is in no sense a religious book. The name of God is not once mentioned; and a narrow and fanatical patriotism everywhere takes the place of genuine religious feeling. Instead a concern for outward practices, such as fasting and sitting in sackcloth, suggests that our author regarded these forms and rites as the sum total of religion. And even these can obviously be set aside when they stand in the way of distinctly worldly ambitions.

The reasons for its inclusion in the canon of the Scriptures are discovered in its evident purpose. That purpose was to intensify the patriotic fervour of the Jews and their hatred of all Gentiles at the time when they were threatened not only by the invasion of Hellenism but by the terror of national disintegration and death. It was also to proclaim the institution of the Jewish feast of Purim, a yearly feast established to commemorate this story of the successful slaughter by the Jews of thousands of their Gentile enemies.

There are two chief theories as to the date of the writing of Esther. The book has been most commonly placed not long after the fall of the Persian Empire to Alexander in the third century B.C. and assumed to have been written in the East where, because of their aloofness, their religious arrogance, and their rise to economic power, the Jews had incurred hatred and opposition. The distinctly Oriental colour of the story aids in bearing out this assumption. There is, however, more than a slight basis for placing it much later, at the time of or shortly after the wars of the Maccabees when, in revolt against the frightful persecutions of Antiochus Epiphanes in 168–165 B.C., the Jews were swept by a wave of intense nationalism and of violent hatred of their Gentile enemies.

Whatever the date, the purpose remains the same; and one hundred years more or less cannot lessen or increase the atmosphere of hatred and lust for blood which runs throughout the book. Whether the author lived in Persia, as the first theory would assume, or in Jerusalem, as the second would contend, he is a novelist first and an historian second. For he is guilty of the use of completely incredible material which he claims to be historical. As examples of his rampant imagination, he tells us that the royal feast at Shushan lasted for six full months, that the gallows on which the wretched Haman met his death were eighty-three feet high, that in but one day the Jews without a loss to themselves slew 75,510 Gentiles, and that hundreds of "fair young virgins," imported from all the provinces in the kingdom, were given a full year's beauty treatment with every variety of ancient cosmetic! He apparently has no conception of historical time, for he places the date of his King Ahasuerus, or Xerxes, who actually ruled between 485 and 465 B.C., shortly after the First Captivity in 597, in which year, he tells us, Mordecai was deported from Jerusalem. Or, if he is aware of the correct date for Ahasuerus, he is not disturbed over the fact that Mordecai is a mere one hundred and twenty years of age at the opening of his story! Nor does he seem at all doubtful that a Persian monarch would have chosen a Jewess as his wife even with her alleged beauty.

After making all possible allowances for the barbarous character of an ancient age and for those excesses which intense nationalism often encourages, most readers will find little in Esther to commend it except the technical and literary excellence of its structure. Extreme devotion to one's race and kindred hardly atones for such implacable hatred toward one's enemies. And yet we must guard against the unfair conclusion that it portrays in general the Jewish mind of that day even in a time of bitterness and turbulence. It is far more fair to say that its author was as intolerant, dogmatic, and nationalistic as the authors of Ruth and Jonah were tolerant, liberal, and international. He was a good writer, but a small man.

The yearly feast of Purim, which perhaps was not so much chronicled as actually *invented* by the fervid author of Esther,

201

is still celebrated by orthodox Jews in the early spring; but, although the book is used as the Scripture lesson of the day, it is safe to say that, as they feast and give gifts to one another, they pay relatively little attention to the actual origin of the festival and less to the bloodthirsty spirit that animated its story.

9

The Book of Job

The Old Testament poem known as the book of Job is the incomparable literary masterpiece of our Bible. So far as I know, this statement has never been questioned by critics, scholars, or common readers; it merely repeats what numberless men and women of many centuries have gratefully acknowledged. Moreover, in its surpassing excellence the book has joined the company of the greatest masterpieces in the literature of the world. It is ranked with Dante's *Divine Comedy* and with Milton's *Paradise Lost,* both of which it deeply influenced, with Homer and with the great Greek tragedies, with Lucretius, Vergil, and Shakespeare. With them it shares the qualities of all complete and perfect art in its noble and exalted conceptions, its superb style, its sensitive apperception of the physical world, its profound thought, its compassionate illumination of human experience. And yet, unlike many of them, it seems to have placed small if any reliance upon earlier poetry. Perhaps, indeed, these earlier poems were neither known to its author nor accessible to him. At all events, his book is perhaps the most original work in the literature of mankind. It fits into no sphere or category. The abundance of its literary forms and of its moods and its thoughts defies any classification devised by the critics. It is not exclusively a lyric poem, nor a didactic, nor a reflective; it is all. And yet it might as well be termed a spiritual epic. Dramatic though it is in much of its movement, it is not intrinsically a drama; nor is it primarily a symposium. Nor with all its philosophy does it belong to that form of literature. All these classifications, specific or general, fail either to define or to do justice to it. It leaps the boundaries of them all to dwell in a place by itself, secure in its own peculiar and unparalleled genius.

Countless scholars, critics, and poets, writing about the book of Job, have brought to its interpretation their own wide and acute knowledge. With this fact in mind it is with a profound sense both of incompetence and of humility that I attempt in this chapter to make the reading of it more clear and the appreciation of it more profound. And yet, since obviously no book on the Bible can neglect to emphasize its distinctive and superlative contribution and character, I have no other choice than to do the best I can in introducing it to my readers.

The book should, I think, be considered from four points of view: its structure and form; its meaning and significance in relation to its time; its literary art; and its triumphant conclusion. Before beginning with the first of these, it should be said that the author of the book is unknown by name and that no definite place has been attributed to him by most scholars. The great majority believe that he was unquestionably a Jew, who lived in Jerusalem or at all events in Judea, although there are those who contend that he may have been of Arabian or Edomitic nationality. The date of his book has never been discovered nor is even its approximate time generally agreed upon. It has been variously placed from the time of Jeremiah in the seventh century to three hundred years later. Perhaps more critics place it between 500 and 400 B.C. than at any other date. All scholars unite in claiming the possession of great learning by its author. The sureness of his style, his command of language, the independence of his thought, and his amazing familiarity with the natural world assume an extraordinary intellectual capital as well as a consummate imagination. The knowledge that we have of him, however, is only that gathered from his book. Although he shed light upon the darkness of the minds of men, the actual facts of his life and character remain forever in obscurity.

The form of the book of Job is careful in plan and orderly in structure. It is comprised of five well-defined parts. The first and the last of these parts are in prose; the second, third, and fourth are in poetry. The first and last parts known as the *Prologue* and the *Epilogue* occupy, respectively, chapters 1 and 2 and chapter 42, from verse 7 to the end of the book. The second part, which consists of a long and sometimes repetitious debate between Job and his three friends, extends from chapter 3 to chapter 32. Part three, which records the speeches of a pompous young man named Elihu and which is very likely an interpolation by an editor, includes chapters 32 to 37. Part four, in which the book reaches its height as poetry, reveals the answer of God to Job out of the whirlwind and Job's reply, and extends from chapter 38 to the seventh verse of chapter 42.

The prologue and the epilogue form the prose framework within which the great poem is set. They tell, or perhaps retell, in vivid and picturesque language the story of a "perfect and upright" man who lived in a land called Uz and whose name was Job; they recount how Satan wagered with God that Job's piety and faith could not endure disaster and pain, how God accepted the wager, how Job bravely suffered the loss of his children and of his health, and how, after his three friends had failed to comfort him, God gave him twice as much as before and caused him to live happily ever after. This story has all the characteristics of an ancient folk tale and may well have been still current at the time of the writing of the book. There is a reference in the 14th chapter of the book of Ezekiel to a famous character in Hebrew legend named Job, who with Noah and Daniel has long been remembered for his righteousness; and it is obvious that the author seized upon his name and very likely much if not all of his traditional story. At all events by whatever means he made the story his own, he used it admirably as a charming, simple, and almost naive framework for his poem.

The poem, which we shall consider first in its meaning and its significance in relation to its time, begins with chapter 3, when Job, after having sat upon the ground in silence for seven days and seven nights with his three friends, Eliphaz, Bildad, and Zophar, curses the day in which he was born. Thereupon his friends begin their cycle of arguments with him upon the meaning of his cruel fate. There are three cycles of arguments, in all of which each friend has his say; and to each friend Job replies.[1]

The arguments are long and frequently wordy and redundant largely because the friends are given to repeating what they have to say for want of fresh points and premises; but the wise reader will omit no part of the three cycles, partly because the affirmation of the poem rests largely upon Job's refutation of his friends, partly because interspersed with Job's replies are some of the most beautiful passages of the poem both in the form of monologues and soliloquies and in shorter passages of his arguments themselves.

The specific subject of the argument is the explanation of Job's misfortunes. Why is he, a just man, seemingly punished for sins of which he is innocent? The broader subject arising from the specific is the justice of God in His dealings with human beings on this earth. And arising from this wider statement of the question is the whole philosophical problem of the presence of evil in the world which seems not consonant with the existence of an omnipotent and a just God. The problem may be stated as simply as possible in these words: Since God, having created all things, is responsible for all that is, He must be re-

[1] The three cycles are contained in chapters 3–14; 15–21; 22–27. It will be obvious to the reader that, in the last speeches in cycle 3, because of mistakes in editing, certain portions of Bildad's and Zophar's arguments are wrongly attributed to Job.

sponsible for evil; unless then one can prove that evil has rational explanation in human affairs and behaviour, God cannot be looked upon as either benevolent or just in His dealings with men.

One sees from the outset of the long argument that there is a great mental and spiritual gulf between Job and his three well-intentioned friends. Their purpose in talking with him is to explain and to justify his sufferings. Within their explanations they are entrenched and completely satisfied. No broader aspect of the subject of suffering disturbs them, and they become angry and vituperative when Job not only refutes their arguments but goes more deeply into the problem. For Job is not satisfied either with their weak and reiterative arguments or with his own initial assumption that God is omnipotent but not just. Out of his own anguish he sees with newly opened eyes a suffering world in which there seems no relation between man's conduct and his fate, where men pay too dearly for sins and shortcomings apparently inherent in them, where the righteous suffer and the wicked prosper, and where even death is denied a man who longs for it. The explanation of his own suffering is not enough. He must ask for other men, for a whole tortured world, why these things are so, who and what God is, and why He deals thus with all men everywhere. His friends are concerned only with Job's suffering and would help him if they could; Job is concerned with the pathos of human life, as well as with his own state, and with the questioning of other men. His friends seek the reason for Job's suffering in Job himself; Job seeks the reason in the nature of human life and in God. And throughout all his questioning he remembers as a never-to-be-forgotten assurance those days that are past when he walked by God's light through the darkness of life and when God's visitation had preserved his spirit.

When Eliphaz, the Temanite, opens the debate, he does so with great tact, complimenting Job on the comfort which in the past Job has given to others. He is, therefore, surprised at Job's cursing of his birth and at his longing for death. This is weakness in Job, and it must be corrected. He reminds Job that no innocent man ever perished from affliction and pain; that it is only the wicked who are consumed by the anger of God. Bildad and Zophar continue with the initial assumption of Eliphaz, entrenching themselves within a kind of syllogism: Only the sinful suffer; Job suffers; therefore, whether he is conscious of it or not, Job must be a sinner. They are willing to admit that no man is entirely sinless, that no man is just before the mighty justice of God; but they are not willing to acknowledge that Job's affliction is completely unmerited. As they continue in their arguments, they explain his suffering either as a punishment for natural human imperfection, in him as in all men, or as a disciplinary measure of God designed for Job in order to refine and deepen his nature. In any case God, who is just and merciful, can and will deliver Job from his anguish if Job unreservedly commits himself unto God.

Behold, happy is the man whom God correcteth: therefore despise not thou the chastening of the Almighty:

For he maketh sore, and bindeth up: he woundeth: and his hands make whole.

He shall deliver thee in six troubles; yea, in seven there shall no evil touch thee. . . .

Lo this, we have searched it, so it is; hear it, and know thou it for thy good.

As the friends continue throughout their long speeches, they add little to their initial arguments. They cite various examples of the pain accorded to the wicked man, how his roots are at last cut off, how he loses his good name in the streets of his city; and they bolster up their own argument by citing the faith of former ages and the teaching of their ancestors who believed precisely what they themselves hold to be true. They one and all beg Job to rely upon God, and they remind him that his searching for God's reasons is quite in vain:

Canst thou by searching find out God? canst thou find out the Almighty unto perfection?

It is as high as heaven; what canst thou do? deeper than hell; what canst thou know?

Job in his speeches refutes his friends. Right words, he says, are forcible always, and he is glad to listen to them, but their arguings establish nothing at all. His friends are, in fact, like dry brooks in a desert. They have failed to prove that he deserves his pain. They are forgers of lies and physicians of no value, and he wishes they would hold their peace. He readily acknowledges that God is all powerful and all knowing, just as they have reminded him; but unlike them he maintains that this omnipotence and omniscience of God are not controlled by justice; for it is perfectly obvious to any man who thinks for himself and trusts to his own experience that God destroys the righteous and the wicked alike and makes no distinction between them:

This is one thing, therefore I said it, He destroyeth the perfect and the wicked.

He contends that although, being a mortal man, he is not sinless, nevertheless he has done nothing to deserve such misfortune. He is not only innocent of crimes, but he is also innocent of wicked thoughts. And yet, even although he is innocent, he cannot assail God or contend with Him, much as he longs to do so, for God is not held by man's standards:

For he is not a man, as I am, that I should answer him, and we should come together in judgment.

Let him take his rod away from me, and let not his fear terrify me.

Yet in spite of his fear, Job at last, before the growing horror of his friends, speaks to God and declares his innocence:

Thou knowest that I am not wicked; and there is none that can deliver out of thine hand.

Thine hands have made me and fashioned me together round about; yet thou dost destroy me.

Remember, I beseech thee, that thou hast made me as the clay; and wilt thou bring me into dust again?

I am full of confusion; therefore see mine affliction . . .

Only do not two things unto me; then will I not hide myself from thee.

Withdraw thine hand far from me: and let not thy dread make me afraid.

Then call thou, and I will answer: or let me speak, and answer thou me.

In these speeches of Job to God, which are given in chapters 7, 10, 13, and 14, and in his affirmation of his faith in chapter 19, one becomes aware of four separate and distinct stages through which he passes as he speaks. First of all, in bitter complaint he accuses God of setting a watch over him as He would set a watch over a sea or a whale and of terrifying him by dreams at night. Secondly, he boldly proclaims his innocence which he says God knows as well as he does. In the third stage of self-justification he swears that he will retain his own independence of judgment before God: *Though he slay me, yet will I trust in him: but I will maintain my own ways before him.* And in the fourth, he proclaims not only his faith but his hope that he may be vindicated by God Himself after his own death:

For I know that my Redeemer liveth, and that he shall stand at the latter day upon the earth.

And though after my skin worms destroy this body, yet in my flesh shall I see God:

Whom I shall see for myself, and mine eyes shall behold, and not another; though my reins be consumed within me.

After Job's temerity in addressing God and declaring his innocence, a new element enters into the speeches of his three friends. They have no further arguments to make, but, infuriated by his mocking of them and horrified at his blasphemy in reproving God, they proceed to castigate him for his boldness. His words are not only unprofitable, but they are godless. How does he dare let such speech go out of his mouth? Even though he has not sinned heretofore, he is guilty now of the sin of blasphemy. They are insulted over being called as stupid as beasts, and they proceed to reiterate the fate of the wicked man.

210

By the time the third cycle of speeches begins, their disgust and anger know no limits, and they begin to accuse Job of specific misdeeds, of refusing bread to the hungry, and of injustice to the widows and the fatherless.

Job overlooks the angry accusations of his friends. He is concerned with deeper matters. He longs to appear before God if he only knew where to find Him, but he does not.

Behold I go forward, but he is not there; and backward, but I cannot perceive him:

On the left hand . . . but I cannot behold him; he hideth himself on the right hand, that I cannot see him:

But he knoweth the way that I take: and when he hath tried me, I shall come forth as gold.

Why is it that God has hidden His ways even from the righteous? Why is it that the wicked prosper? Why is it that dishonesty and cruelty seem to triumph in the world? Who shall answer these questions, not only for Job but for all men who like him wonder and are not satisfied?

After Job's friends are finally silenced, not, one gathers, so much by the force of his arguments, which have failed to convince them, as by their own disgust with him and his blasphemy, Job in a series of beautiful monologues reviews his past life, his present affliction, and the ethical code by which he has lived, a code which records compassionate virtues far in advance of the code of his day. This noble apologia, which occupies chapters 29, 30, and 31, apparently has no effect upon his friends; and at this juncture a new character is introduced in the person of a young man named Elihu. In spite of the fact that this third division of the book is considered by most scholars as an interpolation and not by the author of Job, it is well to summarize briefly Elihu's contribution to the argument. Elihu is obviously a bumptious young man who introduces himself by saying that the aged do not always understand matters clearly and that, since he has been given divine inspiration and is full of ideas, he will speak his mind. This he proceeds to do for six chapters until a coming storm silences him. He has nothing new to say whatever and reiterates the old badly. In his opinion, Job has added rebellion to his other sins and, so far as Elihu is concerned, he sincerely hopes that Job will suffer even more in the future than he has in the past.

With the speeches of Elihu, or, if they are interpolated, with the close of the final cycle of the speeches of the three friends, the argument of the book of Job is brought to a close to make way for the sudden and overwhelming appearance of God out of the whirlwind. The chapters which follow overshadow the argument itself not only in their astounding literary beauty but in the vision which they give to Job of the cosmos and of God as its author. Yet the argument itself is of peculiar significance for it sets forth for the first time in any extant biblical records the challenging of a religious and theological theory which before the publication of the book of Job had never been taken into question: the theory that human conduct receives just recompense or retribution from God. Job's three friends are the champions of the theory. They represent the orthodox Jews of their day who believed, in accordance with the Jewish Code of Law, that God had made a covenant with Israel, and that according to the terms of this covenant both nation and individual alike would be blessed if they fulfilled God's will, but cursed if they violated the Law. Certain of the prophets, to be sure, teaching both before and after the establishment of the Law, had attempted to place other emphases both upon the nature of God and upon the relationship of men to Him. They had stressed not so much the punishment for sin as the complete justice and mercy of God. They had encouraged personal communion with God as the highest state to which the individual could reach; and they had enlarged the conception of God as not only the God of Israel but the God of the whole earth. Nevertheless, the Law superseded the prophets, and, in spite of the proof of human experience, this doctrine of strict earthly retribution triumphed in the Jewish orthodox religion until long after the time of Job.

Eliphaz, Bildad, and Zophar are spokesmen for this traditional point of view. To them evil and suffering imply that the man who endures evil and suffering has consciously or unconsciously sinned. They are willing to admit both that a good man like Job may suffer evil because of a natural human weakness common to all men and that this suffering may be not so much punishment as a disciplinary measure sent by God; but, that suffering and punishment are essentially divine and just retribution for weakness as well as for sin, they do not for a moment doubt.

Job, on the other hand, denies the theory. A genuinely religious man by nature, he stands out against the traditional orthodoxy of his day. Intelligence, experience, and observation have proved to him that the theory is false, that there is, in fact, no exact correlation between a man's conduct and his fate. Evil is a taint of human nature, so inherent within it that no human being is free from wrongdoing. Pain and sin are natural laws, and since all laws, natural and divine, proceed from God, the only logical inference must be that God, at least so far as human intelligence can ascertain, is omnipotent but not just. This realization that God is of necessity neither benevolent nor just is more distressing to Job than all his physical anguish; and the knowledge that not only he but all men alike must endure this ironic injustice makes him cry out with insistent and desperate questioning.

The glory of this long and ancient argument lies, not first of all in its poetry, for greater poetry follows in the succeeding chapters, but in the intellectual honesty of Job. Faced on one side with a venerable religious theory and teaching and on the other with the plain, unadorned facts of human observation and human experience, he has the independence and the dignity to insist that the facts must take precedence over the tenets of his ancestral faith. His friends may hedge themselves about with formulas; he will maintain his own mind, his own independence and honesty of thinking even before God. He cannot, like

213

Ecclesiastes at a later date, be indifferent when he sees the ruin of his religious convictions. His deepest need is for faith in God, and yet to him, until his vision, no faith which is rationally impossible can endure. He becomes, therefore, the glorious non-conformist of the Old Testament and, indeed, one of the great non-conformists of history. And although at the close of his book his spirit is so exalted that even faith seems possible, his mind to the end refuses subjection to an untenable, if old and established, explanation which does not explain.

The finest evidences of literary power in the book of Job occur not in the argument proper, although there are occasional brilliant passages in its many chapters, but in those parts given over by the author to the monologues of Job and to the voice of God out of the whirlwind. Together these portions form, without question, the most exalted poetry in the entire Bible.

Before dealing with these several poems as units, it may be well to preface our reading of them by noting those distinctive and peculiar qualities which have made the author of the book of Job so justly renowned as a poet. First of all, his work is marked by intense and highly personal emotion. His language throbs throughout with an honesty and a depth of feeling which dispel any notion of convention, on the one hand, or of self-consciousness on the other. The matters of which he writes are of such importance to him that the reader is carried on from one to another of his varying moods with a sense of complete and immediate reality. Whether he is dealing with the bitter disillusionment and confusion of the world of men or with the magnificent and harmonious world of nature, this underlying perception of that which is real so unites and inflames his words that it is literally impossible not to be transported to his worlds and to live entirely therein.

His knowledge and appreciation of nature in all her manifold aspects render shadowy, indeed, all other poetry on the same subject. The sea, the clouds, the treasures of the snow, the hoar

214

frost, the constellations, the reeds, the irises, the corn, the olive, the lions in their dens, the wild ass and ox, the ostrich, the horse, the hawk, the eagle—all are seen as a vast series of vivid pictures, alive and activated by his amazing powers of acute and devoted observation. Nor are they seen only by themselves, for they are used to clarify the frailties and misery of men, their brief span of years, all manner of human activities, and the activities of God as well. Man's days are as a shadow or they are as the hasting eagle; his cries pour out as water; he comes to his grave like a shock of corn and casts off his life as does the olive its flower. The clods of the valley are sweet to the dead; the life of man faileth as the waters fail from the sea; God destroyeth the hope of man as the waters wear away the stones. Fields and even furrows complain when they are not tilled; God speaks even to the "small rain" and quiets the earth by the south wind; and the morning stars sing together. The poet's imagination so possesses him that in the dull mouths of the three friends he must needs place utterances which we cannot imagine them saying!

The poet's style is marked by great variety of construction and by sudden changes which add to one's astonishment at the breadth and variety of his images and figures. Now he questions, now he cries out in lament, now he sings in the slow measures of an ancient chant:

For now should I have lain still and been quiet, I should have slept: then had I been at rest.

He employs terse and rapid phrases and clauses and heightens their effectiveness by stirring verbs. His horses rejoice; they paw and swallow the ground; they cry *Ha! ha!* in the midst of battle. He loves the sudden expletives, *behold!* and *lo!* We are not surprised to be told by linguists that his Hebrew includes more unique, unusual, and varied words than does any other book of the Old Testament.

The most beautiful poems in Job are those contained in chapter 3, the poem on death; chapter 28, *Where is Wisdom?;*

chapter 29, the remembrance of things past; chapter 38, the glories of heaven and earth; and chapter 39, the wonders of the animal world. These should be read aloud and with the characteristics of the poetry in general clearly in mind.

The poem on death has the slow, measured accents of a dirge with its repeated use of the imperative throughout its first part:

Let the day perish wherein I was born, and the night in which it was said, There is a man child conceived.

Nor does the accent quicken when the imperative gives way to the plaintive questioning:

Why is light given to a man whose way is hid, and whom God hath hedged in?

The imagery throughout is dark and sad with its references to twilight, to the night, and to the shadow of death.

Where is Wisdom?, in chapter 28, is a beautifully constructed poem which shows fine workmanship in each of its verses. The many images of gold and silver and of various precious stones suggest that the poet may have seen his poem in terms of beautiful and delicate work in metal. The use of the refrain: *Where is the place of understanding?* serves as an effective unifying device. The single verses are practically all complete and concrete units in themselves with almost no run-on lines. It is, perhaps, in its tight and uniform structure the most simple in style of any of the single poems, and one surmises that the poet chose this neatness of form in order to allow the vastness of his thought to make its unembellished impression.

The poem in chapter 29 on the remembrance of things past is heartbreaking in its minor tones and its preponderant use of monosyllables. One thinks of Francesca's sad words in the *Inferno:* "There can be no sorrow greater than when in bitter distress one remembers happy days." The succeeding verses with their run-on clauses suggest a succession of now sorrowful memories:

Oh that I were as in months past, as in the days when God preserved me;

216

When his candle shined upon my head, and when by his light I walked through darkness;

As I was in the days of my youth, when the secret of God was upon my tabernacle;

When the Almighty was yet with me, when my children were about me;

When I washed my steps with butter, and the rock poured me out rivers of oil; . . .

Then I said, I shall die in my nest, and I shall multiply my days as the sand.

The poem on the glories of heaven and earth has no equal not only in the book of Job but in the Bible as a whole. One is tempted to say it has never been surpassed in any literature of any age. Its beginning in the whirlwind should not be overlooked nor should the realization that mighty winds have played a dramatic part throughout both Old and New Testaments. In the narratives of the New Testament they are used to increase the power of the miracles of Jesus and to describe the coming of the Holy Ghost on the day of Pentecost when "there came a sound from heaven as of a rushing mighty wind." In the Old Testament it was a great wind that assuaged the waters of the flood in Genesis, and a greater which rent the rocks of Mount Horeb when God appeared to Elijah in the still, small voice. This wind out of which God spake is the mightiest on record in the Bible. Its force was inconceivable, and its sudden terrifying appearance with the utter darkness in which it clothed the earth is the fitting setting for the voice of God.

The superb literary art of the poem is accomplished in various ways: its range, which begins with the foundations of the earth and continues with the immensity of its four parts, the north, the east, the south, and the west, with the proud waves of the sea and the dwelling-place of darkness and of light, is both tremendous and illimitable; its description of the phenomena of the heavens with their treasures of snow and hail, fog, wind, rain, and thunder, leaves no element undiscovered or untouched;

its form of questioning reveals quick and remarkable insight. The questions in themselves suggest answers, and, since Job can give no answers, they suggest also both the mystery which sweeps his mind and the mystery of God Himself. In its turn this two-fold mystery increases the dignity of the poem by its added implication of the eternal mystery of life.

I have never agreed with the critics who term this awful and majestic questioning of God "satiric and ironic." The questions in themselves, at least to me, deny any such rather paltry and distinctly human adjectives. They are overwhelming surely, but I cannot feel that God is convincing Job of his ignorance so much as He is overwhelming Job with His own power and might. The implication of satire on the part of God is, I think, too negative for the exalted affirmation of the poem itself.

The last poem, that contained in chapter 39 on the wonders of the animal world, reveals God in almost a naive manner. He seems to be taking delight in parading before Job His minute knowledge and care of His various creations. The poem lacks entirely the perfect structural unity of that on the glories of heaven and earth; and, although in its composition the poet evinces an astounding range of scientific information which he records brilliantly, there is far more of subjective pleasure in its wonders than of the objective grandeur with which he clothes his most perfect work.[2]

The fourth division of the great poem closes with God's final words to Job as recorded in chapter 40 and with Job's reply in 40 and 42:

Shall he that contendeth with the Almighty instruct him? he that reproveth God, let him answer it.

Then Job answered the Lord, and said,

Behold, I am vile; what shall I answer thee? I will lay mine hand upon my mouth.

[2] The added poems on behemoth and leviathan, charming though they are, are, in the opinion of scholars, interpolated and not by the author of Job.

218

God then concludes His addresses to Job by affirming that Job must take upon himself the majesty and power of God before he can dare to judge Him. And Job in his turn, now not only contrite and humble, but satisfied, repents in dust and ashes with the illuminating cry:

I have heard of thee by the hearing of the ear; but now mine eye seeth thee.

It is to the epilogue that we owe not so much the extravagant story of all the blessings now heaped upon Job as the reassuring vindication by God of His servant:

And it was so, that after the Lord had spoken these words unto Job, the Lord said to Eliphaz the Temanite, My wrath is kindled against thee, and against thy two friends: for ye have not spoken of me the thing that is right, as my servant Job hath. In these words of God are clearly evident His approval of the ways and of the speech of His servant Job. Man's right is to question rather than to accept blindly the teaching of other men; he should maintain his own ways before God; his confusion and bewilderment, even his complaint and his cursing, are more right and even more pleasing to God than is his unthinking acceptance of a faith handed down to him. There are dignity and worth in his use of the mind which God has given him even although that use leads him to doubt and uncertainty. That he is touched by the lot of his fellow-men, that his compassion enfolds them, that, in other words, he is alive and not dead during his threescore years and ten—these things justify his creation and are not only acceptable but even admirable in the limitless mind of God.

What then is the poet's conclusion of the whole matter? For it is he who has put into the mouth of Job his own bewilderment over the problem of evil in the world and his own desperate questionings; and it is he who at the close of his mighty book has recorded for his own and future generations the reaffirmation, though in darkness, of his own faith.

In his mind, as in that of Job, remains the realization that in view of the transcendence of God and of man's limited understanding of Him there is in this realm of time and space no solution and no answer to the vast and dark problem of human suffering and to the presence of evil and injustice on this earth. His intellectual position, therefore, remains unchanged: God is almighty, but He is not just.

Yet in the light of the vision granted to him of the wisdom and the might of God, of the order of His cosmos and the creation of His creatures, of the beauty of His universe before which man's mind is chastened and quickened, this intellectual position is revealed as not enough. He becomes aware of his own finite mind and nature before the infinite mind and nature of God. His spirit is exalted through what he has seen and heard; and he is swept by the profound conviction that his rational answer to the problem cannot be final and that, although man can never pierce the mystery of God's inscrutable ways or discover their meaning, there must be nevertheless beyond time and place and man's imperfect understanding an explanation and an answer. Like the blind man in St. John's Gospel who has received his sight and whose joy and faith are untouched by the querulous questions of the Pharisees, he knows but one reality: *One thing I know, that, whereas I was blind, now I see.* His own words echo those of him born blind when he cries:

I have heard of thee by the hearing of the ear; but now mine eyes seeth thee.

Upon this conviction he rebuilds his faith, a faith based upon vision rather than upon sight and no longer needing or asking a sure and certain answer to the sad questions of this earth.

10

Two Anthologies of Biblical Poetry

1

THE SONG OF SONGS

In our Bible the Song of Songs is known as the Song of Solomon or, in its full title given in verse 1, "The Song of Songs which is Solomon's." This title was given to it by some editor who was prompted to accord the book to Solomon probably because that king is so often mentioned in its verses and because in the book of I Kings Solomon is said to have written one thousand and five poems. The suggestion in the title is, of course, that this one is the best of that vast number.

The attribution of these poems to Solomon, however, is as fictitious as is the assumption through other descriptive titles that he wrote Ecclesiastes, Proverbs, and portions of the Apocrypha. Opulent and magnificent he was as a king, but there is no valid reason whatsoever to believe that he ever wrote a poem; in fact, all that we know about him dispels rather than contributes to that idea.

The Song of Songs, whose author or authors are quite unknown, is a short anthology of love poems. They are of various lengths, and their beginnings and ends are often difficult to determine, since in the form in which we now have them they are arranged without any clear and definite plan. They are sung by various characters, chief among whom are a bride, a bridegroom, their friends and wedding guests. For example, in chapter 1, verses 2 to 7 inclusive, the bride is yearning for her sweetheart. She is also worried over her coat of tan, which she has gotten from her work in the hot sun, and she is planning, as she ponders over the effect of her complexion upon her lover, a meeting with him:

I am black, but comely, O ye daughters of Jerusalem. . . .

Look not upon me, because I am black, because the sun hath looked upon me: my mother's children were angry with me; they made me the keeper of the vineyards; but mine own vineyard I have not kept.

Tell me, O thou whom my soul loveth, where thou feedest, where thou makest thy flock to rest at noon.

And in the same chapter, verses 8 to 11, the bridegroom sings the praises of her who to him is "fairest among women":

I have compared thee, O my love, to a company of horses in Pharaoh's chariots.

Thy cheeks are comely with rows of jewels, thy neck with chains of gold.

These first songs in their exchange of love and compliments are really arranged in the form of a duet, the girl singing, the boy answering her.

Interspersed with the exchange of songs and sometimes separate from them, for we must always remember that the present arrangement of the book is capricious and probably not as it was originally set down, are certain other poems and songs. These tell, as in chapter 5, a story of a search for the bridegroom through the city by the bride, who is treated roughly by the horrified watchmen, or, as in chapter 2 beginning with verse 8, recount reminiscences of the bride of a song sung to her one night in spring by her serenading lover:

Rise up, my love, my fair one, and come away.

For, lo, the winter is past, the rain is over and gone;

The flowers appear on the earth; the time of the singing of birds is come, and the voice of the turtle is heard in our land.

Arise, my love, my fair one, and come away.

Sometimes the friends and wedding guests sing of her beauty as she dances before them, as in chapter 7:

How beautiful are thy feet with shoes, O prince's daughter:
Thy two breasts are like two young roes that are twins.

Thy neck is as a tower of ivory; . . . thy nose is as the
tower of Lebanon which looketh toward Damascus.

The climax of the collection comes in the last chapter where the bride, beginning with verse 6, sings an eloquent and intensely passionate description of human love as the strongest and most precious of all things on earth:

Many waters cannot quench love, neither can the floods drown it: if a man would give all the substance of his house for love, it would utterly be contemned.

The background and atmosphere of the Song of Songs are idyllic and pastoral as are their images and figures. These latter are so much more elaborate and rapturous than elsewhere in the poetry of the Old Testament that one suspects foreign influences on the author or authors. For example, the term "my sister" used in addressing the bride is an Egyptian expression. The overwhelming admiration for doves, gazelles, lavish gardens, foreign fruits and spices, and the many other somewhat bizarre and overdone images are also seemingly Egyptian or in places Persian in origin. The graceful and beautiful descriptions of the awakening of the world in the spring show a far more aesthetic appreciation of natural scenery and a far greater elaboration and variety in literary method than is characteristic of Hebrew poetry, where the images are much more simple and the expression, even at its most lyrical as in certain of the Psalms, far more restrained. These traits, together with the use of certain Egyptian, Persian, and Greek words, prove the date of the book to be late, surely after the conquest of Palestine by Alexander and probably around 250 B.C.

The early Christian Fathers and scholars interpreted the Song of Songs as an allegory signifying the love of Christ for the Church. But it is clearly a most beautiful collection of poetry extolling the quite natural and even physical love of human beings for each other. The atmosphere of fields, orchards, and vineyards, the delight in colour, sound, tastes, and fragrance, the elaborate and impassioned imagery, and the tender descriptions of the coming of spring—all these prove the vivid and prodigal imagination of the poet or poets to whom we are forever indebted. The Song of Songs, completely different though it is from any other poetry in the Old Testament and not in any sense religious, nevertheless adds immeasurably to the richness, variety, and humanity of our Bible.

2

THE PSALMS

No portion of our Bible, whether of Old Testament or of New, is so familiar to most persons, so reverenced, and so loved as is that part of it known as the Psalms. These ancient songs have been used for centuries in both Jewish and Christian worship; they have been repeated over and over again to express every variety of religious thought and feeling; and they have been rightly regarded in their English form as among the most deathless contributions to our literature.

What then are the Psalms? They are, first of all, the most profound revelation in the Old Testament of the life and the character of the Hebrew people, both in the outward and inward manifestations of that life and character. In them are displayed those racial and hereditary qualities which we have seen elsewhere in the Old Testament but which here are presented and suggested in the heightened form of poetry. The qualities preserved here are, therefore, those most strongly marked and felt, salvaged from the whole and preserved as those most full of meaning and reality to the Hebrews themselves. In these poems one finds their patriotism and their glowing, fervent faith, their intense love of life with all its pain, their hatred of their enemies, their sense of human worth and dignity and of the wonder of human creation; one finds, too, that intimate knowledge of mountain and desert, the hills to which they lift their eyes, their love of pastures and of flocks, their gratitude for water, for the shadows of great rocks, and for the bounty of the harvest, their knowledge of the swallow and the sparrow, of the hart who panteth in thirst, and of the fields dry and wet by rain. And over all their familiar landscapes there rise again and again the bulwarks, the towers, and the gates of Jerusalem, their actual and mystical home, the outward and visible sign of their inward and spiritual grace and strength, toward which pilgrims come from afar chanting their hymns of praise. The Psalms are, then, the spiritual epic of the Hebrew people, the yearnings of their souls after what is alone real to them; and they possess as their most outstanding and beautiful quality the natural and uncontrolled expression of all which lay deep within the hearts and minds of their writers.

The Psalms are also perhaps the most perfect blending in all literature of poetry and of religion. Into their words and music is translated that inner rhythm of the soul which only the most profound depths of human emotion can conceive and express:

Whither shall I go from thy spirit? or whither shall I flee from thy presence?

If I ascend up into heaven, thou art there: if I make my bed in hell, behold, thou art there.

If I take the wings of the morning and dwell in the uttermost parts of the sea;

Even there shall thy hand lead me, and thy right hand shall hold me.

The Psalms are one of the richest collections of poetry in any language because literally every emotion is within them. They complete the whole wide range of human desires, the longing for security and peace, for food and drink to sustain life, for companionship both human and divine, for approbation and for praise. They mirror in their words and images not only those highest reaches of which the soul is capable but all the more inglorious qualities of human nature, for complete frank-

ness and sincerity are among their chief attributes. The writers
hate as well as love, curse as well as praise; they do not conceal
their anger even before the Lord nor do they forget to call
upon Him for revenge and anger on His part: *O daughter of
Babylon, happy shall he be that taketh and dasheth thy little
ones against the stones. . . . Let burning coals fall upon them:
let them be cast into the fire; into deep pits, that they rise not
up again.* They freely acknowledge their periods of doubt, their
personal shame, nor are they upon occasion slow to assert their
self-righteousness. Again and again in the Psalms are reflected
the loneliness of the human spirit which no earthly comfort can
assuage, the solitude of mental pain, the waves and the billows
upon which men's souls are tossed; yet more often are voiced
the wonder of life itself, the incomparable mercies of God, and
His constant care for His children. Joy, sadness, revenge, praise,
hope, faith, gratitude, fear, anger, hatred, and love in all its
forms—these together make possible those utterances of the
Psalms which discover, and *uncover,* human nature in all its
attitudes and aspects.

The word *Psalms* comes from the Greek word *psalmos,* which
means the playing of a stringed instrument and which suggests
that the Psalms were songs intended to be sung to accompaniment. The Hebrew title of the book is *tehillîm* or *tillîm,* which
means *praises* and which defines the *contents* of much of the
book just as the Greek and English titles define its form. In
actuality, however, the Psalms are not strictly a collection of
hymns, even although many of them were doubtless sung in
the services of the Temple, for within their pages are many
poems which were obviously not composed for singing and
several others which are not entirely of a religious character,
such as Psalm 45, a song in praise of a king and of a royal
wedding. We are on safer ground if we call the Psalms an
anthology of Hebrew poetry, devotional in its nature, written
and collected for the daily help and enjoyment of the Jewish
people rather than for the performance of rituals in the Temple.

Few of the psalms were written before the Exile or probably even before the year 400 B.C. An exception is made of Psalm 24, or at least a part of it, with its familiar words: *Lift up your heads, O ye gates; and be ye lift up, ye everlasting doors; and the King of glory shall come in.* This may well have been sung in the early days of the monarchy, and it is often associated with the bringing in of the Ark to the new Temple of Solomon. But its probable age is rare among practically all the psalms in the collection; in fact, there is no evidence that there was singing in connection with Temple worship until at least a hundred years after the Return to Jerusalem, when guilds of Temple singers began to be organized and when probably much of our Psalter originated, or at least that part of it obviously liturgical.

We should, then, think of the Psalter as largely the product of three centuries, from 400 B.C. to 100 B.C., when it was completed. In style it represents the literature after the Exile. One can easily see how completely different are its language and its imagery from those of the ancient Hebrew poems like the Song of Deborah and David's Lament. This ancient poetry is simple and concise in style and far more restrained than is that of the Psalms, which have much in common in their quicker rhythm and in their ecstatic, unrestrained outpourings with the poetry of the Second and the Third Isaiah. We have already seen that the theory of the David authorship is entirely impossible. That his name provides the titles for so many of the psalms can be ascribed to the addition of titles by editors who, of course, remembered his fame as a poet and as a musician.

A careful examination of the book of Psalms will discover that it is made up of five clearly defined collections of songs and hymns. These may well have been separate anthologies, compiled at different times and joined together only when the final edition of the book was made. Each collection is separated from the one following by a kind of doxology which forms the final verse of the last psalm. The first book, or collection, ends with Psalm 41, with the words: *Blessed be the Lord God of Israel from everlasting, and to everlasting. Amen and Amen.* The second book closes with Psalm 72: *The prayers of David the son of Jesse are ended.* Psalm 89, with its doxology similar to that of Psalm 41, concludes book three as Psalm 106 concludes book four. The final anthology includes Psalms 107 to 150 and ends in the same manner.

There is obviously no unity of subject matter in each of the five collections. Each comprises psalms on all manner of subjects and reflects every sort of human emotion. But since the various authors have not assisted us by grouping their poems in any clear and definite way, we may well, for the purpose of better understanding this most beautiful of religious anthologies, make our own distinctions within the mass of unrelated material.

The book of Psalms may, then, be considered under two main divisions: (1) those psalms which primarily have to do with the nature and with the works of God; (2) those which present the various emotions of the individual. Sometimes, of course, these subjects will overlap in a single psalm, but, on the whole, the division will, I think, prove helpful. Nor can we obviously expect to consider more than a few of the finest psalms in each division.

(1) Many of the most beautiful psalms extoll the greatness and glory of God in the physical world. Two of particular excellence are Psalm 19 with its familiar beginning: *The heavens declare the glory of God; and the firmament showeth his handiwork,* and Psalm 104 with its exultant, ecstatic outpourings in praise of God's manifold creations, from the clouds which are His chariot to the trees which He has made "full of sap," from the volcanoes and the earthquakes to the conies who live in the rocks and even to the bread "which strengtheneth man's heart." This psalm, one of the loveliest in the entire Psalter, is supposedly based on the Egyptian hymn of King Ikhnaton. The poets' contemplation of the heavens in certain psalms leads, as

in Psalm 8, another especially fine one of this first division, to the question: *What is man, that thou art mindful of him? and the son of man, that thou visitest him?*

This contemplation of the glory of God leads the psalmist to consider the justice of His judgments and the assurance of His mercy. Of all the many psalms, which include, as outstanding examples of this interpretation of God, Psalms 1, 34, 77, 91, and 95, I am inclined to think that Psalm 91 is the richest in its wealth of beautiful figures, in its mystical symbolism, in its various forms of parallelism, and in its skillful change of the personal pronouns to include all men:

He that dwelleth in the secret place of the Most High shall abide under the shadow of the Almighty.

I will say of the Lord, He is my refuge and my fortress: my God; in him will I trust.

A thousand shall fall at thy side, and ten thousand at thy right hand; but it shall not come nigh thee.

(2) The second division, those psalms which present the manifold emotions of the human heart and mind, is much larger than the first and of a far more varied character. The first group of these distinctly personal psalms includes those which express the individual's gratitude and praise to God for His many blessings. Among them are Psalms 40, 103, 111, 116, 138, 145, and, perhaps finest of all, Psalm 107, with its summary of God's gifts to man and with its repeated refrain: *O that men would praise the Lord for his goodness, and for his wonderful works to the children of men.* The refrain, of course, suggests that it was a hymn used in congregational singing in temple or synagogue, and yet it is, first of all, a personal hymn of praise.

Among the psalms of this division are many which may be called pilgrim songs, for they were evidently composed to be sung while people were journeying to Jerusalem from their distant homes for religious festivals. One can imagine a long line of such pilgrims nearing the Holy City and bursting forth into the exultant words of Psalm 121 as they reach the first foothills: *I will lift up mine eyes unto the hills, from whence cometh my help. My help cometh from the Lord, which made heaven and earth. . . .* Or of those of Psalm 125: *They that trust in the Lord shall be as mount Zion, which cannot be removed, but abideth forever. As the mountains are round about Jerusalem, so the Lord is round about his people from henceforth even forever.* And when they have once arrived in the city before the Temple, what more likely than that they should sing Psalm 48: *Great is the Lord, and greatly to be praised in the city of our God, in the mountain of his holiness. Beautiful for situation, the joy of the whole earth, is mount Zion, on the sides of the north, the city of the great King.* Or Psalm 122: *I was glad when they said unto me, Let us go into the house of the Lord. Our feet shall stand within thy gates, O Jerusalem.*

In this second division are the so-called occasional poems which recount the sufferings of Israel or which draw inspiration from her triumphs. These were apparently written in the interests of national pride and patriotism or for the purpose of instruction. Psalm 78, for example, in its many verses is perhaps not so noteworthy for its literary expression as for its long account of God's wondrous "signs in Egypt," His revenge upon Israel's enemies, and His everlasting understanding of His chosen people. Without doubt the best illustration of these occasional psalms is Psalm 137 with its quick shift of emotions from heartbreaking sorrow to bitter hatred and its corresponding change in style. There are few more perfect examples of later Hebrew poetry at its best than the opening verses of this psalm:

By the rivers of Babylon, there we sat down, yea, we wept, when we remembered Zion.

We hanged our harps upon the willows in the midst thereof.

For there they that carried us away captive required of us a song; and they that wasted us required of us mirth, saying, Sing us one of the songs of Zion.

How shall we sing the Lord's song in a strange land?

230

Other psalms reflecting distinctly individual and personal emotion are the many poems of private lamentation over grief or over sin. The most heart-breaking of these in its simplicity and broken rhythms is, perhaps, Psalm 130, known as *De profundis: Out of the depths have I cried unto thee, O Lord. Lord, hear my voice; let thine ears be attentive to the voice of my supplications.* Another, Psalm 51, forms the confession of a contrite heart and reminds us in many ways of passages in Jeremiah's confessional chapters: *Have mercy upon me, O God, according to thy loving-kindness. . . . Wash me thoroughly from my iniquity and cleanse me from my sin. . . . Purge me with hyssop, and I shall be clean: wash me, and I shall be whiter than snow.* Still another is Psalm 22 with its agonizing cry: *My God, my God, why hast thou forsaken me? . . . I cry in the day time; but thou hearest not; and in the night season, and am not silent.* And a unique psalm belonging rather to this category than to any other is Psalm 102, which forms the prayer of a man who is so critically ill that he can neither eat nor sleep. This is, in fact, one of the most vivid and interesting of all psalms although it is less well known than many others. The description of sickness itself, the fear of death while one is young, the range of comparisons and images from the homeliest to the most poetic combine to give it a unique character of its own:

My days are consumed like smoke, and my bones are burned as a hearth. . . .

I am like a pelican of the wilderness: I am like an owl of the desert.

I watch, and am as a sparrow alone upon the housetop . . .

I said, O my God, take me not away in the midst of my days: thy years are throughout all generations.

Of old hast thou laid the foundation of the earth: and the heavens are the work of thy hands.

They shall perish, but thou shalt endure: yea, all of them shall wax old like a garment; . . .

But thou art the same, and thy years shall have no end.

In a mood directly opposite from this one are those psalms which express personal confessions of faith and of complete trust in God's protection from all dangers and His nearness at the time of death. The best known and loved of these is, of course, Psalm 23 with its succession of connotative words and its images drawn from the life of the hills and pastures. Psalm 27 is another example of this type and second only to the 23rd in its widespread familiarity: *The Lord is my light and my salvation; whom shall I fear? the Lord is the strength of my life; of whom shall I be afraid?*

And, finally, in this group of personal psalms are those which consist of meditations and reflections by the individual on his own sense of God. Sometimes he reflects upon God's demand for uprightness of life, as in Psalm 15: *Lord, who shall abide in thy tabernacle? Who shall dwell in thy holy hill? He that walketh uprightly, and worketh righteousness, and speaketh the truth in his heart.* Sometimes, as in Psalm 90, he meditates on his own personal sense of the allness of God: *Lord, thou hast been our dwelling place in all generations. Before the mountains were brought forth, or ever thou hadst formed the earth and the world, even from everlasting to everlasting, thou art God.* Sometimes, as in Psalm 139, he is so filled with wonder over God's knowledge of him, over the very fact of his creation by God, and over God's constant presence beside him that he is overwhelmed both by amazement and humility. There are few, if any, more beautiful psalms than Psalm 139. The sense of artless, childlike wonder in it is almost humorous in its complete simplicity and wide-eyed astonishment. It reminds one of Thomas Traherne's lines in his poem *Wonder:*

> *How like an angel came I down!*
> *How bright are all things here!*

Of all the many unknown poets who wrote the psalter this poet of Psalm 139 is to me, at least, the most sincere, ingenuous, and charming of persons.

It is easy to be so affected by the religious fervour of the Psalms and so touched in personal ways by the emotions which they express that one is inclined not to study them critically as works of literature. Similar as they are in style and in the use of common imagery, they differ widely in originality of thought and in the range and depth of their appeal to the imagination. Many of them are repetitious; some, like Psalm 119, are of inferior literary quality; and not a few are superficial in their thought. We must guard against considering them as one book rather than as a combined anthology of some three hundred years of literary endeavour.

The greatest psalms from an artistic point of view are those which give spur to our imaginations, which lead us to unusual conceptions and ideas, which enlarge our thoughts and our vision through their appeal to mind as well as to heart. On this basis of criticism, for example, the 23rd Psalm, lovely and assuring as it is in its word pictures and in its expression of faith and trust, is not in any sense so fine a piece of literature as are many other psalms, for example the 19th, the 104th, the 90th, the 91st, and the 139th. In the 23rd Psalm the poet is actually limited to one emotion, that of his own trust in God, and even in that trust his emphasis is on himself and his safety quite as much as on God who is the giver of that safety. In the 91st Psalm, on the other hand, the vision of the poet is bigger and more objective. He is not concerned with himself and his safety so much as he is imbued with the thought of all men and of their need. In the first half of the 19th Psalm, which was originally probably two separate poems, the poet is not thinking of himself at all, or, indeed, of other men. It is the speech of the day and the knowledge possessed by the night, the course of the sun and the breadth of the heavens which overpower him with mystery and wonder. Obviously his imagination and vision are of a higher quality than are those of the poet of the 23rd Psalm.

Since it is true that the greatest of literature illuminates and heightens human experience and does so in proportion to the number and depth of thoughts and emotions which it arouses within us, we should evaluate the psalms as we evaluate other literature. Some in this respect are clearly far greater than others; and it is the discovery and appreciation of these which should make our reading and study of this unrivaled anthology of Hebrew poetry of consuming interest and importance.

I I

The Proverbial Wisdom of Israel

The book of Proverbs like that of the Psalms is a collection of collections, accumulated and without doubt issued as separate books over a long period of time. The earliest portions of it are probably not earlier than the sixth century B.C. and the latest, which comprise the first nine chapters, date not earlier than the third century. It is, then, an anthology arranged under separate collections or units and published as a whole not before 400 and not later than 200 B.C.

The eight separate collections in our present form of the book are clearly marked by sub-titles suggesting their actual or traditional origin. Thus, collections 1 and 2, which, since they include the first twenty-two chapters, form the largest portion of the book, are called *The Proverbs of Solomon*. Other shorter collections are known as *The Words of Agur,* given in chapter 30, and *The Words of King Lemuel, the prophecy that his mother taught him,* given in the first nine verses of chapter 31. The book concludes with a famous poem, originally written in alphabetic and acrostic form, on the price of a virtuous woman.

Solomon's reputed wisdom gave his name to the larger part of the book, but the title is purely conventional. There was surely no known collection of proverbs made so early as Solomon's time, and, although his biography in I Kings claims that he wrote three thousand of them, there is no reliable proof that he did so. One may remark, however, that the sort of wisdom shown by him, that of diplomacy in making commercial agreements with Hiram, King of Tyre, and that of shrewdness in judging the claims of two women, each of whom professes to be the mother of the same child, is not at all at variance with the greater part of the wisdom extolled in the book of Proverbs.

For much of this proverbial wisdom of Israel has seemingly little to do with the more idealized meaning of the word, vision and spiritual richness. This higher interpretation of wisdom occurs, it is true, and lends to the book a dignity and beauty without which it would be barren indeed; but by far the larger portion of it throughout all its collections, or units, sounds quite a different note. As a matter of fact, the so-called wise men, or sages, of Israel were ethical and moral, rather than religious teachers. Successors to the prophets in point of time, they seem to have translated the lofty and inspired ideas of men far wiser than themselves into the vernacular of getting on successfully in life, or, in another figure, to have debased prophetic gold, transforming it into the current coinage of small change. Since they could neither rise to the spiritual conceptions of the prophets nor share their exalted enthusiasm, they insisted, for the most part, on a far different application of a far different sort of wisdom.

Before we begin to study the writings of these wise men in the book of Proverbs, we must become aware that in this book there are two quite different approaches to life and two entirely different interpretations of wisdom. On the one hand, there is the realistic view of life, the sponsors of which inculcated through their proverbs the obvious lesson that success, happiness, and material prosperity are gained through common sense, intelligence, respectable living, and, above all else, diligence. On the other hand, there is the more ideal attitude toward one's brief span of existence. The holders of this attitude, although they did not minimize happiness and success as goals of human endeavour, nevertheless believed and taught that such blessings are gained only by a knowledge of God and His wisdom and are, in fact, a reward of righteous and godly living.

These two conceptions of wisdom occupy by far the largest portion of the book of Proverbs and are obvious in the numberless maxims and aphorisms which make up its contents. There is, however, another and loftier conception; for among the second group of wise men there were apparently some, if we can judge from at least two noble and exalted poems in the book, who glimpsed this higher conception of wisdom—men who, like Job, saw beyond the moral law of life and even beyond the orthodox religion of their day not only to the mystery of God and of His creation but also to the refining and spiritual influence of a sense of that mystery upon human life and thought. To these few wisdom was both an end in itself and a means to communion with God who alone had possessed wisdom "in the beginning of his way." It is to these unknown poets that we owe certain beautiful passages placed among the mass of proverbs like gems set in comparatively cheap and tawdry metal.

But before considering these saving passages we must attempt to understand something of the book as a whole; and it is, first of all, the realists among the wise men who will engage our attention. The sayings of these realists, who interpret wisdom in terms of sagacity and common sense, have little or nothing to do with religion. Their business is to teach the art, or rather the craft, of life by shrewd observations upon it drawn from their own experience. These teachings cover a wide range. They include good manners as well as morals, honour to one's parents, the bringing up of children, the right attitude toward friends and enemies, the conduct of business affairs, the escape from sinners who will do one harm, the avoidance of strange women whose "feet go down to death" and whose "steps take hold on hell," the decent treatment of animals, the diligent attendance upon one's business so that one may "stand before kings," the efficacy of a soft answer, the dangers of intoxication. The ideals of such wise men are not high. Their motives are always those leading to personal security and happiness. There is little in their teaching that concerns the welfare of others. Kindness brings a reward; therefore it is better than unkindness:

If thine enemy be hungry, give him bread to eat; and if he be thirsty, give him water to drink:

For thou shalt heap coals of fire upon his head.

These realistic teachers advise following the letter of the law requiring sacrifice, for its observance will bring a plentiful reward:

Honor the Lord with thy substance, and with the first fruits of all thine increase:

So shall thy barns be filled with plenty, and thy presses shall burst out with new wine.

The dominating motive of these purely secular thoughts is self-interest. The realistic purveyors of them in their proverbs do not advise justice and sacrifice for their own sakes or even for the sake of others. They are emphasizing as a fundamental principle of human life that just dealing is rewarded and that unjust dealing is followed by discomfort and unhappiness.

The book of Proverbs is filled with hundreds of such teachings, most of them expressed in the couplet form common throughout the book. They comprise without doubt a veritable mine of good counsel for sensible and judicious living; but they are dispiriting in their selfish emphasis upon material gain and success in life. Nor have they any literary value aside from their graphic, terse language and their balanced form.

It is a relief to turn to the more religious of the wise men, for although they do not stress virtue as an end in itself and although they conceive of God as hardly more than the dispenser of rewards and punishments, they do, nevertheless, recognize His existence, teach that only through His pleasure can man be rewarded, and interpret wisdom as dwelling only with Him. Their proverbs are far more idealistic than the purely

238

secular proverbs of the realists. They stress the difference between the religious observances of the wicked man and the humble prayer of the upright:

The sacrifice of the wicked is an abomination to the Lord: but the prayer of the upright is his delight.

The Lord is far from the wicked: but he heareth the prayer of the righteous.

They even emphasize the value of self-discipline and the cultivation of the inner man:

All the ways of a man are clean in his own eyes; but the Lord weigheth the spirits.

Every way of a man is right in his own eyes; but the Lord pondereth the heart.

And in the first part of the book, chapters 1 to 9 inclusive, they glorify wisdom as the secret and the source of a good life, and they identify this wisdom with "the fear of the Lord."

These first nine chapters of Proverbs are, in fact, those in which wisdom is extolled. Here there is less emphasis on the realistic, materialistic approach to life and more on the religious, orthodox though it is:

Wisdom is the principal thing; therefore get wisdom: and with all thy getting, get understanding.

Exalt her, and she shall promote thee: she shall bring thee to honor.

When wisdom entereth into thine heart, and knowledge is pleasant unto thy soul;

Discretion shall preserve thee, understanding shall keep thee.

For the Lord giveth wisdom: out of his mouth cometh knowledge and understanding.

Two poems among these first nine chapters lend a graciousness and beauty to the book as a whole which without them would seem barren and utilitarian enough. Some wiser men must have composed them, poets of imagination and larger understanding, who saw beyond both the purely materialistic ideas of the realists and the more idealistic conceptions of the religious teachers. The first and lesser of the two poems occurs in chapter 3, verses 13 to 20 inclusive. Its words set among those of mere good counsel and advice give lift to one's spirits and make one grateful that among the sages of Israel there were those who saw and felt beyond the narrow confines of earthly prosperity or of religious bargaining:

Happy is the man that findeth wisdom, and the man that getteth understanding:

For the merchandise of it is better than the merchandise of silver, and the gain thereof than fine gold. . . .

She is a tree of life to them that lay hold upon her: and happy is everyone that retaineth her.

The Lord by wisdom hath founded the earth; by understanding hath he established the heavens.

By his knowledge the depths are broken up, and the clouds drop down the dew.

The second is in chapter 8, the one chapter in the book of Proverbs entirely given up to the subject of wisdom. Although the first two-thirds of it, written in rather undistinguished couplets, is not impressive, except for the rhythmic and arresting questions at the beginning, it should be read throughout as a preface to verses 22 to 31 inclusive, which form one of the noblest poems in all Old Testament literature. Here are Job and the best of the Psalms; here are thought and vision which make the rest of the book of Proverbs barren and almost futile. The monotonous style of most of its chapters is here relieved by stateliness, dignity, and grace; and the conception of wisdom as that power before the creation of the world, "set up from everlasting," reduces the drab notions of the other sages to dust and ashes:

The Lord possessed me in the beginning of his way, before his works of old.

I was set up from everlasting, from the beginning, or ever the earth was.

When there were no depths, I was brought forth; when there were no fountains abounding with water.

Before the mountains were settled, before the hills was I brought forth:

While as yet he had not made the earth, nor the fields, nor the highest part of the dust of the world.

When he prepared the heavens, I was there: when he set a compass upon the face of the depth: . . .

Then was I by him, as one brought up with him: and I was daily his delight, rejoicing always before him.

After such satisfaction as this, it seems unnecessary and even redundant to comment further on the book of Proverbs. Yet something might well be said in favour of chapter 7, verses 6 to 23 inclusive, where the advisory couplets again give way to make room for a vivid story told of a harlot who practises her wiles upon "a young man void of understanding." This is fine narrative, interspersed with lines of poetry strongly suggestive of the Song of Songs. Nor should the reader miss in the words of Agur in chapter 30 the distinctive poem beginning with the latter half of verse 15 and closing with verse 31: *There are three things that are never satisfied, yea, four things say not, It is enough.* This makes the few sayings of the unknown Agur worth many times those of his fellow sages. And finally in the words of King Lemuel of the desert country of Massa we are given the famous portrait of the virtuous woman who used to be a discouraging model for all brides, and whose prodigious talents have the effect of wearying one in well-doing. The picture is an Oriental one suggesting that this superwoman is extolled, not so much for her good works in themselves, as for the relief they quite rightly afforded her husband from all tedious labour!

The book of Proverbs makes difficult reading because of its lack of order, its repetitious quality, and its sameness of style; and although many of its sayings have entered into our language and speech more than have any other portions of the Old Testament, it should be not too highly regarded as a work either of literature or of thought. Its chief value, to me at least, lies in its two beautiful poems already commented upon and quoted in part. Both are worth many readings, and the latter, that contained in chapter 8, lends to the book a distinction which it certainly needs and without which it would merit little admiration.

12

Ecclesiastes, or Koheleth, the Preacher

The man who wrote the book of Ecclesiastes around the year 200 B.C. called himself Koheleth and identified himself as a preacher. From his identification comes the Greek name Ecclesiastes. In his introduction to his essay, which we may call "The Meaning of Life," he says that he is "the son of David, king in Jerusalem." This statement which, of course, suggests Solomon as the author, is a mere literary device, not seriously considered even by the editors who prepared his book for insertion among the other books of the Old Testament.

Koheleth wrote his book after many years of what was apparently a fairly happy existence filled with many experiences which had taught him many things. He may be thought of as a radical of his day who had discovered through keen observation of the processes of nature and of the life of man and through his own reflections upon both that the Jewish orthodoxy of his time had little meaning and less truth for him and that, on the whole, traditional religion is but wishful thinking. Although his rather magnificent descriptions of his life given in chapter 2 of his book cannot be taken literally, as he is apparently here continuing his fictitious assumption of Solomon as himself, the tone and atmosphere throughout his twelve chapters would certainly suggest that he was in no sense a poor man. His brilliant command of language and the worldliness evident throughout his sophisticated reflections on life characterize him rather as one who had the means to live comfortably and pleasantly, who was most acceptable socially, and who may well have travelled beyond his native city of Jerusalem. Perhaps, indeed, he knew Alexandria or had even been to school there, for it is evident that Greek thought interested and influenced him. At all events, we should think of him as a cultured and cosmopolitan man, not in any sense as one who from under his own vine and fig-tree gave expression to captious thoughts and carping disillusionments.

Disillusioned he surely was, but not to bitterness. Perhaps, like so many others of his race, he was too intensely alive for complete misanthropy. Even although in theory he claims that death, or at least non-existence, is preferable to life, and praises the dead more than the living and even more him "which hath not been," in practice he recommends a full enjoyment of whatever joys life has to offer, bread, wine, clean clothes, marriage, and that work in which one has delight. Nor would he be overzealous for too much wisdom or for too much righteousness, nor for their opposites, wickedness or folly. In a word, since the world is topsy-turvy anyway and since it is plainly impossible to discover, even after much thinking and study, any consistent plan either in nature or in human life, one should serenely and even zestfully enjoy what can be enjoyed before old age and death forever take away the capacities for pleasure.

Koheleth wrote most of his book in prose, although poetry is not lacking in certain portions, notably in his first chapter and in his famous concluding poem. Sometimes, indeed, his prose and his poetry are difficult to distinguish, at least in our translation. Although he was one of the most original thinkers in the Old Testament and has much to say on a great variety of subjects, he rarely arranges his reflections and conclusions in any logical order. The first four chapters of his book have more coherence than the rest, perhaps because within these he has voiced his main conclusions and afterward merely repeats them in one form or another. He states his thesis in the beginning:

244

Vanity of vanities; all is vanity, and he apparently has great fondness for this witty invention of words, for he repeats them again and again throughout his book.

Although he does not doubt the existence of God as a cosmic force and as that inscrutable spirit which gives life to man, he can discover no just plan for human life and in the monotonous round of nature only futility. Not for him the wonder of Job before the mysteries of the world, the treasures of the snow, the singing of the morning stars. In spite of the beauty of the short poem which follows immediately upon his introduction to his book, one is conscious of something akin to weariness in its lines, or perhaps even of the aimlessness and monotony of which he writes:

One generation passeth away, and another generation cometh: but the earth abideth forever.

The sun also ariseth, and the sun goeth down, and hasteth to his place where he arose.

The wind goeth toward the south, and turneth about unto the north; it whirleth about continually, and the wind returneth again according to his circuits.

All the rivers run into the sea; yet the sea is not full: unto the place from whence the rivers come, thither they return again.

To Koheleth God's obvious ruling of the world has no relation to His concern for man and his suffering. Apparently, indeed, He has no such concern. The order and the time of all events are determined by God, and yet He and His activity alike are incomprehensible to human intelligence. So far as Koheleth can see, and he has thought and studied all his life, God is not the God of Israel, nor is He a just and merciful ruler of men; He is rather a blind fate, and not only blind but fickle and capricious. One has only to look about him, says Koheleth, to see that the work of man, his righteousness and his goodness, weigh nothing with God. Pleasures and prosperity may be snatched from him, suffering and poverty may come upon him without regard for his worth as a human being. His success or his failure in life are not governed by justice, but merely by chance, for anyone with his eyes and mind open can see that the same fate overtakes both the good man and the wicked one:

I returned, and saw under the sun, that the race is not to the swift, nor the battle to the strong, neither yet bread to the wise, nor yet riches to men of understanding, nor yet favor to men of skill; but time and chance happeneth to them all.

Nor does Koheleth extoll wisdom for its own sake; in fact, he has tested both wisdom and folly and has discovered that they are equally futile. The search for wisdom cannot give one an understanding of God and of His works, for even "though a wise man think to know it, yet shall he not be able to find it." *For in much wisdom is much grief, and he that increaseth knowledge increaseth sorrow.* The way of folly is equally disappointing, for in wine and women, luxury and wealth, there is but vanity and a striving after wind. As a matter of fact, the man who labours with his hands can sleep for he has no worries, but the rich man must worry in the night hours for fear he will lose his abundance.

Since the future is unknowable, "for who can tell a man what shall be after him under the sun," and since from all appearances it will be but a repetition of what has been for "there is no new thing under the sun," it is worse than useless to look for any better order of things. Nor is there the least hope of any redress after death, for "the dead know not anything," "the memory of them is forgotten," "their love, and their hatred, and their envy" are perished. Therefore, since human beings are powerless to change their destiny and since assuredly there is no knowledge nor wisdom in the grave where all must go, the only wise and sensible way to meet the uncertainties and caprices of life is to live as joyfully as possible, for the light of the sun is sweet to one's eyes, bread and wine increase merriment in one's heart, and there is joy in living with a woman whom one loves even though one's days are vanity. After all, to be "a living dog is better than a dead lion."

With more than a touch of ironic humour Koheleth admits that, though in his search for wisdom he has failed, he has found out one thing: a certain sort of woman whose heart is like a snare and a net is more "bitter than death" and only a fool will not run from her!

Koheleth warns against overseriousness and against that soul-searching which to him is both unwholesome and a waste of time. Just as it clearly does not pay to be wicked or to indulge in foolishness, it is just as clearly a bad investment to be over conscientious:

Be not righteous over much, neither make thyself over wise: why shouldest thou destroy thyself?

Be not over much wicked, neither be thou foolish: why shouldest thou die before thy time?

Koheleth's genius as a poet is shown in the last chapter of his book in his beautiful and justly famous poem on old age. Contrary to the belief of many readers, it is neither a moral nor a religious poem. It is instead a lyric which depicts in startlingly original images and in lines full of cadence and sorrow the pathos of those deprived of their youth by the ceaseless round of time. It begins not with chapter 12 with the well-known words, *Remember now thy Creator in the days of thy youth* (which are, in fact, an interpolation by some later editor and not Koheleth's own), but with verse 9 of chapter 11, and should read, after the later additions and corrections are taken out, as follows:

Rejoice, O young man, in thy youth; and let thy heart cheer thee in the days of thy youth, and walk in the ways of thine heart and in the sight of thine eyes.

Therefore remove sorrow from thy heart, and put away evil from thy flesh:

While the evil days come not, nor the years draw nigh, when thou shalt say, I have no pleasure in them;

In the day when the keepers of the house shall tremble, and the strong men shall bow themselves, and the grinders cease because they are few, and those that look out of the windows be darkened,

And the doors shall be shut in the streets, when the sound of the grinding is low, and he shall rise up at the voice of the bird, and all the daughters of music shall be brought low;

Also when they shall be afraid of that which is high, and fears shall be in the way, and the almond tree shall flourish, and the grasshopper shall be a burden, and desire shall fail: because man goeth to his long home, and the mourners go about the streets:

Or ever the silver cord be loosed, or the golden bowl be broken, or the pitcher be broken at the fountain, or the wheel broken at the cistern.

Then shall the dust return to the earth as it was: and the spirit shall return unto God who gave it.

Vanity of vanities, saith the Preacher; all is vanity.

The beauty and significance of this poem are enlarged and deepened once it is understood in all its rich symbolism and allegory. Although there have been many interpretations of its images and metaphors, most scholars are convinced that its vivid descriptions have to do with the physical handicaps and weaknesses of age. The "keepers of the house" are the trembling hands of the old; the "grinders" which cease are the teeth which are gone; the darkened windows are the blinded eyes. The old "rise up at the voice of the bird" because their sleep is so light; they take no pleasure any longer in music; they are afraid of high places and of crowded streets; their hair is as white as the blossoms on the almond tree; and all the desires of youth and its passions have failed and gone from them. Their hands can no longer carry the pitchers to the well, nor can they draw water, nor safely care for the golden bowls and silver cords of their lamps.

This poem is unique in biblical literature because of this very richness of imagination and wealth of symbolism, which, once understood, endows it with a meaning hitherto obscure. The haunting echoes of its musical notes in a distinctly minor key lend to it a peculiar charm and sadness; and in the possession of anything so lovely we can easily overlook Koheleth's cynicism, since in this poem he reveals the compassion which he felt for all who live from birth to death.

Nor is his cynicism necessarily disillusioning or unpleasant. There is evident throughout his book a light humour which relieves it from darkness; and one can certainly detect, in spite of his skepticism, a keen enjoyment of life. He is neither moping in a corner nor announcing grim facts from house-tops.

Many readers and students of his book see in it the influence of Greek thought which by 200 B.C. had surely made itself strongly felt in Palestine. The philosophy of Koheleth may well be tinged with the Epicurean doctrine of making the most of the pleasures of life without overindulgence and possibly with that of the Stoics in his poem on time and the cosmic flow of things. He surely was out of sympathy, as was Job, with the Jewish orthodoxy of his day, with its interpretation of life in terms of rewards and of punishments according to goodness and to evil; but his skepticism, unlike that of Job, stopped short of distress, nor in his hands did it become a stepping-stone to impassioned and noble questioning concerning the mysteries of life and of God.

We may well wonder why it was that the book of this Omar Khayyam of the Old Testament should have been allowed inclusion in the Jewish Scriptures. One reason was doubtless that of its popularity in its day. Perhaps, too, the fictitious assumption that it was written by Solomon bore weight with the scholars and editors who made up the Old Testament in its final form. But it assuredly would not have found a place had not certain annotators changed its emphasis in places and added certain passages and ideas of their own to Koheleth's original work. Worried over his denial of God's retribution on earth, they took upon themselves the responsibility of interpolating their own words in his text. Such an interpolation occurs, for example, in verse 9 of chapter 11, which verse introduces Koheleth's great poem on old age: *But know thou, that for all these things God will bring thee into judgment.* Such a thought is directly opposed to his teaching, and lends, as do various other interpolated portions, a note of perplexity to his book. Again in verse 17 of chapter 3 the editors, disliking Koheleth's cynical statement in verse 16 that wickedness is in the place of judgment, added their own words, *God shall judge the righteous and the wicked.* Several of these interpolated passages lend an annoying note of inconsistency to the book; and we can imagine how they would have annoyed and angered Koheleth himself.

The worst instance, however, of this tampering with his work occurs at the close of the symbolic poem with which Koheleth, of course, planned to end his book and in the perfection of which, one can assume, he took great pleasure and satisfaction. Not content with adding the first line of chapter 12 in order to sound a pious note, the revisers and editors proceeded to tack on to the poem five dull and moralizing precepts. There were apparently two of these meddling annotators. The first in verses 9 and 10 strives to explain that, after all, the Preacher was wise and wrote words of truth. The second, not yet convinced that Koheleth's book will not do more harm than good and possessed of a sardonic, if grim, humour, admonishes its readers that of making of many books (like this unfortunate one!) there is no end and that, in his opinion, nothing is to be gained except weariness from so much study. He himself has a safe and sane conclusion to the whole matter—and he proceeds to give it!

13

The Story of Daniel

The book of Daniel, together with the final edition of the Psalms, is the last complete book of the Old Testament. In time of publication it belongs to the second century B.C. and can be dated with accuracy around the year 165. It is a most unusual and fascinating book comprised of stirring narratives, of prophetic history, and of a series of visions, which in their words and thoughts have exercised a profound influence both on Christian literature and on Christian thought. Since to most cursory readers of the Bible or to those who remember only some of its stories, Daniel means at most a lions' den with the possible addition of a fiery furnace, it is well at the start to describe as clearly as possible the background from which the book arose.

To understand the origin of the book and the part played by it in the world of its day, we must recall certain facts of history. We shall, I hope, remember that the date of the book is contemporary with the life of that Antiochus Epiphanes, the Seleucid king of Syria, who tried so hard and so cruelly to force Hellenistic culture and religion upon the Jews of Palestine. We shall recall, too, that in the year 168 B.C. his army besieged Jerusalem, placed a Syrian garrison there, and that there then followed an era of bitter persecution of those Jews who refused to bow to the commands of Antiochus. It was at this time that the Wars of the Maccabees took place and that incredible victories were won by Judas Maccabeus against the armies of Antiochus.

It was at this crisis in the history of the Jewish nation that the book of Daniel appeared. It was obviously written to lend faith and courage to those who were fighting what seemed to many inevitably a losing battle. The author of the book, much of which is prophecy, chose to give a fictional name to it and took that of Daniel, who held a traditional fame among the Jews as one of the great figures of their past and who had been listed by Ezekiel with Noah and with Job as a holy man. He apparently chose to employ this name for his book in order to gain a hearing for his prophetic message, since he realized that the time and influence of the prophets were at an end and that the people of his day, for the most part, believed that prophetic inspiration had ceased. His implication was, of course, that his book had actually been written in full or at least in part by the ancient traditional prophet and that he had only now discovered it.

Who the author actually was we do not know, but from the nature of the stories and of the prophecies in his book we can gain certain fairly accurate knowledge concerning him. He was obviously a very learned man with a wide range of reading and a great deal of more or less reliable historical information. He apparently belonged to a group of intensely religious Jews of his day who called themselves the Hasidim, or the Pious, to distinguish themselves from their more worldly contemporaries, and who were the forerunners of the sect of the Pharisees in the New Testament. These Hasidim were governed, or governed themselves, by certain strict rules of fasting and prayer and by the avoidance of certain foods proscribed by the tenets of their religion. They were even fanatically devoted to the Jewish Law of God, and infinitely preferred martyrdom to the idolatry which Antiochus was attempting to force upon them. In the first book of the Maccabees in the Apocrypha the story is told of many who were slaughtered with their families rather than defend themselves on the Sabbath. They were, in fact, pacifists on principle and only rose to the standard of Judas Maccabeus because of the intense gravity of the situation which faced their nation and their religion. And they surely believed with the author of Daniel that the triumphant and irresistible intervention of Jehovah in their cause was certain and imminent.

The book of Daniel may be looked upon as a kind of manifesto of the Hasidim since it was written to encourage those who were suffering persecution under Antiochus. Throughout its pages run certain thoughts characteristic of these Jews as a group of zealous men bent on preserving their religion at any cost and relying upon the supernatural aid of God. It is clear that the author of Daniel shares their convictions and their faith. Everywhere in this book, in stories, prophecies, and visions alike, is discernible his unassailable belief in God's mighty power of salvation which, together with His wisdom, always takes precedence over His moral attributes of justice and of love.[1] Such a theology is without doubt explained by the bitter situation of Daniel's day. Surrounded by empires which were to him and his fellow Hasidim entirely heathen and persecuted by Antiochus, they could see small possibility of human help. God was their only hope, and, in order to save them, He must be omnipotent, able to intervene miraculously on their behalf.

It is necessary to understand clearly the background both of history and of thought which brought forth the book of Daniel in order to understand the book itself. Two parts almost equal in length comprise it: the first six chapters which form a collection of stories about Daniel and his friends; the last six chapters which record visions and revelations given to Daniel by God. The author set the scene of his book in the Babylonian empire of Nebuchadnezzar, at which time he evidently believed Daniel to have lived. He wrote much of the first part, not in Hebrew, but in the Aramaic of his own day. He was not a great writer from a purely literary point of view, as even the English translation bears proof; but he was a vivid story-teller largely perhaps because he chose such exciting stories to tell.

[1] It is interesting in this connection to read certain psalms which are of Hasidim origin and probably written about this time: Psalms 74, 79, and 83.

The heroes of his book are four young men of Judah brought into Babylon among the captives, Daniel himself, Hananiah, Mishael, and Azariah. Called to live in the king's palace in order that they might be taught "the learning and the tongue of the Chaldeans," they are given new names: Daniel is to be called Belteshazzar, and the other three are to be known as Shadrach, Meshach, and Abednego.

From beginning to end of the series of miraculous deliverances accorded by God to these faithful young Jews, we see clearly the influence of Hasidim theology and thought. They will not defile themselves by eating the king's meat or by drinking his wine; they flourish on pulse and water; they refuse to bow down to Nebuchadnezzar's image of gold just as the Hasidim had forfeited their lives rather than do homage to the image of Zeus, set up in the Temple by Antiochus. When the outraged Nebuchadnezzar commands that Shadrach, Meshach, and Abednego be thrown into a "burning fiery furnace" so hot that it slew those men that threw them in, an angel of the Lord delivers the three so untouched that not a hair of their heads is singed nor is there any smell of fire upon them. The same supernatural deliverance is accorded to Daniel, who because of his divine genius in interpreting the dreams of Nebuchadnezzar has been made "ruler over the whole province of Babylon" and who continues his interpretations in the court of Belshazzar by deciphering the mysterious handwriting upon the wall of the king's palace. A removal of Daniel to the Persian court of Darius does not seem to bother the author, since the flaming purpose of his stories is greater than their historicity. Here in Persia the preference shown to Daniel angers the princes of Darius, who induce the king to make a decree forbidding petition to any god or man except to Darius himself. But Daniel, looking toward Jerusalem, kneels three times a day upon his knees. In persecution for his unconquerable faith he is cast one evening into a den of lions whose mouths are straightway shut by the angel of the

Lord. The import of the story is clear: the faithful Jews should continue their private worship in spite of Antiochus just as does Daniel in spite of the laws of the Medes and the Persians.

The second half of the book records the prophetic visions of Daniel, already prefaced in chapter 2 by Nebuchadnezzar's dream of the image made of various metals and broken to pieces by a stone "cut out without hands." This image according to Daniel's interpretation of it before the king represents the four world-empires, Babylonian, Median, Persian, and Greek. The stone which breaks the image in pieces is the nation of Israel. In his visions which follow he sees these same heathen empires under the guise of four great beasts, a lion, a bear, a leopard, and the unnamed fourth beast with ten horns, which symbolize the ten kings of Syria. The "little horn," which in chapter 7 is described so ominously, is none other than Antiochus Epiphanes himself, with his "mouth speaking great things."

In verses 9 to 14 of chapter 7 which follow immediately upon Daniel's sight of the "little horn," Antiochus, we move from the symbolic interpretation of a dream to the realm of mystical and apocalyptical literature:

I beheld till the thrones were cast down and the Ancient of days did sit, whose garment was white as snow, and the hair of his head like the pure wool: his throne was like the fiery flame, and his wheels as burning fire.

A fiery stream issued and came forth from before him: thousand thousands ministered unto him, and ten thousand times ten thousand stood before him: the judgment was set, and the books were opened. . . .

I beheld even till the beast was slain, and his body destroyed, and given to the burning flame. . . .

I saw in the night visions, and, behold, one like the Son of man came with the clouds of heaven, and came to the Ancient of days, and they brought him near before him.

And there was given him dominion, and glory, and a kingdom,

that all peoples, nations, and languages, should serve him: his
dominion is an everlasting dominion, which shall not pass away,
and his kingdom that which shall not be destroyed.

It is impossible to know and even difficult to surmise precisely
what Daniel had in mind by such an exalted description as this.
Of a meaning which has been argued by countless scholars for
many years, it would be both arrogant and valueless for me to
attempt any clear or certain explanation or even to give an
opinion of any importance. But to even the common reader
certain things are relatively clear in the light of the book itself.
Daniel is surely visualizing the future in terms of the destruction
of the great empires and of the restoration of the Jewish people
through God, the Ancient of days. The Son of man, which was
to mean to so many the Messiah, probably did not mean that to
him any more than did the suffering Servant to Deutero-Isaiah.
To both, these epithets probably meant the Israelitish nation
which, after all its sufferings, is through God to be assured of
"everlasting dominion." In the verses following Daniel's first
great vision he speaks of the possession of the kingdom "by the
people of the saints of the Most High"; and this term also doubtless refers to those Jews of Jerusalem who are steadfastly keeping
their faith even amid the horrors of persecution.

The following visions recorded by the author in chapters 8 to
11 inclusive possess difficulties equal to the first. Many of them
are repetitious and practically all of them are embellishments
or variations of the first with much the same significance and
meaning. The most elaborate and detailed vision is given in
chapter 10 and followed by a prophecy in chapter 11 in which
the author sketches with great accuracy the history of the time
of Antiochus Epiphanes and even of the Greek kingdoms preceding him. The blunders which are so obvious in his stories of
Babylonia and Persia here give way to fact, since he is writing of
his own time and of those things which he has seen with his own
eyes.

These last chapters of the book of Daniel, particularly chapter

12, exerted a profound influence on later literature and on later conceptions of religion. For the first time in the Old Testament we hear of the princes of heaven, Gabriel and Michael, one the angel of revelation, the other the champion of Israel, whose appearances in Daniel introduced into Christian literature and thought that hierarchy of the ministers of God. For the first time also in Hebrew literature the doctrine of the resurrection is stated as a dogma:

And many of them that sleep in the dust of the earth shall awake, some to everlasting life, and some to shame and everlasting contempt.

And they that be wise shall shine as the brightness of the firmament; and they that turn many to righteousness as the stars for ever and ever.

The zealous and patriotic Jews under the terror and persecution of Antiochus Epiphanes evolved the new doctrine, for to them in their anguish it seemed inevitable that, unless God were guilty of injustice, He must, by a promise of life to come, justify and recompense His saints and martyrs who had given their lives for His cause. In this new and comforting hope, of which Job in his mental and physical pain had dreamed, there was established that faith which was to come into its fruition in the New Testament.

The author of Daniel was in no sense a great literary artist. The prose of his book is wordy, and even in his stories he rarely writes with vividness or drama. The stories themselves were used to substantiate and encourage the religious dogmas of the Hasidim, and it is clear that their author cared more for his message than for his manner of disseminating it. The characters are in no sense visualized as are those in David's biography, in the Samson tales, or in the Jacob-Joseph saga; and there is far too much of the pompous and the ceremonious in their dialogue. Whatever atmosphere there is, is mere stage-setting; and the sense of reality throughout is hurt by exaggeration on the one hand and by abstraction and obscurity on the other.

And yet there are portions where the author, taken out of himself, achieves great poetic and dramatic power. There is an epic grandeur in the contrast between the four horrible beasts with their monstrous physical features and the luminous figure of the Ancient of days with the flames playing about His throne and ten thousand times ten thousand standing before Him. It is these scenes, together with the "voice of a multitude," the lightning and the lamps of fire, the presence of angels, the "glorious holy mountains," and the opening of the books of judgment, which were to enter nearly three hundred years later into the imagination of St. John and, more than any other portion of the Old Testament, make possible the writing of his beatific vision of the New Jerusalem, the City of God.

PART III

THE NEW TESTAMENT

I

An Introduction to the New Testament

In general, I think it is safe to say that to most readers of the
Bible, careful or cursory, or at least to those of Christian lineage,
the New Testament is more familiar than the Old. The reasons
for this fact are not difficult to find. The New Testament is at
once the foundation and the corner-stone of Christianity, to
some branch or sect of which most of us either nominally or
actually owe some measure of allegiance, if not by conviction, at
least by family tradition. The New Testament seems less remote
than the Old; it is woven into our civilization as the Old Testament is not; it has had more to do with our institutions, our
society, our ways of thought. Our ethical, social, religious, and
even certain of our economic ideals spring from its teachings.
Although it is based upon the Old Testament, without which
it would not have its being, it nevertheless exists in our minds
and our imaginations largely by itself.

Between these two parts which make up our Bible there are,
of course, wide and radical differences. The first is that of space
and of time. The New Testament is only one-third as large a
book as is the Old; its writings all belong to the same age and
cover a period of only one hundred years, whereas the Old Testament reflects the life of at least eleven centuries. Moreover,
the literature of the New Testament is confined to one subject,
the life and the teachings of Jesus and of His followers, for even
the apocalyptical drama of Revelation arises from and is dependent upon that material; the literature of the Old Testament,
on the other hand, includes every type and every subject. Except

for the few songs and hymns interspersed among the narratives of the New Testament and inherited in every case from the Old, its medium of expression throughout is prose, whereas the Old Testament contains practically every form of poetry. The New Testament is concerned only with a scattered Christian community and has comparatively little relation to the wider life of its time; the Old Testament is concerned with the life of a nation from its legendary beginnings to its tragic close and cannot be understood without at least some knowledge of the history of the world of its day. The purpose of the New Testament is overwhelmingly religious, and its literary excellence arises almost entirely from the religious fervour of its authors; the Old Testament is a work of literature as well as one of religion, and as literature it is vastly superior to the New.

The name *New Testament* is, of course, distinctly religious in its origin and refers, in contrast to the Old Testament, to that new covenant which, as Jeremiah records in the 31st chapter of his prophecy, God has promised to make with the house of Israel, a covenant not like that made with His chosen people whom He led from bondage, but written instead in their hearts. When the earliest Christian writings were assembled, they came to be called *The Books of the New Covenant*. The word *covenant* in legal phrase is also the word for a *will* or a *testament*, and it was because of this confusion in terms that the title *New Testament* came to be generally accepted.

The New Testament, like the Old, is a collection. It is made up of twenty-seven books which, with other writings less valuable, comprised the literature of the primitive Christian Church. These books existed quite separately at first as documents copied on rolls of papyrus, and they were circulated among the important early churches as a means of instruction. Probably very few, if any, churches possessed all of them until at least a century had elapsed after they had all been written. The earliest of the twenty-seven was St. Paul's First Epistle to the Thessalonians written probably in 50 or in 51 A.D.; in fact, the nucleus of the

New Testament was the letters of St. Paul, which in date are all considerably older than the four Gospels as we know them today. Most of the twenty-seven books were composed during the sixty years between 50 and 110 A.D. Only one, in fact, is of demonstrably later date, the Second Epistle of Peter, which was, of course, not actually written by him, as it appeared about the year 150 A.D.

These sixty years in which the books of our New Testament came into being may be looked upon because of this sole achievement as one of the richest literary periods in history. There are such periods or times in the history of every literature, times which seem peculiarly ripe for the lavish flowering of prose, or of poetry, or of both, times when seemingly almost of its own accord creative work of the highest order comes suddenly into being, when the imaginations of men seem almost miraculously touched with new and fresh power. Such a period was the age which produced the New Testament; and the power which brought it forth was the wonder of the new revelation of God, a revelation which men believed they had found in the life and the teachings of Jesus.

The men who wrote the New Testament were not men of great literary genius like many of those who wrote the Old. They had little of the creative power of Deutero-Isaiah or of the unknown authors of the biography of David, the Song of Deborah, and the book of Job. They were in no sense the Shakespeares, the Dantes, or the Miltons of their age. But they were men on fire with a new idea, with a fresh and a young enthusiasm, with an exalted hope for mankind. They were stirred by new emotions in an old and tired world, and because of these living waters welling up within them, these unquenchable and glowing fires burning in their souls, they were able to transfer to their pages a zest, a newness, an eloquence, a perennial freshness, and a vigour, which, even without learning and long practice in literary art, gave to their work the charm, the eagerness, and the fervour which mark all great literature. They may not have been able to lend to their compositions the artistic distinction of the most memorable books and passages of the Old Testament; but they were able to place upon their rolls of papyrus an undying ardour which has made their literature peculiarly beautiful and their messages to mankind immortal.

We must remember, too, that, unlike many of the writers of the Old Testament, they wrote with a definite purpose in view. To write with an object or an intention is, in fact, characteristic of the Jewish mind; and yet the purpose of the New Testament is much more obvious than are those discernible in many of the books of the Old. Without in the least underestimating their contributions to the art and to the thought of the world or undervaluing their worth as literature, we may truly think of the writers of the New Testament as propagandists, as men with a message, and a message far more important than the manner in which it was clothed. Their books were, to use perhaps a dull and uninspired word, text-books of their time. Thus the Gospels were written to acquaint those whose knowledge was lacking or insufficient with the facts of the life of Jesus, with His teachings, and, perhaps, above all to clear Him in their minds from the charge of conspiracy against the Jewish religion and against the Roman state, which had unjustly sent Him to an ignominious and undeserved death. These Gospel writers were possessed with the belief and faith that God had spoken to men through the divine life and thoughts of Jesus, and their work was to picture His life on earth in such a way that its divine significance should be made clear. The book of the Acts of the Apostles was written by St. Luke to acquaint the early Christians with the zeal, the labours, and the success of the first missionaries. St. Paul wrote his masterly and inimitable letters to various churches to warn them against the dangers latent in their localities or to instruct them concerning their own special needs and difficulties as the pioneers of a new religion. Since he could be with them but seldom, he employed this method of keeping in touch with them and of encouraging them in the new life which they had undertaken. St. John, whoever he may have been, the author of the gospel by that name or quite another man, wrote his incomparable book of Revelation to lend courage to those who must die as martyrs for their new faith, to keep alive in them the knowledge that, regardless of torture and of pain, a glorious triumph awaited those who could overcome the bonds of earth and of suffering.

Thus the purpose behind every page of the New Testament is religious, and no page will reveal its meaning unless we keep that fact clearly in mind. Whatever literary value its books may possess, and certain of them possess a great deal, they were surely not written with that aim and purpose in mind. Their artistic value arose, as we have said, from the flaming hopes and ideals of their writers who never for a moment thought of themselves as literary artists, but rather as the workmen of God who must write as best they could in order to perform under Him the tasks assigned to them. What is more, they were not addressing a fanciful or even an impersonal audience. They were writing for those persons who, like themselves, had discovered a new truth to enliven and to transform their daily lives. Because of this necessity and aim, they rarely, if ever, deal with abstractions or even with the general, but rather with the concrete, the specific, and the real. And because of this very fact they managed to transfer to their pages a reality and an immediacy not to be found in most of the pages of the Old Testament.

The writers of the New Testament were not only propagandists; they were also controversialists. Each maintains stoutly his own point of view, and his own interpretation of the Christian message. St. Luke, for example, wrote his Gospel because he was dissatisfied with that of St. Mark and perhaps with that of St. Matthew, which he may or may not have known. Their emphases were not his own. St. Mark had omitted too many details in the life of Jesus to suit St. Luke, who was by nature a biographer and a dramatist. He also was too much imbued with the teachings of St. Paul and had, for St. Luke's taste, too much interest in theological problems and in the purely Messianic character of Jesus. St. Matthew had wished, perhaps above all else, to demonstrate, on the one hand, with St. Mark, that Jesus was the promised Messiah of ancient prophecy and, on the other, that He had come to found an ecclesiastical institution, the Church, which should not only give new life to Judaism but should also provide all things for all men. St. Luke was not primarily interested in doctrine. What concerned him, since he was a born story-teller, was first of all the character of Jesus, and, secondly, the fact that His gospel is for all men, regardless of race or of country. The Epistles of St. Paul and, in a lesser degree, of the other mostly unknown epistolary writers bristle with controversial material and with matters of theological dispute. This spirit of controversy, of the value to each writer of his own cherished thoughts and conclusions, runs throughout the New Testament and adds immeasurably to its variety and to its interest.

We must guard also against the assumption that the New Testament as we have it today is in precisely the form in which it was originally written. We must understand that for a great number of years at the beginning of our Christian era the books of the New Testament were in no sense regarded or treated as scripture. They were instead considered the property of the early Christian Church, of the people for whom they had been written; and, although they were valued the most highly of all churchly possessions, the Church felt entirely free to deal with them as it wished. For instance, whenever they were copied, as they often were, certain changes were without doubt made to make them more effective for a given time, place, or situation. We do not know what all these changes were, but that they were made seems not only inevitable but certain. Also we must remember that in the various exigencies of copying by many hands and in the work of ancient book-making, mistakes from the original must have been made. Some of St. Paul's letters now bound together as one letter, or as two, may well have originally been several in number. Possibly some small roll of papyrus of uncertain or unknown authorship, seemingly too valuable to lose, may have been inserted into the work of some author recognized and known. In other words, probably no single book in the New Testament of today is precisely as it was when it left the hands of its original writer.

Nor must we fail to remember that the definite and final form of the New Testament was not concluded and put into circulation as a book until more than three centuries after its first portions were written by St. Paul. During these centuries the twenty-seven books were necessarily in competition with many other writings, most of which we do not know even by name. The twenty-seven survived because, as years went on, they became the most valued and beloved by the growing number of persons who had become familiar not only with them but with many other early Christian documents. It was not, in fact, until the year 367 A.D. that Athanasius, Bishop of Alexandria, who had come to be acknowledged as the most brilliant theologian and most important man in the entire Church, sent out a famous letter at Easter time to the now many congregations scattered throughout the Mediterranean world and in his letter not only listed the twenty-seven as we now have them, but declared that from henceforth these books together were to form the New Testament.

In our succeeding study of certain portions of the New Testament we shall, wisely I think, employ the selective method used in the presentation of the Old. Obviously it would be most confusing to attempt to distinguish among the four Gospels those things most valuable in each. Since to me that of St. Luke is not only far superior as literature but far more interesting as narrative, I shall limit my presentation of the Gospels to that one written by him; and since no knowledge of the New Testament or pleasure therein can be gained without a reading of the dramatic and brilliant stories contained in the book of the Acts of the Apostles, I shall include a chapter on that fascinating book, also written by St. Luke. Since St. Paul is far and away the greatest writer of the various Epistles in the New Testament, I shall try to present his letters, not merely as epistles to the various churches of Asia Minor, Greece, and Rome, but rather as separate letters on a variety of subjects. And, lastly, the attempted understanding and evaluation of the unique book of Revelation, or rather the *Apocalypse* as I like better to call it, will conclude not only our study of the New Testament but my book as a whole.

2

St. Luke: His Gospel

The Gospel of St. Luke has been called by more than one discriminating reader the most beautiful of all books, not only in the New Testament or even in the Bible, but literally of all books in any language. Such praise seems not only extravagant but more than a little absurd. Why endow with such superlative admiration this brief account of a series of happenings mostly simple even although imbued with extraordinary significance, this one book of four on the same subject and constructed from much the same material? The answer, I think, lies in the singular attractiveness of its author. True it is that his language is more apt and graceful than that of the other gospel writers and that his appreciation both of the homely and of the unusual in human life is more sensitive and dramatic than theirs; nevertheless, it is not these superior qualities which in themselves can account for the peculiar and distinctive charm of his book. It is beloved by all who know it because its author was in himself so lovable, because he was content to lose himself completely in One greater than he, and because he loved men and women with a tenderness which at times is almost heart-breaking in its genuineness. St. Luke was, of all writers of the Bible, the simplest of men, and simple in the fine and literal sense of that word, as having but one thought, one purpose, and one desire in contrast to many. It was that radiant simplicity which made him able to go to the heart of a situation, to cast away everything unnecessary and redundant, and to lay bare the throbbing reality not only of the life of his time but of that Truth which had shorn from his life everything but Itself.

There has existed a persistent tradition since early Christian times that St. Luke was a Greek; but there seems little reliable basis for this attractive assumption save that his name is of Greek origin and that the Greek in which he wrote his books is more natural and more lucid than that of much of the New Testament. He was probably Jewish in origin, as were all the other writers of both the Old and the New Testament. Although his personality shines forth from his work so that we know him better than we know any other writer of the New Testament, we possess few actual facts about him. St. Paul mentions him as his companion on his missionary journeys and as one of his "fellow labourers," and in his epistle to the Colossians describes him as a "beloved physician." If he had, indeed, been trained as a physician of his day, we may safely assume that he was a man of relatively superior education and training which may, in a measure, account for the literary excellence of his writing.

St. Luke wrote his Gospel about the year 90 A.D., some twenty years after that of St. Mark had appeared and about the date of that of St. Matthew.[1] From his rather stilted and conventional introduction we know that he had sources for it other than the many oral stories current about the life of Jesus. The chief of these sources was, of course, the Gospel of St. Mark; but it is clear from the four verses in his introduction that there were others. He, in fact, suggests that there were "many others" and that some had been written by "eye-witnesses." It is now generally accepted by scholars that there existed an early source, now lost, of the sayings of Jesus and perhaps an account of His life upon which all the gospel writers drew for their work. There may even have been more than one such document, since St.

[1] It must be remembered that St. Matthew's Gospel could not, in point of time, have been written by the disciple of Jesus known as Matthew. Its unknown author obviously either possessed or assumed the same name.

Luke speaks of many who have "set forth in order a declaration of those things which are most surely believed among us."

It is not, however, with the long-disputed subject of gospel sources with which we as readers are primarily concerned, but with the book itself, its charm and richness, and with the man who could endow his pages with such interest and appeal. He was not content like St. Mark to deal only with the most striking events of the life and ministry of Jesus. The abundance and the vitality of his imagination urged him on to tell everything possible, the simple, homely details as well as the more stirring episodes and anecdotes. His object was evidently to write a life of Jesus modelled upon that form of writing very much in vogue in his age, which among other biographical works produced the *Lives* of Plutarch. He also knew and obviously loved the most picturesque and vivid of the Old Testament narratives which may well have inspired him to go and do likewise. He dedicated his book to a friend of his, one Theophilus, "a lover of God" by his name, in order that Theophilus might know the "certainty" of those things which so filled his own mind and heart.

Many readers of the four gospels regret that from his book St. Luke has omitted certain passages written or incorporated by one or more of the other three authors and, through long association and familiarity, become of especial value. For example, they wish that he had included the Sermon on the Mount in the complete form given by St. Matthew; or that his version of the Lord's prayer did not differ from the accepted one; or that his Beatitudes had mentioned the peacemakers and the pure in heart. To him, however, the Sermon on the Mount in its entirety was apparently less important than certain parables and stories unique with him; and perhaps his failure to bless the peacemakers and the pure in heart lay in the fact that his own heart was so pure and his own motives so peaceful that he was slow to recognize that everyone was not like himself. These omissions and emendations seem slight enough when we once realize what greater things we owe to St. Luke. The incomparable richness of his book will, I hope, become apparent as we consider him as one of the greatest literary artists of the first century, not overshadowed even by the writers of Rome.

At the outset we become aware that he is no theologian in spite of his companionship with St. Paul. He is, instead, a storyteller and a biographer. His purpose is to present the character of Jesus so that readers and hearers may become aware not only of His divine nature and message, but also of its meaning and necessity for all men throughout the world. He does not mention the founding of the Church, nor is he so much interested in Jesus, the Messiah of prophecy, as in Jesus, the man among men; in fact, it is *people* who interest St. Luke above all else, and it is through them that he reveals the personality and the nature of Jesus.

He is like Boswell in his avidity for experience, and he finds it in all manner of persons: the rich and the poor, the sinful and the good, fishermen, centurions, and the rulers of synagogues; the sick in body and the troubled in soul; women and children, Pharisees, publicans, and hated Samaritans. They fill his pages with their problems and personalities: Zaccheus, who, because he was small of stature, climbed a sycamore tree in order to see Jesus; Jairus, whose little daughter was ill; Jesus at twelve in the Temple; the old man Simeon and the old woman Anna.

He is particularly interested in women, whom he pictures with a consideration and an interest not so evident in the other gospels. He begins his story with Mary, her wonder and perplexity over the words of Gabriel, her visit to Elisabeth in the hill country, the rejoicing of the two together, and Mary's song sung in Elisabeth's house rather than in the presence of Gabriel. He emphasizes Mary's remembrance of all the wonders told by the shepherds, her pondering of them in her heart. He carefully identifies women by their names as though individually they meant something to him: *It was Mary Magdalene, and Joanna, and Mary, the mother of James. . . . Certain women,*

Mary called Magdalene . . . and Joanna, the wife of Chuza . . . and Susanna. To him we owe the picture in Bethany of Martha, "cumbered about with much serving," irritated at her sister's lack of willingness to help her, and of Mary's "good part which shall not be taken away from her." But it is the unidentified women who are perhaps even more appealing: the woman who touched the border of Jesus' garment and then lay trembling before Him; the woman who was so "bowed together" that she "could in no wise lift up herself"; the girl looking "earnestly" upon Peter by the fire in the high priest's house; the Galilean women who followed after the body of Jesus so that they might know the place of the sepulchre in order to return at dawn; the women in the parables with their yeast and their lost silver; and, above all others, the woman in the Pharisee's house with her alabaster box of ointment, whose extravagant devotion called forth perhaps the most wise and beautiful of all the sayings of Jesus: *Her sins, which are many, are forgiven; for she loved much: but to whom little is forgiven, the same loveth little.*

One has but to read St. Luke's version of this story given in chapter 7, verses 36 to 50, in comparison with the same story told by St. Mark in his 14th chapter and by St. Matthew in his 26th to see how much more vividly the woman herself is pictured in St. Luke's description of her. The others emphasize her sacrifice and the lesson which Jesus drew from it. It is St. Luke alone who lets us clearly see the woman herself, who places the emphasis upon *her,* and who tells of each of her various acts of unrestrained love.

The genius of St. Luke had unquestionably a deep emotional quality which in less skillful hands might well have fallen into sentimentalism. This emotional quality is shown again in his presentation of Jesus as a friend of the poor and of those ostracized from society by sin or by disease. In all his scenes are evident his warm and generous sympathy, his pity and compassion, his sense of human worth: in his story of the blind man begging by the wayside, of the wretched servants beaten by the husbandmen, of Lazarus, the beggar, whose sores the dogs licked, of the poor widow casting her two mites into the treasury, and of the thief on the cross, to whom Jesus promises companionship in Paradise. In his pages more than anywhere else in the New Testament "the blind see, the lame walk, the lepers are cleansed, the deaf hear, the dead are raised, to the poor the gospel is preached." And if one seeks the thesis of his book, it is to be found in verse 18 of chapter 4, when in the synagogue at Nazareth he pictures Jesus as reading from the book of Isaiah, a passage upon which St. Luke has surely placed his careful hand:

The Spirit of the Lord is upon me, because he hath anointed me to preach the gospel to the poor; he hath sent me to heal the broken-hearted, to preach deliverance to the captives, and recovering of sight to the blind, to set at liberty them that are bound.

That St. Luke knew and loved the Old Testament is plain. His frequent quoting of it, as well as his obvious familiarity with its narratives, proves that fact. He tells the story of the famine at the time of Elijah, of Elijah's service to the widow, and of the cleansing of Naaman by Elisha; he refers to Elijah's calling down fire from heaven and to Jonah as a sign to the people of Nineveh. The hymns which he alone of the four includes in his Gospel, the *Magnificat* of Mary, the *Benedicite* of Zacharias, and the *Nunc Dimittis* of Simeon, have a distinct Old Testament atmosphere in style, language, and imagery and were unquestionably adapted from ancient material, as we have already noted in the obvious similarity between the songs of Mary and of Hannah, the mother of Samuel.

These hymns, which have become a part of the liturgy of the Christian Church, are not only one of the most beautiful of St. Luke's contributions to Christian literature, but they add immeasurably to that sense of drama which is so characteristic of him. All, it will be remembered, are sung under most moving circumstances by persons under the influence of profound emotion: Mary, conscious that God hath done to her great and holy things; Zacharias, miraculously cured of his dumbness; the old man Simeon, understanding suddenly that he in his last years has seen the Christ. There is small wonder that they speak in dramatic words: *For he that is mighty hath done to me great things. Blessed be the Lord God of Israel. Lord, now lettest thou thy servant depart in peace.*

St. Luke loves to make other men and women speak in moving and dramatic tones and words: *Behold, thy father and I have sought thee sorrowing. Wist ye not that I must be about my Father's business? Master, we have toiled all the night, and have taken nothing. Lord, I am not worthy that thou shouldest enter under my roof. Foxes have holes, and the birds of the air have nests; but the Son of man hath not where to lay his head. Jesus, thou Son of David, have mercy on me. For this my son was dead, and is alive again; he was lost, and is found. Were there not ten cleansed? but where are the nine? Why seek ye the living among the dead? Lord, remember me when thou comest into thy kingdom. Zaccheus, make haste and come down; for today I must abide at thy house.*

He loves also to set scenes for his stories: the house of Elisabeth and Zacharias in the hill country; the field at night with the stars above the watching shepherds; the long road to Emmaus with the two sad men walking and talking together; the house of the Pharisee on the Sabbath with all the company there watching Jesus in suspicion; the corn field through which the disciples walk and rub the ripe ears with their hands.

Another dramatic device is his use of the double form of address. It is as though to him the thing to be said is of such importance that the hearer's name must be spoken twice: *Martha, Martha, thou art careful and troubled about many things. O Jerusalem, Jerusalem, which killest the prophets. Simon, Simon, behold, Satan hath desired to have you.*

The greatest single dramatic achievement of St. Luke is without doubt his account of the last days of Jesus, of the crucifixion, and of those miraculous happenings on the road to Emmaus and in Jerusalem. This narrative begins with chapter 22 and continues to the end of the book. More than any other gospel account of the story this one is told largely in dialogue, or perhaps more accurately, in the succinct statements of bystanders and participants. Not a word here is unnecessary. The story is carried almost entirely by verbs of sight and sound and by the most concrete of nouns. Read aloud it is seen to be, by all standards, at once the most moving and the most dramatic narrative of the four gospels.

All these qualities of St. Luke as a man and as an artist unite to make his life of Jesus the most distinctive and the most lovely of the four accounts given to us. Like other biographers of his day and of our own he draws upon a wealth of typical anecdotes and incidents in order to bring forth the personality of his subject. Since he plans to treat the life of Jesus as completely as possible, he begins even before His birth with the angelic announcement to His mother and with the birth of John the Baptist. Nor does he omit the boyhood of Jesus, he being the only one of the four writers to give us the appealing story of Him among the doctors in the Temple, which, we may be sure, was the one anecdote discoverable by him of that period of Jesus' life. And yet it is for the parables of Jesus that we owe St. Luke our greatest debt, for no other gospel writer records with such art these symbolic and yet realistic stories, several of which are peculiarly his and his alone.

The word *parable* comes from two Greek words which together mean *to throw across*. Thus parables are stories which bridge the fanciful and the real and by their intrinsic truth convey a teaching to those who listen. There is no written source known for these parables of St. Luke. There may have been one, now lost, but it is far more likely that he gathered his material for them from oral tradition, for in their form and language they show his own peculiar style. Although St. Mark says that Jesus spoke many parables, he records but few of them, and St. John even fewer. Those in St. Matthew's Gospel are about equal in number to those told by St. Luke, but, fine as they are, especially those of the Wise and Foolish Virgins and of the Ten Talents, none equals in dramatic effectiveness and literary perfection the two told only by St. Luke: the Prodigal Son and the Good Samaritan. St. Matthew's best parables are longer and more diffuse; one feels that their author is perhaps overly anxious that their teaching shall not fail, that their meaning must at all costs be driven home. St. Luke, on the other hand, with his all-embracing trust and confidence in people, tells his with great compression and thereby gains a far finer effect. His parable of the Prodigal Son has been many times extolled as the most perfect narrative in any literature, with that of the Good Samaritan a close second. Moreover, in St. Luke's parables there is evident that sympathy and tenderness, that understanding of human nature at its best and at its worst, that eager tolerance and acceptance of all men regardless of race or nation. The one leper of the ten who returns to glorify God and to give thanks for his healing is a Samaritan, the bitter enemy of the Jews, as is the one compassionate man of the three who journey from Jerusalem to Jericho.

It was mainly upon his parables that St. Luke relied, not only for his interpretation of the teachings of Jesus, but for the revelation of His influence upon men and women. We must remember that at the time he wrote Christianity was under suspicion as a revolutionary movement against the Roman state. Persecutions had already broken out, and countless Christians had gone to their death by martyrdom. St. Luke intended that his life of this man who had been condemned by a Roman court as the perpetrator and the agitator of unrest should refute the charges against Him and reveal Him, not as one who spent His life in political interference, but rather in healing the minds and the souls of men. He wrote it also not alone for Palestine, but for the great Gentile world outside, for those people of Asia Minor whom he had come to know through his missionary journeyings with St. Paul. To whatever race or nation they belonged they were familiar with foolish young men who spent their substance in riotous living, with shepherds who lost their sheep in the wilderness, with unjust judges and stewards, with beggars full of sores by many waysides, and with rich men clothed in purple and fine linen. In an age of too little compassion and too great injustice they would gladly hear of one who ate with sinners, who loved the poor, and who had given His life as a ransom for many.

St. Paul might set himself the task of proving by logical arguments and theological reflection the universal truths of the gospel; St. Luke was content to show by means of his own freshness, simplicity, and enthusiasm its world-wide appeal through the boundless humanity and compassion of its Founder.

3

St. Luke: His Acts of the Apostles

The book of the Acts of the Apostles is a continuation of St. Luke's Gospel, conceived by him probably as a second part and without doubt originally published with his biography of Jesus. Its present title seems to have been added at a later time, perhaps when the Acts was first detached from the Gospel. What St. Luke himself called it we unfortunately do not know, but that he intended it as a complement and conclusion to his "former treatise" and that he dedicated it also to his friend Theophilus is clear from its opening sentences.

The book of Acts is our one surviving account of the earliest Christian age and of the establishment of Christian communities and churches throughout Asia Minor, in the Aegean Islands, in Greece and at Rome. It is therefore of supreme value as history. That much of it is inaccurate is without doubt true, for just as St. Luke was a story-teller and not a theologian, so he was a dramatist first and an historian second. Also we must remember that he was writing it some decades after his experiences with St. Paul, who died about the year 64 A.D.; and that his memory of the matters of which he writes had inevitably become relatively dim with the passing of years. These facts have given rise to many questions and problems concerning the book, its sources, whether or not St. Luke wrote the whole of it, in how far it is reliable as sober history, and what relation it bears to the Epistles of St. Paul.

We must at the outset determine not to confuse our minds in a space so brief as this with problems still unsolved and with

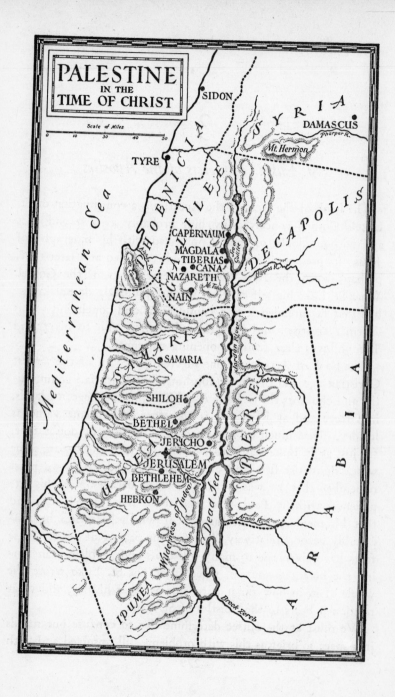

PALESTINE
IN THE
TIME OF CHRIST

Scale of Miles

0   10   20   30   40   50

SIDON

SYRIA

DAMASCUS

Pharpar R.

Mt. Hermon

TYRE

PHOENICIA

DECAPOLIS

Mediterranean Sea

CAPERNAUM

MAGDALA

TIBERIAS

CANA

NAZARETH

Mt. Tabor

NAIN

Sea of Galilee

Jordan River

Hippos R.

SAMARIA

SAMARIA

Jabbok R.

SHILOH

BETHEL

JERICHO

JUDEA

JERUSALEM

BETHLEHEM

HEBRON

Wilderness of Judea

Dead Sea

PEREA

Arnon R.

Brook Zereb

IDUMEA

ARABIA

matters of little interest to us as common readers. It is sufficient to be assured by the scholars that St. Luke was unquestionably the author of the Acts. This being known, we can proceed to our main business: the book itself and its value both as fairly reliable history and as a dramatic and charming piece of literature.

Part of the book was obviously written as a kind of diary since the first person is used in certain of its sections; and it is very likely that these portions formed originally a journal kept by its author as he travelled with St. Paul. This journal was preserved by him and formed the nucleus of his book when many years later he had time and opportunity to write the whole.

Just as in the first part of his book, the life of Jesus, he had attempted to portray the appealing and compassionate personality of his subject in order to show that the influence of Jesus was neither dangerous nor revolutionary toward the Roman State, so, in this second part, he is obviously writing to portray that widening influence throughout the world of his time. Here, as in the first part, his spirit of universalism is evident. The new religion is a religion, not for the Jews alone nor for Palestine, but for all men and for the Gentile world. There is apparent in the Acts, as perhaps its most outstanding and embracing quality, the sense of excitement on the part of its author in the knowledge that this obscure faith of Galilee has spread in ever-widening circles until it has at last become established even in the imperial capital of Rome.

This sense of excitement pervades and lends its drama to the series of episodes and incidents which comprise the book. For it is made up of a blocking or grouping of these dramatic episodes into six sections or units, which are contained approximately within the following chapters: chapters 1 to 6, those taking place in Jerusalem; 6 to 10, in other places in Palestine; 10 to 13, from Palestine to Antioch in Syria; 13 to 16, in districts of Asia Minor; 16 to 19, in Macedonia and Greece; and 20 to 28, those incidents that precede St. Paul's arrival in Rome. It is in no sense necessary to keep clearly in mind these respective sections, but it is interesting to note them, since their arrangement proves St. Luke's careful designing of his book and since they serve to show both the wide extent of its background and the spread of Christianity in terms of geography.

It is rather the nature of the episodes themselves which is of paramount interest to the reader. They may be compared to highly coloured or brilliantly illuminated vignettes in prose, such as those which Laurence Sterne gives us in *A Sentimental Journey* and in which he highlights either the main character or the dramatic instant; or to some of the finely lined portraits of Rembrandt by means of which one's imagination is spurred on not only to reconstruct characters but actually to see those characters in fancied situations. It is easy to understand why so many of the incidents in St. Luke's Gospel and in his Acts of the Apostles formed the subjects for numberless artists in the Middle Ages and in the Renaissance.

Once the book of Acts has been read as a whole in order that the reader may become aware of the extent of its background and of its value as history, perhaps the best means of appreciation of the best of these single dramatic episodes is to lift them out of their context and to look at them as units of narrative. For unless one employs this method, many of them are likely to be lost among material of relatively little value as literature. St. Luke in common with other ancient historians, such as Livy and Tacitus for instance, and the earlier Herodotus and Thucydides, reports long speeches presumably uttered by his characters but obviously largely made, or remade, by himself. A large part of the book of Acts is consumed by such addresses, now ostensibly made by Peter, now by Stephen, now by St. Paul. They without doubt show St. Luke's ability to use eloquent and moving language, but they by no means contribute to the book its peculiar value as literature. For a sense of that value it is to the single episodes which we must look.

As a means of further clarification we may well group the episodes about the various characters with whom they are connected. Among the finest of them are those which have to do with Peter. In chapter 3 there is the touching story of the "man lame from his mother's womb" who was "laid daily at the gate of the temple which is called Beautiful." This incident, comprised of only ten verses, for it should close with verse 10, is an excellent example of St. Luke's compression of material, his cutting off of non-essentials, his dependence upon one significant or dramatic utterance, such as, here, the words of Peter: *Silver and gold have I none; but such as I have give I thee,* and his swift and lively use of finite verbs and of participles, often repeated or used in a series for added effect: *And he leaping up stood, and walked, and entered with them into the temple, walking, and leaping, and praising God.*

Another of especial vividness and reality occurs in chapter 5, verses 1 to 12, the story of the lies told by Ananias and Sapphira, his wife, concerning the price of their land. Here again much of the power of the story lies in the sharp questions and fateful warnings addressed to both by Peter; and its atmosphere is darkened by the grim and repeated action of the young men who bury the guilty pair. The same compression of material marks this story as well as the first.

A third story of those centering around Peter is the account given in chapter 12, verses 1 to 19, of his miraculous deliverance from prison with its careful and detailed setting designed, of course, to increase the drama. For the third time the author employs the same use of excited and exciting exclamations to heighten his tenseness of atmosphere and the same lively verbs. The sound of the knocking, of course, contributes its note of mystery and of ominousness and keeps the close of the story on as high and taut a level as the beginning.

The one story of Stephen, upon which so much Christian tradition has come to be based, is among the most perfect examples of St. Luke's art if we are wise enough to consider it as a story only in its last verses given in chapter 7, verses 51 to 60 inclusive. The long account of the accusation and trial of Stephen with his good but long-winded speech will dim the real strength of the story itself if we allow these portions to intrude their prolixity. We should begin to read the story proper with Stephen's courageous and biting words to the council. From there on the story itself leaps into wonderful being with the fury of his enemies and the serenity of himself. Perhaps, indeed, this episode is among the richest of all those in the Acts because of its variety of swiftly changing passions and emotions, the noise of anger and revenge giving place to the calm of a vision of God and the serenity of death. Its artistic and climactic triumph occurs, of course, in the terse and ironic announcement: *And the witnesses laid down their clothes at a young man's feet, whose name was Saul.*

None of the stories of St. Paul contends for excellence with the famous scene on the Damascus road in chapter 9, verses 1 to 9 inclusive, which should for fuller understanding be prefaced by the first four verses of chapter 8 and followed by the remainder of chapter 9 as far as verse 30. The story itself, however, should be lifted even from these explanatory and interpretative additions and read for itself alone. Here again are the concrete and graphic verbs and nouns, the short and weighted utterances of the voice from heaven and of Saul himself, the wonder of the speechless men who watch and help, the blindness of Saul.

The story of Philip and the eunuch of Ethiopia in chapter 8, verses 26 to 39 inclusive, is of a different order in its complete and almost ingenuous simplicity. One surmises that it was a special favourite of St. Luke's own since so much of his nature is within it. The picture of Philip running after the chariot in which the eunuch sits with the prophetic book in his hands is lovely and the conversation between them even more appealing. The author shows a sensitive discrimination in omitting Philip's explanation of the scriptural passage and proceeding at once to the "certain water." The story, filled with naive surprise and wonder, cannot be read without a smile of sympathy and pleasure.

But of all these striking episodic stories, which show so completely the distinction of their author, none is so fine or so moving as that which begins the 2nd chapter of his book. There is a mounting effect here from the first words to the rightful close and climax of verse 11. Nowhere in the entire Bible is better narrative than this. The suddenness of the wind and of the fire, the clamorous, unfamiliar words echoing throughout the house, the amazement of the thronging multitude of men with their questions, the piling up of the names of races and of countries, and at the very end the climactic, pregnant phrase, "the wonderful works of God." The temptation to quote the story complete is irresistible:

And when the day of Pentecost was fully come, they were all with one accord in one place.

And suddenly there came a sound from heaven as of a rushing mighty wind, and it filled all the house where they were sitting.

And there appeared unto them cloven tongues like as of fire, and it sat upon each of them.

And they were all filled with the Holy Ghost, and began to speak with other tongues, as the Spirit gave them utterance.

And there were dwelling at Jerusalem Jews, devout men, out of every nation under heaven.

Now when this was noised abroad, the multitude came together, and were confounded, because that every man heard them speak in his own language.

And they were all amazed and marvelled, saying one to another, Behold, are not all these which speak Galileans?

And how hear we every man in our own tongue, wherein we were born?

285

Parthians, and Medes, and Elamites, and the dwellers in Mesopotamia, and in Judea, and Cappadocia, in Pontus, and Asia,

Phrygia, and Pamphylia, in Egypt, and in the parts of Libya about Cyrene, and strangers of Rome, Jews and proselytes,

Cretes and Arabians, we do hear them speak in our tongues the wonderful works of God.

It is these dramatic episodes which give to the book of the Acts its appeal and its literary distinction. St. Luke was not a young man in years when he wrote his two-fold work, but his vitality was apparently unquenchable and his imagination undimmed. We cannot be sufficiently grateful for this legacy of his to the literary and spiritual treasures of the world. It is pleasing also to note in the Acts the same traits which in his Gospel reveal him so gracious and so winning a person. The same interest in women is here: in Joppa there is Tabitha, or Dorcas, who has given her name to countless church sewing-circles, a woman of good works and of many coats and garments; in Thyatira there is Lydia, who opens her home to the apostles; in Corinth there is Priscilla, who, with her husband Aquila, goes with St. Paul by ship to Syria and to Ephesus where she expounds the Scriptures "more perfectly" than even the learned Apollos; there is the miserable damsel possessed with a spirit of divination and compelled thereby to bring her masters ill-gotten gain; and there is the impulsive and attractive girl Rhoda, who loses her head completely when she hears Peter's voice and runs in to tell everybody the good news instead of opening the gate for him.

Throughout the book of the Acts, in spite of suffering, martyrdom, and shipwreck, there is a radiance of spirit even brighter than in St. Luke's Gospel. He loves to use the words *wonder, amazement, astonishment,* and *gladness.* People go on their way rejoicing, tell good tidings as did the angels in the fields without Bethlehem, see visions of great joy, break bread and eat meat with "gladness and singleness of heart," are filled with faith

286

and power and with the Holy Ghost, dispense glad hospitality, and give thanks to God. It is the glory of the light on the Damascus road that remains with St. Paul to make his sufferings and hardships as nothing. The face of Stephen before his accusers shines like that of an angel; and on the day of Pentecost tongues of flaming fire appear in that room where the apostles are gathered "all with one accord."

This latter half of St. Luke's great book is most surely to be valued for the light it throws upon the early Church and for its descriptions of the spread of the new faith throughout the Mediterranean world; but it is to be cherished for that brighter and more radiant light glowing throughout its pages in the spirits of men and women, who, in common with that many-tongued multitude on the day of Pentecost, hear for the first time "the wonderful works of God."

4

The Letters of St. Paul

The very name of St. Paul, even to persons who know little about him, immediately gives rise to a variety of impressions: that he wrote many books of the New Testament known as Epistles; that he once persecuted Christians and later converted multitudes to the religion which he formerly suspected and abhorred; that he was a man of prodigious vitality and contentious character; that he was ugly to look at; that he went on many missionary journeys; that he had small use for women and disapproved of marriage; that he loved argument and theology and caused more than a little controversy concerning the doctrines of the Christian Church. There is some measure of truth in all these notions concerning him; and our purpose in this chapter will be to construct out of these and others perhaps more accurate a picture of him as the most brilliant figure among the Christians of the first century and as one of the most remarkable and vital personalities of any age or time.

Although Saul, or Paul, of Tarsus himself leaves us in little doubt as to what manner of man he was, the reliable facts concerning his early life are few. We owe these to St. Luke, who in his Acts of the Apostles has told us the story of Paul's conversion (a story which the great apostle himself loves to tell), and who by his inclusion of Paul's speeches has allowed us to gather from them certain other details. According to these sources, the Apostle to the Gentiles was born in Tarsus, the chief city of the province of Cilicia, which lay just northwest of Syria on the Mediterranean. We have no knowledge of the exact date of his birth, but since we know that for seventeen years after his conversion he lived and worked largely in the neighborhood of Tarsus and of Antioch in Syria and that he did not begin his wider missionary journeys until the year 48 or 49 A.D., he could not have been born very long after the beginning of the Christian era.

He speaks proudly in Jerusalem of his birthplace as "no mean city." In this he spoke truly, for Tarsus was a rich and cosmopolitan center connected with the Mediterranean by the river Cydnus. In its streets could be heard the tongues of many nations and peoples, for it was not only a place of trade and commerce but also a cultural center of its day and renowned for its schools and its thinkers. Moreover, the people of Tarsus had been granted under Pompey the supreme protection and privilege of Roman citizenship, to which St. Paul more than once refers and which allowed him to plead his cause in Rome.

As a boy he apparently learned the trade of the tent-makers, who wove the material for tents from goats' hair and whose craft is known to have formed one of the chief industries of Tarsus in his day. From references in the Acts and in his epistles it is clear that he continued to support himself by this trade during his longer stays in the various places of his missionary journeys. From his own account we know that he went as a young man to the famous Rabbinical school of Gamaliel in Jerusalem to be trained there in the Jewish Law, or Torah. He is in his letters explicit in his statement that he was trained in the strictest sect of the Pharisees. It was during these years in Jerusalem that he witnessed and, in his own words, "consented to" the martyrdom of Stephen. He was at first violently opposed to the Christians and their teachings, and because of this violence, which was apparently not infrequently physical, he incurred the fear and suspicion of the Christian community there. After his conversion the hatred and suspicion of the Jerusalem Jews followed him because of his apostasy from his traditional faith. Nor was he seemingly at any time in his life free from contentions within the Church itself, since the strictly Jewish Christians represented by Peter objected strongly to his liberalism toward the uncircumcised Gentiles.

That he was a man of great learning and of extraordinary intellectual gifts is evident not so clearly in his scant references to his education as in his remarkable fund of theological knowledge, his genius in logic and argument, and his distinguished use of language. He seems, however, surprisingly enough, to have been a poor speaker. In his letters to the church at Corinth he refers twice to the lack of excellency in his speech, which, he quotes his opponents as saying, is "contemptible." Nor in this connection does one forget St. Luke's succinct and graphic episode in chapter 20 of the Acts of the young man Eutychus, who fell asleep "as Paul was long preaching" and fell out of the window! Tradition has heightened his reference to the weakness of his "bodily presence," also given in the second letter to Corinth, and has pictured him as short of stature, defective in eyesight, and ugly in countenance. That he was subject at times to sudden attacks of illness, which were due apparently to some form of epilepsy, is, however, well substantiated by his own words and may account for the fact that he took St. Luke with him as a physician as well as a fellow labourer.

The prodigious vitality of St. Paul, both mental and physical, was perhaps his most basic and outstanding characteristic, for upon that excessive vitality and energy depended most of his other attributes. Although he may have been weak in bodily presence, he was anything but weak in bodily activity. Throughout his astounding career as a missionary he spent thirty years in travel and in adventures which might speedily have put an end to many men stronger than he. After seventeen years of preaching and teaching in Syria and Cilicia, he embarked upon those wider travels which took him to Macedonia, to Greece, back to Asia Minor, and back again to Greece. During these almost incredible journeys he founded the various churches which became the recipients of those letters destined to make him famous throughout the world for nearly two thousand years. When he finally reached Rome some three years before his death, he arrived there as a prisoner for his faith, proclaiming his right as a Roman citizen to appeal to Caesar. Since the book of the Acts, after its fine account of the adventurous voyage, leaves him in Rome, we are left in the darkness as to the result of his trial. But there seems to be little doubt that, after he had been detained there for three years, he was condemned to death about the year 64 A.D.

Before considering the letters themselves, it is well to understand just which of those ascribed to St. Paul were actually written by him. If we examine our New Testaments, we shall see that the title of every book from that of Romans to Hebrews inclusive is "the Epistle of Paul the Apostle," that, in all, fourteen letters are assigned to his pen. Only ten of these were actually written by him. The great Epistle to the Hebrews, with its thrilling chapter 11 on faith as "the substance of things hoped for, the evidence of things not seen" and its echoes in other chapters of the beautiful language of the prophets, was not written by him, much as we should like to give him credit for it. Even the early Christian Fathers recognized this fact, one of them, Origen, saying that "the author is known to God alone" and none of them, in common with later scholars, being able to discover its writer. Nor did St. Paul, much also to our disappointment, write the so-called Pastoral Epistles, the pleasant personal letters to young Timothy and Titus. In their style and diction they bear no resemblance to the language of St. Paul; they obviously reflect a life within the Church far different from that of his day; and their teaching is not that of St. Paul. They were very probably built up around some notes of instruction sent by him to his various fellow labourers and constructed in their present form by some later teacher into whose hands the notes had fallen. They were probably written about the year 100 A.D., more than thirty years after St. Paul's death.

We have left, then, ten letters or groups of letters, which are without doubt genuine, those written to the churches in Thessalonica, Galatia, Corinth, Rome, Colossae, Ephesus, and Philippi, and that one written to his friend Philemon. All were composed during a space of about ten years, from approximately 50 to 60 A.D.

If these letters of St. Paul possessed no intrinsic merits in themselves as great pieces of literature, they would still be of boundless value as the earliest documents of the Christian religion and as the nucleus of the New Testament. Yet it was perhaps their very excellence as works of art rather than their historical and theological value which ensured their preservation and immortality. Nor must we overlook the fact that together with their literary distinction they contain, perhaps more clearly and vividly than in any letters ever given to the world, the portrait of their writer. All of St. Paul is within them: his brilliant powers of argument, his scorn of idleness, his intolerance of evil, the amazing agility of his mind, his sense of the beauty of language, his passion for order, his almost humorous prejudices, the ups and downs of his volatile nature, now dejected in utter misery, now uplifted to the heights of joy, his saving common sense and his care for practical details, his encouragement of the young, his understanding of the various gifts allotted to men, his never-failing courtesy and gratitude, his almost boastful pride in his sufferings, and, above all else, his astounding and flaming faith.

His letters are not epistolary tracts, even though they are filled with anxiety concerning the problems facing the churches for whom he wrote them and although in each he has some clear purpose in view. They were apparently not written with any thought of publication, perfect as most of them are as models of literary composition. The extreme care which is evident in each of them arose from his desire to express as accurately as possible the things which he wanted to say; and throbbing within and beneath the words of each, whether in

292

exhortation, or in brief anger, or in approval, or in warning, or in explanation, or in self-revelation, are his friendship, his solicitude, and his love. In many respects among the loneliest of men, he looked upon these struggling communities of early Christians not only as his charges but as his families of children; and throughout his letters to them this evident fact lends at times an almost pathetic quality of concern and anxiety to his style:

Let all bitterness, and wrath, and anger, and clamor, and evil speaking be put away from you, with all malice.

And be ye kind one to another, tender-hearted, forgiving one another, even as God for Christ's sake hath forgiven you.

The personal references to those men working with him, often made at the close of the letters, together with the definite statement at the conclusion to the epistle to the Romans, *I Tertius, who wrote this epistle* and at the end of the first epistle to Corinth, *The salutation of me Paul with mine own hand,* surely suggest that St. Paul found the mechanics of writing irksome if not difficult and that he therefore dictated his letters. One can surmise in this connection that the men who took them down for him must have known some trying hours! For the perfection of them assumes not only meticulous care but constant polishing of the style and diction. Gifted as their author doubtless was in the use of language, letters such as these were not completed without hours of careful rewriting. They were, of course, designed to be read, probably in public, to the entire church community to which they were addressed; and it is evident at the close of the letter to the Colossians that they were also circulated among neighbouring churches. The studied art of the greatest passages in all of them shows a careful and deliberate choice of words and an even cautious molding of sentences which bear proof of the tireless and conscientious labour in their construction.

Each of the communities to which St. Paul addressed his letters was marked by traits distinctive and peculiar to itself; and this fact must be borne in mind when the letters are read and studied. The church at Thessalonica, the modern Salonica, to whom he writes his first letter, was a new church about which he was especially anxious. We shall perhaps recall from St. Luke's account in chapter 17 of the Acts that there had been an uprising in Thessalonica of certain Jews who had stirred up a riot against Paul and Silas and expelled them from the city after a stay of some weeks. St. Paul had journeyed into Greece, but he could not get from his mind his anxiety over his new converts in Thessalonica and would have attempted to return there, had not one of his peculiar seizures, his "thorn in the flesh" or "the messenger of Satan" as he vividly describes these attacks, hindered him from so doing. He had, however, sent Timothy to them to lend encouragement and to bring him word of how they were getting on. Now that Timothy has returned with good news of them, he writes his letter, which, like his second, probably written shortly afterward, has to do with the special problems of the Thessalonians, who are making a stout stand in an old and pagan city to hold fast to their new faith.

Apparently, however, they have not fully grasped the moral requirements of Christianity which, indeed, must have seemed especially rigorous to them in the Macedonian city in which they lived, with its Hellenistic culture and its frank enjoyment of sensual pleasures. At all events, St. Paul takes this occasion to warn them against brothers "that walk disorderly," against "busy-bodies," and "pleasure in unrighteousness." He reminds them that, while he and Silas were among them, both worked night and day in order that they might support themselves and not become a charge to their hosts. There is, in fact, suggested in these two letters a rather amusing repercussion of St. Paul's first preaching to the Thessalonians. We are told in the Acts that he had laid especial emphasis not only on the Resurrection of Jesus but on His imminent return to bring in His Kingdom. This teaching has evidently been taken somewhat too literally by certain of the brethren in Thessalonica, who have apparently decided that, in the light of St. Paul's wisdom, one need not worry overmuch about assiduity in business since the Day of the Lord is at hand; and now St. Paul feels it necessary to warn them against a too literal interpretation of his words. They must be sober and watchful, he tells them, refrain from sensual pleasures, and not become overly excited in the thought that the Day is close upon them. Above all else, he warns them against idleness. If any man will not work, he commands, that man shall not eat! One wonders if Captain John Smith, who announced the same law to the early colony on the James River, realized that he possessed good Pauline authority for so doing!

St. Paul's letter to the Christians in Galatia is of especial importance and interest, not only because of its wonderful vigour of expression and its reflection of the many-sided character of its author, but also because it contains the account of the beginnings of the Christian Church and of one of its fundamental controversies. The Galatians to whom St. Paul writes in this letter belonged, not to the region known as Galatia in the north of Asia Minor, but rather to the newly-formed Roman province of Galatia, which included a large section of central and southern Asia Minor and in which St. Paul had first preached to the Gentiles. This epistle, written some time between 52 and 58 A.D., contains in its six passionate chapters the chief clue to St. Paul's understanding and interpretation of the basic meaning of Christianity. Obviously trouble had arisen among the several churches of Galatia, and such grave trouble that they had forsaken his teachings and gone over to a far narrower type of thinking which taught that Christianity must not be separated from the fundamental precepts of the Jewish Law.

It has been suggested earlier in this chapter that certain strongly Jewish Christians had been opposed to St. Paul's teachings because he insisted that the teachings of Jesus recognized all men, that He had set aside the Law by His revelation of God, and that certain Jewish rites such as circumcision were unnecessary and even meaningless. To St. Paul Christianity is a new religion, not a revised Judaism, and founded, not on the

Jewish Law, but on an idea and principle entirely different from its meticulous observance of that Law. The news that certain teachers from Jerusalem who were opposed to his interpretation and who were upholding the Law as fundamental to Christianity had gone to the cities of Galatia, sincere in their zeal to undermine his teaching, was a crushing blow to him; and his angry, reproachful, argumentative, and yet tender letter is the result. Throughout its zealous pages he is defending both his own name and his ideal of that Christian freedom which liberates men from the old Law and writes in their hearts the Higher Law, not of works, however good they may be, but of faith. *O foolish Galatians,* he cries, *who hath bewitched you, that ye should not obey the truth?*

This letter of St. Paul to the churches of Galatia has been called the Christian declaration of independence because of its bold assertion that this new religion is, indeed, new and not based upon the old. With its bold affirmation of the beliefs peculiar to Christianity, it contains more than does any other of St. Paul's Epistles his fundamental contribution to the early Church. It is interesting to note that those convictions which led to the Protestant Reformation had their beginning in Martin Luther's study of St. Paul's great letter and that he actually launched his reforms with his *Commentary on Galatians.* In certain of his other letters St. Paul has risen to heights of exalted prose not evident in this one; but in none has he shown such honesty and courage and such profound conviction of essentials as here. His short, sharp sentences have a knife-like edge; anger and profound sorrow mingle with anxiety and warning; and through all is the note of unassailable faith.

The long epistle to the church in Rome is different in many ways from St. Paul's other letters. It deals with general rather than with concrete problems; it is in many ways a more finished and even a more consciously literary work than any of the others; and it lacks almost entirely the personal tone which sounds through every sentence of the letter to the Galatians or even of that to the people of Thessalonica. The reasons for these differences are easily explained. St. Paul was not personally responsible for the forming of the church in Rome, where Christianity had found its way earlier and where a sizable church had already established itself in the great capital city of the Empire. He was, therefore, not personally known to the Roman church; and he quite naturally could not write to its members in the intimate manner in which he wrote his other letters. Moreover, he was quite apparently eager to make the best impression possible upon his readers. In his introduction to his letter he makes it clear that he is planning to go to Rome to start missionary work there, and he obviously wishes to enlist the help and support of his fellow Christians. Since he was by this time known by reputation throughout the Christian world, he was anxious lest his doctrines, so assailed in Galatia by those Jewish-Christians grounded in the Law, be taken into question in Rome also and cause controversy fatal to his hopes.

For these reasons, and perhaps also because the thought of Rome itself as the Imperial City had touched his imagination with a sense of her power and position in the world of his day, his letter to the Romans was most carefully and even perhaps deferentially written. In it he does not deal with definite and concrete problems but rather with the basic matters of Christian theology. His aim is clearly to acquaint this church, which has never known him personally, with his position on matters of faith and dogma, and for this reason his letter, written with such care and even caution, resembles a theological dissertation rather than a letter.

The epistle consists of a careful and even elaborate argument, having as its main thesis that salvation is gained through faith and that a man is justified only by that faith. Both the cultivation of so-called wisdom by the Gentiles and the reliance on the Law by the Jews have proved false and hollow, and only the faith revealed by Jesus remains as a way of life. In this way of life man is re-created by the Spirit sent from God and is inspired with new strength and higher desires so that literally no earthly powers can separate him from God. The argument rises to its culmination in the magnificent 8th chapter with its final verses which mount in a crescendo of impassioned conviction and faith.

Nevertheless the Epistle to the Romans is a genuine letter, perhaps indeed, when one considers how much was at stake, written with deeper emotion than were several of the others although the emotion was of a different nature. And to his readers of the present day its appeal is deepened by the knowledge, then closed to him, that he would go to Rome for the first time, not as a free man, but in chains, and give his life for his faith.

The letter to the Romans was written about the year 56 A.D. In the years following, mostly between 59 and 61 A.D., St. Paul was to write his brief and charming letter to Philemon and his longer ones to the churches at Colossae, Ephesus, and Philippi.

The letter to Philemon is on a distinctly personal matter and reveals its author in a different mood from that of the rest of his correspondence. Philemon was one of the Christians in the Phrygian city of Colossae, who had apparently formed a warm friendship with the apostle during his work at Ephesus one hundred miles away. Philemon owned a slave named Onesimus who had robbed his master and then run away. Apparently he had finally sought refuge in the crowded city of Rome and in desperation had sought out St. Paul, already a prisoner there, to ask for help. The help generously given, Onesimus had attached himself to his benefactor as his devoted servant.

This letter to Philemon written from Rome concerns Onesimus. The one purely personal letter of St. Paul which has been preserved, it is of great value, for it shows clearly those magnetic and winning qualities in him which brought devotion and loyalty in their wake. It is a charming letter filled with courtesy, and even with humour. It is delicately and lightly written with an undertone almost of playfulness. In it he begs forgiveness for Onesimus and asks Philemon to receive him again "not now as a servant" but as "a brother beloved." *If thou count me therefore a partner, receive him as myself. If he hath wronged thee, or oweth thee aught, put that on mine account. I Paul have written it with mine own hand, I will repay it: albeit I do not say to thee how thou owest unto me even thine own self besides.*

We can be sure that Philemon received Onesimus. Few friends could resist so gracious and persuasive a letter. And linked with it went the epistle to the church at Colossae, the one letter of St. Paul which, in its first two chapters at least, is both difficult and obscure.

The letter to Colossae was written to combat a peculiar heresy of which nothing is known save from the letter itself. Apparently, from what one can gather from its pages, the religious beliefs of the people of Colossae were suffering from the lure of certain speculative problems having to do with the relation of the mysteries and wonders of the visible world to the religion of Christ. The letter shows St. Paul's ability to rise to all manner of situations. Here for the first time in his letters he borrows a new doctrine, that of the Logos, or the Word, which is contained within the being of God as a divine principle and which, going forth from Him, brings about His work of creation. St. John was later in his Gospel to identify the Logos with Christ as the Word which was in the beginning with God. The doctrine had been conceived by the great Jewish philosopher, Philo of Alexandria, and St. Paul is quick to adopt it as a logical means of quieting the uneasy, would-be philosophers of Colossae who are apparently worried lest their Christian faith be too restricted.

The first two chapters of this letter are so obscurely written as to suggest that St. Paul himself felt somewhat insecure, and it is a relief to continue with chapters 3 and 4 where he is on

299

far more solid ground with his practical advice. There is more than a suggestion in the close of the letter with its injunctions to masters concerning their servants that he is giving Philemon an extra bit of encouragement as to his reception of the repentant Onesimus.

The Epistle to the Ephesians shares in certain respects the obscurity of that to the Colossians with which it is connected in probable date. It was doubtless not actually addressed to Ephesus, since in the early manuscripts the words "at Ephesus" do not appear, but that it was written by St. Paul and to one of his churches in the neighbourhood of Colossae and Ephesus there seems little doubt. The letter is not in any sense controversial, nor does it deal with any specific situation, nor does it, except in very scattered instances, enforce the ideals of Christian behaviour. It is, in fact, more than anything else a religious meditation on the timeless Reality of religion in general and on the Church as the outward and visible sign of that Reality in particular. It is almost as though its author, a prisoner in Rome and now perhaps seized by a vision or presentiment of death, is gathering together in his mind those deathless things for the life of which in this world he has given his own life. In other words, in order to apprehend more clearly the actual and spiritual significance of the Church, he is trying here to express his sense of the ultimate meaning of the work of Christ on earth as the fulfillment of the great original design of God. To him such an understanding means the apprehending of the divine plan, the ability to comprehend "what is the breadth, and length, and depth, and height."

The letter is a difficult one because of the difficulty of its subject and the vein of mysticism which runs throughout; and yet in certain of its passages, notably in the prayer at the conclusion of chapter 3 and in verses 10 to 17 inclusive of chapter 6, it contains some of the most beautiful and fervent writing of the New Testament.

In many ways the letter to the church at Philippi is the most satisfying of all those written by St. Paul. Its tone of informality and trust in a group of people whom he apparently sincerely loves gives a peculiar warmth to its chapters and makes it unique and distinctive among all the epistles. Except for chapter 3, where for a short space he speaks in bitter tones and words of enemies who are trying to undermine his work, the entire letter sounds a note of mutual friendship and confidence. It is almost wholly lacking in theology, and even its advice is that of the sharing of common problems. It is instead filled with those daily ordinary matters which among friends are not actually so ordinary as they are reassuring, heartening, even rare and precious, because they are so seldom understood in their true meaning.

St. Paul had a special affection for the church in the Macedonian city of Philippi. He had begun there his work in Europe and had early felt the generous nature of its people. Although he had made it a principle to take no money for his service and had instead worked at his tentmaker's trade in whatever place he was in order to be independent of help, he had showed his especial confidence in the Philippians by accepting occasional gifts from them as his letter proves. It was, in fact, one of these gifts which caused him to write to them in gratitude; for, knowing that he was a prisoner and very likely in need, they had sent money to him by a man called Epaphroditus, one of their number, who upon his return home bore the letter to them.

There are few more thoughtful and considerate letters written at any time than this one. In it St. Paul is at his best as a friend rather than as a pastor or preacher. He speaks feelingly of Epaphroditus' serious illness while with him and of his homesickness. He assures them that he himself is in no dire distress and that he hopes soon to be free. Aware from what Epaphroditus has told him that they have suffered certain doubts and misgivings, he assures them that their troubles will soon give way before their faith in which he has complete confidence. He calls them "my beloved" and urges them to rejoice always in God. He so constantly repeats the words *rejoice* and *joy* that his entire letter shines with their light. And when in chapter 4 he concludes with the beautiful and familiar verses on the healing and inspiriting power of thought, it is as though he were sharing with them a common discovery rather than exhorting them to action.

There is no sure evidence as to where the letter to the loyal people at Philippi was written. If it was sent from Rome as seems likely, it has added significance and meaning in that it was probably the farewell letter of St. Paul before his death by martyrdom. It is pleasant to think that the great apostle spoke his last words to the best loved of all his friends:

I rejoiced in the Lord greatly that now at the last your care of me hath flourished again. I have all, and abound: I am full, having received of Epaphroditus the things which were sent me from you.

Just as no other church gave so much joy to St. Paul as did that at Philippi, no other afforded him so much trouble as did that at Corinth. Owing to its position on the isthmus connecting the two halves of Greece, the city of Corinth had always been a place of utmost significance and importance. It was a center, not alone for Greek trade, but for Mediterranean commerce; it was a world-renowned seat of Greek culture; and its somewhat sinister reputation as a city given over to pleasure made St. Paul enter upon his work there "in weakness, and in fear, and in much trembling."

Corinth presented difficulties to the apostle, but lack of vitality was not one of them. His main trouble seems to have been to instill into the lively and effervescent Corinthians rudimentary Christian ideals, which, in spite of their fervour toward their new faith, seemed odd to them and not entirely necessary. Keenly interested like all Greeks in the speculative aspects of religion, they were discouragingly blind to its more practical demands. They loved to think deeply about Christian truths, but they found tiresome and awkward the practice of them in daily life. The strong individualism in the Greek character was likely to be disastrous to a sense of community responsibility. All in all, St. Paul had his hands full in Corinth.

Although St. Paul's letters to the Corinthians were written around 54 A.D., some years before most of the others, it is well to close our study of him and of his work with these two long epistles, which together comprise the largest part of his complete correspondence. The letters as we now have them probably include portions of at least two others, since radical changes of mood in their present form suggest unrelated insertions. Within these long and composite letters to Corinth there is hardly a trait of St. Paul which is not contained or suggested; within them also are the noblest of his literature and the purest of his religious thought.

As might easily be imagined, a large portion of the correspondence is given over to strong advice and warnings to the lively and sensuous Corinthians, who, according to their sometimes distracted teacher, are "babes in Christ." They are stoutly warned in the first letter against sins of the flesh, unseemly lawsuits, and idleness. Chapter 7 complete is given over to the question of marriage which, one assumes, they may have taken lightly. Here the apostle stoutly admits that he would by choice have all men single like himself. Still, "better to marry than to burn!" Chapter 11 threatens women who go with uncovered heads on the streets or, worse, enter the church in such an unseemly state. And in the same chapter he reiterates his somewhat annoying conviction that women are created for men, not men for women!

In the second epistle, some of the chapters of which are evidently out of order and others inserted from a previous letter or letters, there is a variety or even a confusion of material, ranging from St. Paul's delight in the restored faith and behaviour of the Corinthians as recorded in chapter 7 to his begging them in chapters 8 and 9 to be more generous with their collections of money, from a touching account of his

303

physical infirmities in chapter 12 to the glorious enumeration of his willing sufferings in the last half of chapter 11.

These verses in chapter 11 form one of the three finest passages in all the collected letters of St. Paul. All three, in fact, occur in the two letters to Corinth, perhaps because, in his wise understanding of the combined weakness and strength of the Corinthians and in his sense of their need, he is emotionally more profoundly moved than in his letters to the other churches. Whatever the cause, we possess in these Corinthian epistles the unexcelled literary treasures of the New Testament, in all respects worthy to be placed among the best and the noblest of the entire Bible.

Whether the glorious description in II Corinthians 11, verses 22 to 31 inclusive, of St. Paul's willing sufferings is finer than the poetic prose which extolls charity in I Corinthians 13, or whether either quite equals chapter 15 of I Corinthians on immortality is a matter of personal taste and individual criticism. In all three the greatest of the apostles proves himself among the greatest of literary artists in his translation of that inner rhythm of his spirit into the perfection of words:

Charity never faileth: but whether there be prophecies, they shall fail; whether there be tongues, they shall cease; whether there be knowledge, it shall vanish away.

In journeys often, in perils of waters, in perils of robbers, in perils by mine own countrymen, in perils by the heathen, in perils in the city, in perils in the wilderness, in perils in the sea, in perils among false brethren;

In weariness and painfulness, in watchings often, in hunger and thirst, in fastings often, in cold and nakedness. . . .

Who is weak, and I am not weak? who is offended, and I burn not?

There are also celestial bodies, and bodies terrestrial: but the glory of the celestial is one, and the glory of the terrestrial is another. . . .

So also is the resurrection of the dead. It is sown in corruption, it is raised in incorruption:

It is sown in dishonor, it is raised in glory: it is sown in weakness, it is raised in power: . . .

For this corruptible must put on incorruption, and this mortal must put on immortality.

So when this corruptible shall have put on incorruption, and this mortal shall have put on immortality, then shall be brought to pass the saying that is written, Death is swallowed up in victory.

5

The Vision on Patmos

The small island of Patmos lies at the entrance to the Aegean Sea between the coasts of Asia Minor and Greece and among those many other islands, once remembered only for their ancient and poetic associations, now suddenly recalled and become familiar because of the tragedy visited upon them by the present war. Patmos is a steep and rocky island upon whose wooded heights now rise the white walls of a Greek monastery. Toward the close of the first century of the Christian era it was the scene of a mighty vision granted to a man whose name was John and recorded in his book known as the Revelation, or as the Apocalypse of St. John the Divine.

Except for his name we know almost nothing about him, for, lost in greater matters, he tells us little concerning himself. His statement that he was a "brother and companion in tribulation . . . for the word of God" suggests that he was suffering on Patmos for his faith. At his time the island was used by Rome as a place of detention for prisoners who worked in its quarries to procure stone for the mighty building projects of ambitious emperors. It is probable that this John was condemned to labour there as a form of Christian martyrdom.

Although he has been naturally confused with the John who wrote the Fourth Gospel, it is not likely that he was the same man. The language of the two books is not similar, and the interests of the writers of them have little in common. The Greek in which John of Patmos wrote his vision was apparently not a familiar language to him. His use of Hebrew idioms within it suggests that he composed his book first in his own tongue and later did his best to translate it into Greek. Since, if he had lived in Asia Minor all his life, he would have known Greek better than Hebrew, it is safe perhaps to assume that his home was in Palestine.

His strange and even fantastic book, which because of its mysterious nature is, unfortunately, perhaps the least read of all the New Testament, becomes simpler when we understand its purpose and its place in the world of its day. It should not be thought of as mysterious, nor should we share the opinion of an old commentator who once said of it: "This is a book which either finds a man mad or leaves him so." Most readers who vaguely know it only as a description of the New Jerusalem where God shall wipe away all tears will find in it, not only material of deepest interest, but literature of the highest dramatic and poetic quality, once they become aware of its meaning.

For it was written, not for the mad or even for the mystical, but rather for plain men and women who found in it a glorious meaning for their own bitter times. The author had a special message for that time, and he chose to give it in a form common to his day and known as vision, or apocalyptic, literature. To those who knew his book, not only was the form familiar, but the material held no strangeness, since they themselves believed in visions and in the imminent intervention of God in the desperate and sorrowful conditions under which they were called upon by God to live.

The date of the book of Revelation reveals its historical background. It was written about 95 A.D. in the midst of the horrible persecutions of the Emperor Domitian, who had enforced upon all the people of his empire, regardless of race or religion, the worship of the emperor as a god. Those who refused to observe this gross official cult were condemned either to death or to some other form of martyrdom like that which John himself was enduring; and Jews and Christians alike, to whom such an idea was revolting and blasphemous, were the chief sufferers.

These cruel persecutions were at their height between the years 93 and 96 A.D., when the welcome death of the emperor put an end to them; and they were especially widespread in the rich and prosperous Roman province of Asia, to the seven churches of which John addresses his encouraging and prophetic words.

Our book is then a tract for its time. The immediate purpose of its author, writing from Patmos of the vision accorded him when he "was in the Spirit on the Lord's day," is to encourage the people of the seven churches of Asia by imbuing them with new fortitude and faith. Even although they must suffer martyrdom for that faith, their sufferings will soon be past, he tells them, for the glorious triumph of Christ is at hand. The terrible and widespread evil of the world must reach its height before the great deliverance of God can come. To him this evil has now reached that height, the world is enduring its last days of agony and of pain, and the dawn of a new and perfect day is at hand. The tone of the book, in spite of its dire prophecies of the fallen Babylon of Rome, its horrors, and its plagues which now are visiting the earth, is one of exultation and of certain hope.

The thrilling character of the book of Revelation lies not in its opening messages to the seven churches which comprise the first three chapters and in which the churches are warned of their sins and shortcomings, but in the great dramatic vision of the scenes in heaven. For John's book, in order to be understood in all its grandeur and awfulness, must be read as a heavenly drama constructed in three great acts.

The Prologue to this mighty drama opens with chapter 4 in which the stage is set and the vast background for its action assembled. The scene is the limitless space of Heaven where God sits upon His throne:

And he that sat was to look upon like a jasper and a sardine stone: and there was a rainbow round about the throne, in sight like unto an emerald.

Around about the throne are ranged four and twenty seats, and upon the seats sit four and twenty priests, or elders, in white garments and crowned with gold. High in the midst above the throne stand four cherubim like great beasts, each with eyes before and behind and each with six wings. Before the throne and the elders there burn seven lamps of fire, and extending in the distance beyond it is a sea which sparkles like crystal.

This is not a setting of silence, for out of the throne come lightnings and rolls of thunder and the voices of the cherubim, which rest not day nor night but sing amid the thunder: *Holy, holy, holy, Lord God Almighty, which was, and is, and is to come.*

Once the scene is prepared the Prologue begins. In His right hand God holds a great book sealed with seven seals which no one among the priests or the cherubim is found worthy to open. But suddenly there appears in the midst of them all a Lamb having seven horns and seven eyes, who takes the book from the right hand of God. His act is the signal for worship by the priests and the cherubim, who fall down before Him and before the throne. They burst into new and triumphant song, singing with ten thousand times ten thousand angels who suddenly come from the vast spaces of heaven:

Thou art worthy to take the book, and to open the seals thereof; for thou wast slain, and hast redeemed us to God by thy blood out of every kindred, and tongue, and people, and nation.

This mighty burst of song is echoed from the far distant earth and from the sea where all creatures that are therein cry:

Blessing, and honor, and glory, and power, be unto him that sitteth upon the throne, and unto the Lamb forever and ever.

The great drama is then enacted upon its vast and awful stage: its first act, recorded in chapters 6 and 7, is *The Opening of the Seven Seals;* its second, in chapters 8, 9, 10, and 11, is *The Sounding of the Trumpets;* and the third, from chapter 12 through 17, is *The War in Heaven and on Earth.*

Those that take part in the first act, as the Lamb opens one by one the seven seals to the noise of thunder, are beings mounted upon gigantic horses: the white horse of the eastern barbarians, the red horse of revolution and civil strife, the black horse of famine, and the pale horse of death, each of whom comes upon the scene in order and in awful prophecy. With the opening of the fifth seal rise the souls of the martyrs slain for the word of God. With the opening of the sixth, the vaults of heaven are shaken with an earthquake which moves mountains and islands and before which kings and captains and mighty men hide themselves and cry to the mountains and to the rocks:

Fall on us and hide us from the face of him that sitteth on the throne and from the wrath of the Lamb.

Between the opening of the sixth and the seventh seals there is a solemn interlude in the action during which the suffering servants of God receive His sign in their foreheads, while four angels hold the four winds so that they may not blow until the martyrs have received the sign of God. And after the signs have been given there appears a great multitude which no man can number "of all nations, and kindreds, and people, and tongues" to stand before the throne. *These are they which came out of great tribulation. . . . Therefore are they before the throne of God and serve him day and night in his temple . . . They shall hunger no more, neither thirst any more; neither shall the sun light on them, nor any heat. For the Lamb which is in the midst of the throne shall feed them, and shall lead them unto living fountains of waters: and God shall wipe away all tears from their eyes.* With a mighty cry of praise the multitudes sing with the heavenly host:

Amen: Blessing, and glory, and wisdom, and thanksgiving, and honor, and power, and might, be unto our God for ever and ever. Amen.

The first act then closes with the opening of the seventh seal. No action whatever follows, nor is there sound in heaven. The choirs of angels, the multitude of the saints, the cherubim, the elders are still. . . .

310

And when he had opened the seventh seal, there was silence in heaven about the space of half an hour.

The second act, *The Sounding of the Trumpets*, follows with seven angels, to each of whom is given a trumpet, as the actors. As they prepare to sound their trumpets, incense rises from the golden altar, which for this act has been erected before the throne, and throughout heaven there are again "voices, and thunderings, and lightnings, and an earthquake." With the sounding of six of the trumpets in succession the prophetic end of the world is enacted with hail and fire, darkness and death. The sea becomes blood; the light of the sun and moon and the stars gradually dims; hell is opened, plagues visit the earth, and hideous insects like horses prepared for battle appear upon the earth to torment with the torment of scorpions those men who have not known God.

Again as in Act I there is an ominous and solemn pause between the sounding of the sixth and the seventh trumpets. The blast of the seventh trumpet is halted by the appearance of a mighty angel, clothed with a cloud and with a rainbow upon his head, who lifts his hand and swears that there shall be time no longer once the seventh angel has blown upon his trumpet. In the interlude which follows before the trumpet sounds, a series of obscure and symbolical happenings takes place through which John, as witness to these wonders, is commanded to prophesy and which continue to describe the end of the world.

When the seventh angel at last sounds, time stops—and with lightnings and thunderings, earthquake and hail, the life measured by earthly days and years comes to an end. The mystery of God is finished, and the multitude of voices in heaven shout in wonder and in worship.

The final act of the drama, *The War in Heaven and on Earth*, is filled with noise and confusion. One scene follows another in almost breathless succession and with increasingly symbolic meaning. For there is war in heaven between the hosts of Michael, the archangel, and those of Satan, the great dragon,

311

called the Devil, which deceiveth the whole world. He, a flaming Lucifer, falls to the earth with all his Satanic hosts of angels and there fights a losing battle against the hosts of heaven. In these scenes of the third act the prophecies of John are uttered one by one as wickedness consumes the earth. The great beast of the Roman Emperor, with his seven heads, ten horns, and ten crowns, before which the world wonders and worships, opens his mouth in blasphemy and commands that his image be worshiped. But, with a voice of many waters and of great thunder, those sealed with the seal of God sing a new song before the throne, a song which reaches to earth and sounds the prophecy of death to Rome and to her empire. *Babylon is fallen, is fallen, that great city.* Angels on clouds wing their way to earth, gather the clusters of grapes, and cast them into the great wine press of the wrath of God. As the faithful who have gained their victory over the beast and his image stand upon the sea of glass before the throne and sing in praise to God, seven angels open seven golden phials filled with the wrath of God, with plague and blood and fire, darkness, drought, and death.

Again there is an interlude before the seventh angel opens his phial. Then the voice of God Himself cries, *It is done,* and from the phial of the seventh angel falls a final earthquake, before which every island flees away and the mountains are no more found.

The Epilogue of the great drama is contained in the remainder of the chapters, which depict a series of scenes, first on earth and then in heaven, as they are given to John in his vision. He sees the destruction of Rome as a whore in purple and scarlet sitting upon a scarlet beast, arrayed in the gold and precious stones of her wicked wealth, and wearing upon her forehead *The Mother of Harlots and Abominations of the Earth.* He sees the merchants of the earth mourn over her destruction, for no man longer buyeth her merchandise of silk and ivory, cinnamon and ointments, frankincense and chariots, slaves and the souls of men.

And in the final chapters he is granted a sight of the symbolic New Jerusalem coming down from God out of heaven to become from henceforth His City upon earth, having again the glory of God. Her jasper wall is great and high; twelve angels guard her gates of pearl; her foundations are garnished with precious stones; and her Temple has become God Himself and the Lamb. She has no need of the sun or of the moon, for the glory of God brightens her streets of transparent gold. Within her gates enters neither sin nor sorrow, and through them nations bring to her their glory and their honour.

Such was the beatific vision granted on the island of Patmos to the man called John. In his writing of it for the suffering Christians of his day he has drawn upon those Old Testament visions of Daniel, who saw the thrones of earth cast down before the Ancient of days; of the Great Isaiah, before whom in the Temple at Jerusalem God sat upon his throne, high and lifted up, and the seraphim cried one to another; and of Deutero-Isaiah, who called upon the waste places of Zion to break forth into joy and to sing together. Yet, with all the indispensable echoes of them in his mind, he has written a finer work of apocalyptic literature than any composed in former centuries by his people. The splendour of his imagery of sight and of sound, the power of his descriptive passages both of heaven and of earth, the poetic cadence and emotional appeal of his exultant prose, his understanding of the effect upon the receptive mind of hosts and of multitudes and of the mounting succession in which he places them—these accord to his book the distinction of being one of the loftiest works of human imagination that the literature of the world can afford. The abundance of his imagery has made possible many of the most beautiful hymns of the Church and has influenced all the more mystical English poets from John Donne to T. S. Eliot.

That his ten thousand times ten thousand victorious saints, his shouts of *Alleluia,* his sea of glass, his seven trumpets, and his pure river of the water of life meant to even the plain men and women of his age what they cannot mean to us in our own is obvious. Not only were they accustomed to the spectacular, but they believed in the validity and in the reality of visions. To them his heavenly drama meant the concrete and definite realization of a blessed reward in compensation for their earthly sufferings; to us it is a symbol of that hope which forever stirs men's hearts to new life and courage.

It is peculiarly fitting that the New Testament should conclude its pages, not with theology, but with vision, and that this vision should be of the New Jerusalem and of mount Zion, the joy of the whole earth. One likes to think that John on Patmos, homesick for the mountains about Jerusalem, did not forget the Old Covenant in his flaming ardour for those hopes which had framed the New. For, older even than the Christian expectation in his imagination were the long centuries of his people who, deeper than all their devotion to their ancient Law, held in their hearts, as they still hold, the mystical vision and hope of Jerusalem, the City of God. Through the most exalted pages of the Old Testament as of the New that vision shines, binding together thirteen centuries of noble prose and poetry and lending even to our day its imperishable legacy.

And I John saw the holy city, new Jerusalem, coming down from God out of heaven, prepared as a bride adorned for her husband.

And the ransomed of the Lord shall return, and come to Zion with songs and everlasting joy upon their heads; they shall obtain joy and gladness, and sorrow and sighing shall flee away.

BOOKS SUGGESTED FOR READING AND STUDY [1]

(In addition to those especially recommended in the Foreword)

Rand McNally, Historical Atlas of the Holy Land. Chicago, 1938. A good collection of maps is, of course, indispensable to the intelligent reading of the Bible. This comprehensive atlas is the best I know.

W. F. Albright, *The Archaeology of Palestine and the Bible*. (3rd edition) New York, 1937.

Alfred Bertholet, *A History of Hebrew Civilization*. London, 1926. A fine and fascinating book.

Margaret B. Crook, Editor, *The Bible and Its Literary Associations*. New York, 1937. An excellent introduction to a series of essays written by various members of the Smith College faculty on the influence of the Bible on English Literature.

C. A. Dinsmore, *The English Bible as Literature*. New York, 1937.

The Legacy of Israel. Oxford, 1927. A series of fine essays by the best scholars.

John Livingston Lowes, "The Noblest Monument of English Prose," in *Essays in Appreciation*. Boston, 1936. The most beautiful single essay I know on the King James Version. Everyone should read it.

H. Wheeler Robinson, *The Old Testament: Its Making and Meaning*. Nashville, 1937.

---

[1] I have purposely included in this brief list only those books which I value most highly and know will be of deep interest to the common reader.

Sholem Asch, *The Apostle*. New York, 1943. Although this novel would have been more effective if half as long, it is a splendid study of the life of St. Paul.

Elmer Davis, *Giant Killer*. The Readers' Club, special edition. New York, 1943. This is a vivid and fascinating novel on David. I cannot recommend it too highly.

Thomas Mann, *Joseph and His Brothers, Young Joseph, Joseph in Egypt, Joseph the Provider*. New York, 1934–1944. These novels on the Jacob-Joseph story form a remarkable series which all should read. Much of the material may be difficult for the common reader, but the wonderful illumination and interpretation afforded by these novels should not be missed.